Reviews of
'Chasing the Dragons: An Introduction to Draconic Astrology'

'This book provides a fresh approach to a branch of our work every lover of the wisdom and mystery of astrology should explore. It is truly a hypnotizing gaze into the cosmic serpent's eyes. From the minute I tore open the package and started reading, I can't put the damned thing down!'

– **Michael Lutin, former astrologer to *Vanity Fair***

'A gifted speaker and writer, his work on draconic astrology is rich and insightful and he revives a technique of great significance.'

– **Wendy Stacey, Chairperson of the Astrological Association**

'Victor Olliver is a great proponent of using draconic astrology, and his talks on the topic explain it clearly and with great humour, so I'm delighted that he's now written the book on it – it fills a much-needed gap.

– **Chris Mitchell PhD, board trustee of the Astrological Association**

'Victor has the gift of writing clearly, succinctly and most importantly with humour. I feel this book, written by a brilliant astrologer, will be a boon, not only for those who practise astrology, but also for those with an interest in understanding their charts and themselves. I can't recommend this work highly enough.'

– **Sharon Knight MA. QHP. Chair of the Association of Professional Astrologers International**

One of the most challenging tasks of the modern astrologer is developing the ability to explain complex techniques so they are not only easy to understand but also delightful to add to the astrologer's toolkit. No one has done this better for draconics than Victor Olliver.

– **Alex Trenoweth MA (CAA), CAPISAR President and Ambassador for India**

'Victor's background in the legal profession and journalism has brought a welcome clarity, incisiveness and high ethical standard to his involvement in astrology. He brings those qualities to draconic astrology.'

– **Anne Whitaker, author of *Postcards to the Future: Mercurial Musings 1995-2021***

Chasing the DRAGONS

An Introduction to Draconic Astrology

How to find your soul purpose
in the horoscope

To my late mother Giovanna Bozzer

Chasing the DRAGONS

An Introduction to Draconic Astrology

Victor Olliver

How to find your soul purpose
in the horoscope

THE WESSEX ASTROLOGER

Published in 2022 by
The Wessex Astrologer Ltd
PO Box 9307
Swanage
BH19 9BF

For a full list of our titles go to www.wessexastrologer.com

© Victor Olliver 2022
Victor Olliver asserts his moral right to be recognised as
the author of this work

ISBN 9781910531662

Cover design by Andy Jay

With thanks to Astrolabe Inc (alabe.com) for the use of Solar Fire software
in the creation of horoscope charts

A catalogue record for this book is available at The British Library

No part of this book may be reproduced or used in any form or by any
means without the written permission of the publisher.
A reviewer may quote brief passages.

Table of Contents

Introduction ix

Chapter One: Draconic astrology: what is it in outline?   1
The South and North Nodes, and a very brief history of draconic astrology   1

Chapter Two: Soul, the draconic meaning of a life and...how a royal's angst is universal   13
Synastry of self: Prince Charles as our example   17
The timeless quest for life meaning   19
The question of soul   26

Chapter Three: Draconic astrology: the basic technique   33
Draconic transits   35
Draconic interpretation: the spiritual route map   36
Matters to be considered in draconic interpretation   38
Tropical and draconic orbs   43
Aspects   44
The Moon's nodal axis   44
The tropical nodal axis by sign and house: suggested capsule distillations   46
The draconic signs and planets: higher meanings and purposes   49

Chapter Four: The three-step approach to draconic analysis: case studies of notable people and celebrities   59
Queen Victoria: the challenge of independence   60
Karl Marx: the purpose of creating heaven on Earth   67
Hedy Lamarr: a genius talent from nowhere   73
Greta Thunberg: precocious climate activist and her inner struggles   79
Oprah Winfrey: mega-rich, mega-influential – a spiritual figure?   87

Nelson Mandela: overthrowing the status quo	95
Britney Spears: the fight against patriarchy and limitation	101

Chapter Five: Draconic forecasting: transits and solar returns — 111

The Covid-19 pandemic	113
Britney Spears again: a liberation forecast	116
Donald Trump: who wins the US presidential election 2020? Forecasting by draconic solar return	121
Pope Francis I 2020 controversy: sensitivity between tropical transits and draconic natal positions	125
Victor Olliver: a life purpose and the forecast of a death (or transmutation)	129
GlaxoSmithKline: do corporate personalities have souls? A multi-billion-dollar healthcare fraud settlement	134

Chapter Six: Draconic synastry — 143

Harry and Meghan: each other's awakener through Uranus	144
Queen Elizabeth II and Prince Philip, Duke of Edinburgh: an abundance of conjunctions	148

Chapter Seven: Six draconic case studies from my files — 155

Anne Whitaker	156
Margaret Cahill	164
Marie Davis	171
Stephen Gawtry	182
Sue Brayne	188
Alex Trenoweth	196

Epilogue — 205

About the author — 210

Introduction

If you are embarking on a study of astrology, draconic is not the place to start. Nodal or draconic astrology is a specialist technique that can only be utilised once there's familiarity with tropical (or sidereal) astrology. This is because draconic arises out of the tropical birth or event chart – as we shall see. Drawing up a draconic chart is not difficult; the challenge arrives in the form of interpretation. The draconic astrologer seeks to decode the chart for revelations of a person's life or soul purpose, and this requires a very different mindset from that for tropical delineation.

This book is not called an introduction for nothing. I aimed to write a straightforward account of how the system works with plenty of chart demonstrations. It's a starter pack with plenty of opportunity for specialism. Each chapter could be turned into a book in itself (it's tempting), such is the breadth of each subject. And I have left out a lot else.

I am a latecomer to astrology. For the first 40 years of my life, I dismissed astrology as rubbish. Symbols always did fascinate me, the power of icons and logos, but astrology made no sense at all. Then a relationship with media and psychic astrologer Henrietta Llewelyn Davies (now sadly passed) – whose columns and articles appeared in *The Times*, *Cosmopolitan* and other titles – helped open my mind to the idea that astrology is all about symbols. It is a symbolic language. Once this simple truth got past my obtuseness, I decided to learn more. And here I am today.

During my astrology education I never once heard of the draconic zodiac. Even when I became editor of *The Astrological Journal*, draconic meant nothing to me. One day I came across a second-hand copy of Pam

Chasing the Dragons: An Introduction to Draconic Astrology

Crane's *The Draconic Chart* and I was hooked. Coincidentally, around this time, astrologer Patricia Godden sent me an essay on draconic for publication in the magazine – and I am delighted to republish part of it in this book. Life, I felt, was nudging me towards a technique that blends astrology with life purpose as expression of soul or fate. My own draconic self-analysis proved to be peculiarly insightful, and I recount this in one of the chapters. Its truthful resonances made so much sense of an otherwise muddling or muddled life.

As I point out in this book, draconic does not require a faith beyond that in the symbolic codes of astrology. You do not have to believe in reincarnation or even in soul as a manifestation of the divine. But if you understand and are curious about the universal question 'Why am I here?', it is highly probable that draconic astrology could prove very useful to you in your journey of self-discovery and practice.

Chapter One

Draconic astrology: what is it in outline?

The South and North Nodes, and a very brief history of draconic astrology

The word 'draconic' means dragon-like. Once upon ancient times, people thought lunar and solar eclipses were the result of a dragon living in the Moon's nodes which dined on (or even blocked) the Sun and Moon during periods of eclipse. How else to explain the curious dimming and occultations of the luminaries? Astrology starts in myth and its symbols, so in draconic (shortened to 'draco' – itself a Latin word for dragon or serpent) we have fork-tongued dragons.

Historically, dragons as portrayed in mythology have represented an assortment of different energies, often evil and threatening – portents of doom. Think of the Albanian Bolla dragon that consumed people once a year or the Maori taniwha creatures that kidnapped women to take as wives. But as we shall see shortly in this chapter, to ancient Babylonians (the possible creators of draconic astrology) these serpents had a generally benign and life-giving connotation linked to the planet Jupiter.

Draconic is also called 'nodal astrology' and this is our first clue as to draconic's part in the horoscope. We start with the tropical Moon's nodal axis comprising the South and North Node. These are astronomical points in the sky, not celestial objects. These points are markers of where the Moon's orbit intersects the ecliptic – the Sun's apparent pathway – at an approximate angle of 5 degrees. The ascending (or North) node is where it moves into the Northern Hemisphere; the descending (or South Node) into the Southern Hemisphere. A lunar eclipse can occur only when the Full Moon is near either lunar node (within 11°38′ ecliptic longitude). A solar eclipse can occur only when the new Moon is near either lunar node (within 17°25′). These lunar nodes move retrograde and complete one revolution or cycle in just over 18.6 years (known by astronomers as the draconic or nodal period).

So, in a horoscope, a nodal return – that is, when the transiting North Node returns to the same spot as the birth North Node – occurs every 18.6 or so years. The North Node is also known as the dragon's head or *caput draconis*, the South as the dragon's tail or *cauda draconis*.

Later we'll learn much more about the astrological symbolism of these nodes, but for now, let's settle for brief, introductory outlines. The nodal axis (the 180° line of opposition of the two nodes in a chart) represents the pattern and direction of our lives, linking past, present and future. This axis is a symbolic portal to soul themes of the individual – and in the next chapter I'll examine what we mean by 'soul'. Note well, this does not necessarily presuppose a religious faith. 'Soul' may have a secular or atheistic theme in the minds of many.

Traditionally, the South Node is associated with past lives or simply the past in the present life. It has to do with pre-set instincts, with what is reflexively familiar or known experientially and perhaps taken for granted. It is a default position within the self. It may embody our gifts, our potential and/or supposed imbalances arising from past lives or this-life past experiences. In traditional horary, the South Node is called a malefic, but in draconic astrology this is not an appropriate categorisation. It is like the North Node, a zone of experience, of potential and of life direction and purpose.

The North Node is said to represent our destiny, the way ahead. It symbolises the challenges in life that we are set to meet. The life or soul purpose is always to grow, mature, excel, and this process builds on what we know already. Yet it may also involve a painful severance with the past.

Purpose is the focal point towards which we are headed through certain and countless types of challenge. In other words, the hurdles or obstructions we encounter in life are symptomatic of the need to self-explore or self-liberate. Experience helps to uncover what it is we truly want in life in order to get ourselves on the personal growth track.

What sort of life conditions may prompt an interest in the discovery or uncovering of one's life or soul purpose? Here are a few examples taken from my clients' lives:

- A general dissatisfaction with direction of life, a lack of authentic passion for anything or an absence of a galvanising interest. This may also be expressed as aimlessness or boredom.

- Recurring life patterns which are obstructive or frustrating, such as in relationships. You may feel that over and over again you are drawn to similar types of people with whom in the course of time you find yourself in a situation that feels like déjà vu, a repeat of previous relationships problems. Or in one's employment, you're forever coming up again obstructive bosses or managers, no matter where you work.

- A lack of rapport with people around you or in specific situations, perhaps at work. This may be due to a number of other reasons, but one may simply be that you have yet to find like-minds who understand you and your interests and likewise.

- An inner sense that you're not excelling or expressing your optimum potential but just coasting along. Engagement with life purpose should unleash the best we have to offer. The measure of success or failure is not always what other people think or about accumulating awards, degrees or accolades. What matters is what you think of yourself; whether *you* think you have done your best.

- Curiosity. Among my clients are many people who are successful and accomplished, who by the world's usual criteria have lived their dream and earned ample rewards, but who nonetheless have a residual doubt that they have identified the point of their lives. This may be poor self-judgement on their part. Or perhaps a dream or ideal got compromised on or before the career ladder, and now the inner voice is calling louder to be heard. The draconic trip does not always lead to riches and acclaim. Its measure is the sense of self-fulfilment.

- Serious illness. The prospect of death, an intimation of mortality or a sense of vulnerability because of frailty may trigger a questing interest in life in its broader sense, perhaps philosophically or religiously. The individual may review her or his life or desire to search for a greater meaning. Another question might arise: 'Have I accomplished what I was born to do? But what was I born to do?' It is as if the default position of many people in times of crisis is to expand awareness of what might be possible even if there are no words to describe what is sought. This may explain why it is not uncommon for people who survive a health or other serious crisis to want to bring about a fundamental change in their lives that has a more meaningful purpose. For an example of this, read Sue Brayne's story in the last chapter – she underwent a profound alteration in consciousness after escaping death in a plane crash.

None of the above may necessarily or exclusively be to do with the search for one's life purpose – psychological health and the maturation process may play a part – but derive from the reasons given me by my own clients. Draconic astrology addresses the question of what is likely to lead to engaging a sense of purpose towards self-fulfilment. Traditionally, the North Node is known as a benefic, but here again such labelling has no relevance in draconic. The life pathway may be very difficult indeed or punctuated by many moments of glory and accomplishment.

The nodal zones are pointers, not measures of favourability.

But how the nodes align by aspect with chart planets and points of course tells the astrologer the extent to which the course of life will encounter difficulty or experience opportunity.

The zodiac sign, chart house and even degree in which the nodes sit add meaning to the symbols, enabling an astrologer to determine what kind of life and what zones of experience will be the central focus – work, relationships, health etc – on this pathway.

The Moon's nodes, then, are concerned with life or spiritual purposes that are intended to bring out the very best in the individual. This process may be liberating, fraught with challenge or feel the most natural thing in the world. Each life is unique.

Most astrologers examine the tropical nodal axis and leave it at that. There are wonderful books out there demonstrating how to decode this axis – but only at the level of the tropical. The draconic system is specialist in that it invites the astrologer to delve more deeply into the question of a person's life or spiritual purposes. In this book you'll learn how to cast the draconic chart, which begins with shifting the tropical North Node from its natal position to the vernal equinox point, 0° Aries. The rest of the horoscope is then moved by exactly the same number of degrees and minutes as determined by the difference between the North Node's natal position and 0° Aries. But note well: the planets stay in their tropically assigned houses. So, if you have Mars in the 1st house, then in the draconic chart, Mars stays in the 1st house. What have altered are the sign and the degree. The aspects remain the same as in the tropical chart.

The core details I'll go into later, but right now I am offering a flavour of what is to come. If you're not fully comprehending the subject, don't worry. Things will fall into place as we proceed, especially when we explore the charts of notable people and a few of my clients.

One thing to appreciate at this early stage is that the draconic chart is *not* an alternative to the tropical birth or event chart. It is designed to be a specialist supplementary chart. It offers a magnification of themes that may already arise in the tropical chart. The draconic chart in some instances may very well reveal new things about a person's life purpose that are not apparent in the tropical, but for the most part there is a continuation of themes between the tropical and draconic.

The two charts are based on different zodiacs. The tropical is seasonally Sun-based because the Sun starts its annual journey through the horoscope at 0° Aries – the Sun has to do with character, what is known, events. The draconic is Moon-based with the North Node refixed at 0° Aries – the Moon has to do with memory, instinct, past (or past lives), reflexes. It is structured to examine what we call the soul since within it the connections between past and future are laid out with greater clarity and priority. But hold that thought for now and see how draconic works through horoscopes.

There are three stages to a draconic analysis. We start with the tropical chart, then proceed to the draconic followed by examination of the two charts in a synastry biwheel. This biwheel in all probability will have new aspects – the tropical Sun may now fall on the draconic Midheaven – and it is these that bring a whole new dimension to astrological interpretation.

A (very) brief history of draconic astrology

In the late 1970s, the eminent British astrologer Dennis Elwell – author of the highly regarded *Cosmic Loom: The New Science of Astrology* – gave a talk at an Astrological Association (AA) conference on draconic. This was followed up by his essay on this topic published in the 1977/1978 Winter issue of the AA's magazine *The Astrological Journal* titled 'Multi-Dimensional Transits'. Members of the Association can read the piece in its archive at astrologicalassociation.com.

This history journey takes us back to the ancient city of Babylon, the centre of Mesopotamian civilisation, as the possible birthplace of draconic.

In his essay, Elwell starts by expressing disillusionment with 'some of the effects' of tropical transits: in other words, events or characteristics do not always arise in the way one might expect (or at all) from transiting (or natal) aspects in a chart. Then again, astrology is not physics or engineering with literal cause-and-effect processes. Even so, he calls astrology a 'science' and writes that it must be possible to 'perfect' results in a horoscope. He advises astrologers to refine their techniques and look for other approaches to fathom the horoscope's subtler or hidden messages. (It should be explained that Elwell was something of a perfectionist as an astrologer and sought the grail of absolute accuracy in his charts – which to my mind does not accord with reality. No discipline, material or esoteric, can offer perfection or absolute accuracy.)

Among techniques explored is draconic astrology. Its history is scant. Elwell references Ronald Davision who in the 1950s wrote a 'couple of articles' on 'nodal positions' used in conjunction with the birth chart. 'So, I am convinced,' Elwell writes, 'that there is a complete zodiac beginning at the North Node (the ascending node), and that it covers the whole range of functions that we expect from any zodiac. It probably has something to say about character.'

Elwell reaches this conclusion after quoting from a short book, which is out of print at time of writing (but available as a free pdf), called *Zodiacs Old and New* by Cyril Fagan, published in 1950. (Western sidereal astrologer Kenneth Bowser is expected to republish Fagan's book in the autumn of 2022.) Fagan was an expert in astrological antiquities, especially on ancient Babylonian astrological and astronomical texts, and founder of the western school of sidereal astrology. Fagan asserts in his book: 'The astrology of ancient times was essentially lunar', mainly because people 'could trace the path of the moon night after night from the time of the first appearance of the crescent to the last', whereas the sun's path could not be directly observed.

Draconic astrology is a lunar system, and Fagan argues that the ancients classified people not by their Sun sign, but their Moon sign. He uses Roman Emperors Augustus (originally Octavian) and Vespasian as examples of this. Coins of Augustus 'show representations of Capricorn simply because the Moon was in that sign at the time of his birth. The standard of the Flavian legion bore the emblem of Leo because the Emperor Flavius Vespasian was born with the Moon in the 21st degree of the Lion'. Fagan goes so far as to say that the 'names and signatures of the constellations as handed down to us are essentially lunar'.

This area is controversial, especially because there is no agreement on the two emperors' precise birth data, but Fagan's understanding of the lunar nature of this type of ancient astrology has validity.

The key passage quoted in Elwell's piece from *Zodiacs Old and New* reads: 'According to a Babylonian myth, Marduk (Jupiter) created the Great Dragon, putting its head into the Moon's ascending node [North Node], and its tail into the descending node [South Node], making it carry six of the zodiacal constellations on its back and six under its belly...This implies that the Babylonians considered that the positions of the planets in the draconic "zodiac" (i.e. distances from the node) were of consequence.' Fagan goes on to write of the 'astonishing coincidence' that the North Node begins at Aries 0° in the system he analyses.

We have to be blunt here and acknowledge that Fagan reaches his draconic conclusion only by an implication. The truth is that there's no hard evidence that the Babylonians practised nodal astrology. The 'implication' is that they did indeed work with another zodiac other than the tropical, what we now call the draconic. There was sufficient information given for us to explore nodal astrology, especially in the 20th century.

Some people may think this a tenuous basis for a system, and ordinarily I would agree. But the next best thing you can do is to test and practise it to see if it works. Hence this book.

Elwell summarises the formula to create the draconic chart (remember, he wrote this in pre-computer software program days): 'Subtract the longitude of the Moon's tropical North Node from the longitude of each tropical planet and angle'. When we get to the charts, you'll see how easy it is to do the maths (or just press a key).

In passing, I mentioned at the start of this book that to the Babylonians, dragons were far from evil. The Marduk that Fagan discusses above was the protective though feared god of Babylon, patron deity of the city, and its planet was Jupiter. Among Marduk's sacred animals were dragons.

The astrologer and academic Dr Bernadette Brady, in a short essay titled 'The Old Man, Marduk and the Moon God, Sim – a Bright Jupiter is Curtailed', writes:

> 'To the Babylonian astronomer/astrologer Jupiter was "The Bearer of Signs to the World" (Rochberg, 2004:190). Its stations, as well as its times of disappearance in the night sky and then its rising before the sun, were all key times in the Babylonian astrological world view. For the great creator god Marduk was deemed to be, or to be expressed by, the planet Jupiter. He was the god who created order in the world by killing the dragon of chaos, Tiamat, and split her body in two, placing one half in the earth and the other in the sky.'

Brady adds: 'For the Babylonian skywatchers, Jupiter was one of the most important wandering stars, viewed as the protagonist of the heavens. Jupiter was Marduk.'

This is important to remember. The Marduk connection to draconic is mythically a supreme energy set to great, higher and momentous purposes. Our fierce dragons mean to do wonderful things for us if we allow them. Jupiter's association with higher, even divine purposes and protective qualities have survived into our age (albeit minus Marduk).

Elwell gives many persuasive examples of his own draconic research and findings – in predictive astrology, synastry, and so forth – all of which support the notion of a specialist chart that adds nuances to the tropical profile. He gives the example of someone who may be an Aries Sun, yet draconically is a Virgo Sun. Elwell does not spell out how this combination might look to an astrologer, but such a duo of Suns in one individual may point to a more considered or careful cardinal type than the usual combative and impulsive Ram. Or two such Suns may produce a rather bolder Virgin than might normally be the case. Also, the draco Sun could be an indicator of the person's higher calling or a hint as to the energies that could help in achieving a life purpose.

I'll return to some of these examples when I go into greater detail on constructing the draco chart.

The most significant event in the development of draconic astrology in the 20th and 21st centuries has been Pam Crane's definitive and comprehensive *The Draconic Chart*, (an updating of her 1987 title *Draconic Astrology*). It is rich in technical detail and case studies, applying draconic to many other techniques such as solar returns, secondary progressions, synastry, forecasting, rectification and horary, aside from the starting point of tropical nativity analysis. Crane also blends the astrology with her Christian faith and employs the multi-dimensional approach, such as her use of sidereal dwadasamsa in tropical charts.

She also makes an excellent case for suspecting that the American clairvoyant Edgar Cayce (1877-1945) used draconic to discover higher purposes in the horoscopes of clients. She does this by reconstructing draconic charts from given birth data and finding links between his recorded delineations/forecasts and these charts. Very convincing. Yet Cayce – known as The Sleeping Prophet because of his habit of falling unconscious into trance to access higher spirit intelligences – never described his astrology as draconic, so we cannot be absolutely certain.

On the nature of the Moon and draconic, I have selected three key observations in Crane's *The Draconic Chart* worth repeating here:

> 'In the tropical zodiac we find the *human* conditions of the individual journey; in the draconic is found what the *soul* brings to the experience – what it bestows, enjoys or must endure.'

> 'The tropical...maps our individual evolution...the draconic...shows us the pattern of our cosmic purpose.'
>
> 'The Moon herself by tradition is associated with history, roots, inheritance, memory and habit...'

In his Foreword to *The Draconic Chart*, Dr Jacob Schwartz makes a very interesting point about the 'equality' of the Sun and Moon:

> 'So, at last, after five thousand years of a dominant Sun/Earth-based astrology, the Moon, via her nodes, receives overdue recognition as a point of orientation rather than one "planet" among many. The Sun is 400 times larger than the Moon, and the Sun is 400 times more distant than the Moon, a curious coincidence that results in the Sun and Moon appearing to Earthlings to be the same size. Denizens of other planets in our system would never experience this phenomenon. The inhabitants of Earth are the only ones to perceive the equality and hence equal necessity of Sun and Moon. Isn't it about time this balance was acknowledged in the reckoning of astrological orientation?'

My book here sets itself the task of explaining in straightforward terms how to use draconic astrology based on my client and celebrity chart work – it takes the subject much more in the direction of life or spiritual purposes as the *raison d'etre* of draconic, and how in particular it is applicable to natal, predictive, mundane and relationships astrology. This exceeds Elwell's scope for draconic and develops, advances and modulates ideas well expressed in Crane's work. I have stripped away non-astrological factors and focused on a step-by-step treatment to speed up understanding. I have excluded horary, midpoints and rectification (as to the last, I am not persuaded as to its value, though it is for each astrologer to discover the truth of things for themselves once the technique in question is understood).

*

Chasing the Dragons: An Introduction to Draconic Astrology

Before we get to the technical stuff – a lot of which can be side-stepped by use of astrology computer software programs (such as Solar Fire or Astrodienst) which create charts in seconds – we need to take a closer look at what we mean by life purpose and by soul.

Chapter Two

Soul, the draconic meaning of a life and...how a royal's angst is universal

'I am both free and imprisoned...Nor can I *be* the thing for which I was born. I am existing in a timeless and slightly ridiculous abyss...'

These are the ruminations of an anguished Prince Charles. Or rather, a fictional version of Prince Charles as portrayed in *The Crown*, the hit Netflix historical drama series about the epic reign of Queen Elizabeth II. His apparent existential self-pity is actually part of a practical joke on his lover – now wife – Camilla during a dinner à *deux,* but the important point is made for us to understand about his plight through a light-hearted moment. It's a variation on James Joyce's *in risu veritas* (in laughter, truth) or Chaucer's 'ful oft in game a sooth I have herd saye!' – better known as, 'Many a truth is said in jest'.

Many critics of the series have denounced it as one long misrepresentation of events and royal personages and they may be right. Where would showbiz be without dramatic licence – or just contorting the truth for entertainment value? But what can't be denied is that there seems to be a grain of truth, a smidgen of credibility, in this depiction of the heir to the British throne. One could easily imagine him talking like this in a soliloquy of self-reflection (if not self-pity) even if in fact very far from the truth.

Over the decades, his public persona – as glimpsed through caricatures and the Palace memoirs of former aides and servants – all too often has been that of a man frustrated, obstructed, pushed about and compelled by his mother's longevity to be the longest-serving Prince of Wales (Wails?)

in British history. Satirical magazine *Private Eye* regularly sends him up in its joke romantic short story serial titled 'Heir of Sorrows' as a man forever disappointed, forever misled by false reports of Mummy's demise, causing him to run naked from his bath in excited expectation of kingship before making the crushing discovery that she lives and reigns still.

Charles' angst is really to do with perceived life purpose and his frustration at obstruction. His problem at first seems not to be a universal one: after all, he is born of privilege, title and wealth. What has he got to moan about? He has everything! Yet, his *quest* to live his life purpose – and his misery at not being able to do so – is indeed universal, once you strip away crown and ermine. Neither wealth nor poverty has anything to do with the instinct to fulfil the reason why any of us was born. It's as ingrained as any physical or temperamental feature. This profound truth is implicitly understood by the writers of *The Crown*, hence their preoccupation; and if this is doubted, read on...

In one episode of *The Crown*, titled the 'Dangling Man', Charles declares, 'Until [the Queen] dies, I cannot be fully alive.' He compares himself to the central character Joseph in Saul Bellow's first novel *Dangling Man*. Joseph is a man is the existential doldrums, without place or purpose. In one diary entry Joseph writes:

> 'The quest, I am beginning to think, whether it be for money, for notoriety, reputation, increase of pride, whether it leads us to thievery, slaughter, sacrifice, the quest is one and the same. All the striving is for one end. I do not entirely understand this impulse. But it seems to me that its final end is the desire for pure freedom. We are all drawn toward the same craters of the spirit – to know what we are and what we are for, to know our purpose, to seek grace. And, if the quest is the same, the differences in our personal histories, which hitherto meant so much to us, become of minor importance.'

In another entry he writes:

Soul, the draconic meaning of a life and...how a royal's angst is universal

'I am forced to pass judgment on myself and to ask questions I would far rather not ask: "What is this for?" and "What am I for?" and "Am I made for this?" My beliefs are inadequate, they do not guard me. I think invariably of the awning of the store on the corner. It gives as much protection against rain and wind as my beliefs give against the chaos I am forced to face.'

He seeks 'pure freedom' yet...

'We are afraid to govern ourselves. Of course. It is so hard. We soon want to give up our freedom. It is not even real freedom, because it is not accompanied by comprehension. It is only a preliminary condition of freedom. But we hate it. And soon we run out, we choose a master, roll over on our backs and ask for the leash.'

Not all of us do. Pure freedom – or just freedom – may be found in a calling, a passion, a destiny purpose. But the central point – to return to our fictional 'Prince Charles' as our example – here is: Why should the real Prince Charles or his TV fake version *not* wonder as to his actual life or spiritual purpose above and beyond the one assigned him by blue blood to one day 'rule' over us (Brits)? No one is too high or low of social status to ask the question. Most people wonder at some stage of their lives about their direction of travel and whether it's the right one.

As I listened to *The Crown*'s faux Charles drawling out his self-inquiries, I thought: 'Well, Your Royal Highness, perhaps an astrologer could help you out. There is in astrology a system that is geared to enlightening people as to the question of why they have been born and what their life purpose may be. The system is called *draconic astrology*, sir!'

At one point in *The Crown* conversation between Charles and Camilla, he reveals that Joseph in *Dangling Man* must 'serve his purpose' when he is called up to fight for the US Army (in WW2). 'Even if he'll be killed?' she queries. Charles replies: 'Yes. That's how much a human being needs meaning.' The joke that follows this exchange does not deflate the timeless observation. It is one that goes to the heart of draconic astrology.

*

Draconic astrology is new to many stargazers. But as we saw in the first chapter it can be sourced to ancient Mesopotamia, though its history is murky and not its strongest point. There simply is an absence of a documentary trail to be entirely certain of its provenance. History aside, I have discovered for myself – as have a few other astrologers past and present – that draconic has the potential to bring another, revolutionary dimension to chart interpretation. Draconic has its own zodiac, its own ephemeris – and its own 'frequency' which requires an approach that builds on but differs from the tropical chart's in vital ways.

Draconic sets itself the task of identifying higher life purposes in the individual, which we may also call 'soul' or 'spiritual' purposes. And as we have seen, the draconic chart involves a shifting of the tropical nodal axis to the cardinal starting points of Aries and Libra – this I shall explain in much greater detail in the next chapter. This shift in effect produces a chart that brings to the surface themes that may only be hinted at in the tropical chart.

Over and over again in my client work (often conducted 'blind' because I do not know the lives of many of my clients in the main), and in my analyses of celebrity horoscopes, the draconic chart clearly directs the astrologer to what I call the 'headline news' of the subject's life, the major themes that encompass life or spiritual purpose and the kind of experiences that may be expected to serve these ends.

In the last chapter of this book, I publish draconic client case studies and clients' commentaries to illustrate not only how true draconic can be but how it has the power to be catalytic and transformative.

Soul, the draconic meaning of a life and...how a royal's angst is universal

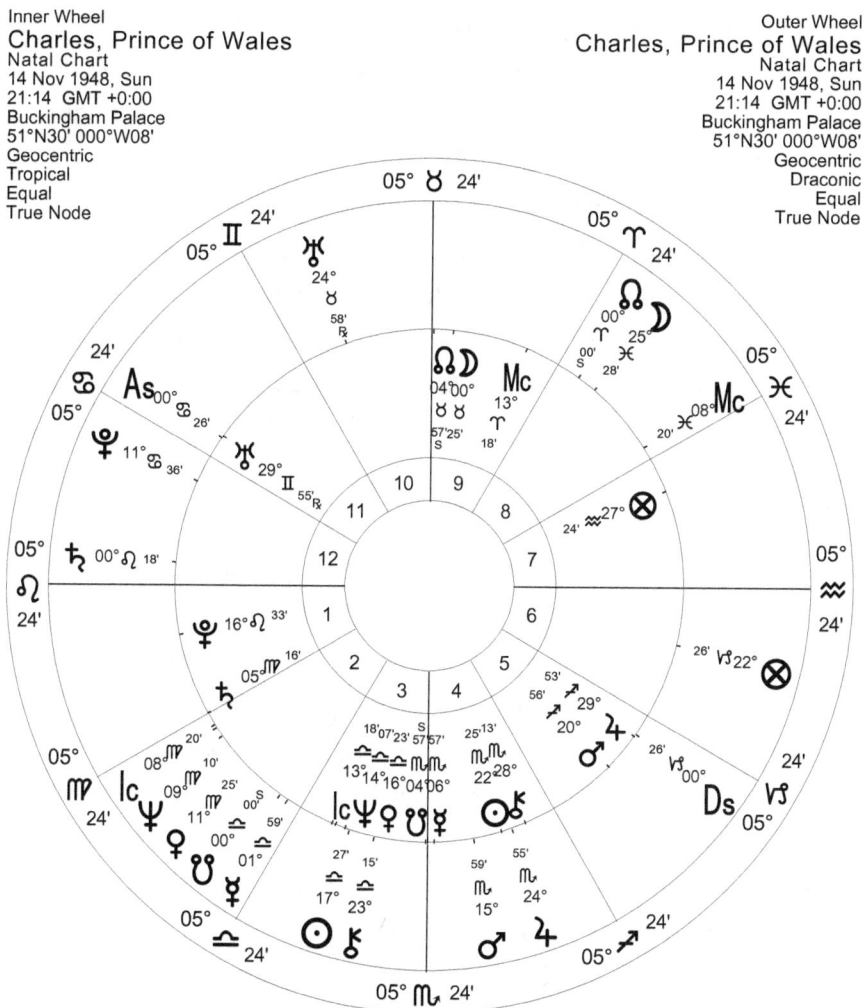

Synastry of self: Charles as our example

A vital part of draconic astrology involves what I call a 'synastry of self' (SOS) analysis in which the tropical and draconic birth charts are put together to discover what interaspects exist between them. Synastry, ordinarily, enables us to assess the strengths and weaknesses of a relationship between two people. A SOS analysis focuses on *one* person and seeks to identify life purposes and challenges at 'lower' (tropical) and 'higher' (draconic) levels.

Chasing the Dragons: An Introduction to Draconic Astrology

How this is done is detailed step-by-step later but for now let's take a glimpse of a draconic SOS. We have said much about 'Prince Charles' as depicted in *The Crown*. So, let's glance at the astrology of the man himself to see what his soul purpose(s) might be.

As we see in the biwheel, the inner wheel is his tropical birth chart, the outer his draconic. His tropical chart is fixed, fiery and angular, his Taurus Moon conjunct North Node leading an individualistic Locomotive chart shape. This already suggests a powerful nurturing and protective life purpose shaped by lunar themes. The tropical Scorpio-Taurus nodal axis does suggest the fateful invitation to turn deeply felt or profound themes and ideas (South Node in 3rd house in Scorpio conjunct Mercury in 4th) into practical expressions (Taurus North Node in 9th – or 10th in Placidus).

His draconic chart is a lot less fixed and fiery: water is now his major element. He is being encouraged to express his emotions, to show empathy, in the demonstration of the things he feels deeply about. His draconic Sun is in Libra, an encouragement to bring his passions (tropical Scorpio Sun) into negotiations and pacts (draco Sun Libra), to be more accommodating and less fanatical or severe, perhaps to be more effective. His draconic Moon is energised by proximity to North Node in cardinal Aries, so there is a capacity to initiate projects which serve his 'lunar' interests – this includes environmentalism and an appreciation of natural laws and cycles in which throughout his adult life he has shown tremendous interest.

Only when we put the two charts together do we get a clearer sense of purposes and circumstances. In his tropical/draconic biwheel SOS chart, abundance of inherited privilege and wealth is more plainly shown (draco Descendant conjunct tropical Jupiter in dignity in Sagittarius, and draco Jupiter conjunct tropical Sun). But I also see the maverick, independent thinking and decidedly troublesome tropical Uranus – aka the 'awakener' – tightly but out-of-sign conjunct his draconic Ascendant in Cancer, sign of nurturing, the land and profound sensitivity (sitting just opposite draco Descendant/tropical Jupiter).

Soul, the draconic meaning of a life and...how a royal's angst is universal

Part of his life purpose is indeed to cause 'trouble', to pioneer new ways of living. And just in case we don't get the message, draco Uranus sits opposite his tropical Sun in the 4th house: somehow or other, taking the world – or part of it – in a new direction is part of his destiny. This can only be achieved by balancing abundant entitlement and natal innovativeness. His royal profile may indeed help him in his labours, yet his true purpose is much more to do with the protectiveness he can bestow on those themes about which he feels passionately – and it is significant that the draconic nodal axis is shifted to the houses of value, values and shared resources, the 2nd and 8th.

With draco Sun conjunct tropical IC in Libra (and other tropical energies) in the 3rd house, it is told that his higher purpose power has to do with ancestry or family (this includes inherited power or influence), possibly the means to an end.

The real or imagined Charles may or may not wonder as to his life purpose and its frustrations. Yet given the range of his known interests and accomplishments in the areas of organic farming and environmentalism, it might be suggested that he has already tapped his soul purpose. Whether he inherits the Crown or not could be viewed as of secondary importance.

The timeless quest for life meaning

Meantime back to the central question at the heart of draconic...

It's a question both universal and timeless: 'Why am I here?' The 'I' is anyone, 'here' is planet Earth. There are variants on the query. Another one is: 'What am I *for*?' Or there's: 'What is my life direction, the reason for my existence?' Those steeped in a religious or mystical faith might wonder: 'What is my spiritual direction in this incarnation?' Or even: 'What does God want of me?' There are people who have lived a full, long, rich life who still wonder what all this experience amounts to, who seek a better understanding of self through memories. No matter how these questions are framed or worded, no matter whether you are atheistic, devoutly religious, philosophical, successful or not in worldly terms, these questions in essence are expressions of a common and fundamental life-driver: to find a way of living that serves an authentic purpose that leads to self-fulfilment.

During the Covid-19 global lockdown of 2020-21, a great many people all at once turned inwards to consider the value and direction of their lives. So many of us became a sort of faux Prince Charles-type. Suddenly, hundreds of millions of people found that they had a lot of time on their hands to re-evaluate their lives. In my own practice as an astrologer, I had personal experience of this phenomenon. I was inundated with client consultation requests to consider the question of life direction from an astrological perspective. Many people were motivated by fear, this is true. Fear of unemployment, penury, disease, losing loved ones and friends. But over and over again I heard something else. The release from routine, professional pressures and obligations created space to reflect on alternative ways of working and living – a great many people were granted a rare moment to consider the question of fulfilment and its absence.

What we call the demands of normal life – a straitjacket of schedules, duties, habits, expectations – were suspended and replaced by soulful self-reviews mixed with anxiety. So many of us had entered uncharted territory. There can be no universal consequence to all this self-searching. One can only speak of each individual – and this book arises from the individuals I have encountered, who shared their life stories with me and who have embarked on a new direction allied to their understanding of life purpose.

The instinct to seek self-fulfilment is not some modern, voguish development. Not in the least. It did not start with the Covid-19 pandemic, though a great many people *en masse* felt compelled to soul-search during lockdown. It is not the product of jaded, consumer or soulless technocratic societies whose populations self-dramatise in front of their looking glasses because they have nothing better to do. It is not self-preoccupation or solipsism or pop psychology. It is indeed timeless. And it is an entirely natural part of who we are and what we are about – essential to personal growth if we are not to live a life of frustration, disappointment or servitude.

Two-and-a-half thousand years ago, the philosopher Socrates said at his trial: 'The unexamined life is not worth living'. This ancient sage understood the value of self-examination to acquire a better understanding of self and life. Similarly, in Mahatma Gandhi's *An Autobiography: The Story of My experiments with Truth*, we witness processes of self-analysis to establish what is true and meaningful to him.

The 20th century American philosopher Alan Gewirth defined self-fulfilment in his book *Self-Fulfilment* as 'carrying to fruition one's deepest desires or one's worthiest capacities'. He added: 'To seek for a good human life is to seek for self-fulfilment.' It's not the intention of this book to blitz you with a plethora of *Reader's Digest*-style wise and worthy quotations, but simply to allude to a library of works by philosophers, sages, psychologists, writers, artists and others on the theme of life purpose and self-fulfilment.

Are self-fulfilled people necessarily happy or happier? That's another question. I won't even attempt to answer that one definitively here. But when I write 'self-fulfilment' and free-associate on the word, these are the synonyms that come to me quickly: passion, talents, realisation, self-expression, heart's desire, self-actualisation, soaring, vividness, engagement, authenticity, satisfaction, fun... 'Rings and jewels are not real gifts but apologies for gifts. The only gift is a portion of thyself...' – Ralph Waldo Emerson.

Happiness is not an inevitable consequence of finding one's purpose in life. Nor is success. There are too many life variables to pronounce on outcomes. But certainty of purpose does provide a directional structure; the sense of mission motivates and inspires. The quality of the life road is what matters, less so the destination, since how you get to a certain point matters more than the point itself. Draconic invites people to invest fully in the life mission that seems ordained for them, and this commitment to self is what matters. The engagement. The dedication. The *trying*.

Draconic does take us in an unfashionable direction. That life is pre-ordained or fated. However, it would be a mistake to suppose that any astrologer can be certain as to the nature of 'fate' (which literally means: 'It has been written') beyond personal belief. Some people will cite a deity as author of our lives. Others will assert confidently that genetics, environment, scale of opportunity, class, ethnicity or wealth are the main determinants of our life course. In this book, you will find no certainty on definitions of fate other than a working assumption that we have come into this life for a purpose and that we will exit it. What lies either end of our hatch and despatch, before this life, after this life, is not addressed in this book.

I like Anne Whitaker's observation in her very insightful book *The Moon's Nodes in Action*: 'There can...be a profound sense in the moment that something "other" is at work, impelling one's actions, one's choices.' So, let's settle for 'other' as the author of our fate. 'Other' is very powerful indeed and operates as a nebulous thing, perhaps as an impulse or feeling whose origin lies in mystery. Call 'other' a god or science. I don't much care. It's up to you.

Draconic does presuppose that the horoscope's nodal axis describes a life narrative, one with a story arc linking past and future via the present. We shall see in this short book that this journey is actually a transition from one state of being to another. There are no doldrums in the world of draconic or of life itself. Movement is constant; something is always happening for a reason. Anne Whitaker again in *The Moon's Nodes in Action:* 'The interface between fate and freewill appears, to our very limited knowledge, to be indeterminate, shifting.'

A cautionary note. It is not for everyone to think of life purposes in a conscious way, not at least in the terms described here. Spiritual inquiry is not for everyone – such an inquiry can presuppose a pre-natal experience that shapes the present incarnation or a purpose set by one's deity of faith or by a precocious talent. The materialist-atheist or existentialist may only register purpose through innate gifts and attribute their sense of purpose to hard graft. In this case, the life purpose question – if any – might be more mundane, such as focused on what kind of career should be embarked upon or the best place to find fame or relationship. Or how to get rich. These are not *per se* draconic questions. The horoscope may provide insights as responses to these questions by reference to other zones of the chart, such as the Midheaven position, but the draconic investigation digs deeper into the soul by casting a specialised birth chart.

There's a great line in 'The Riddle of Strider', a poem in JRR Tolkien's *The Lord of the Rings*, that reads: 'Not all who wander are lost'. Wandering may be part of one's life story, a seemingly aimless succession of experiences that's transient in feel, or 'purposeless'. I have learnt one thing from astrology, and draconic in particular: No life or experience is without purpose. Yet it may be a life purpose to live a life without seeming purpose, to suffer and delight outside of a structured understanding of the self. This kind of life may be a prelude to what Buddhists call 'subitism' (a sudden awakening) or what Christians call 'epiphany' (a moment of great revelation) – when all that has happened is revised by the individual as part of a pattern which points to purpose hitherto unseen. Draconic astrology can distinguish between a life of aims and a life that seems aimless; it can identify a life that must be free of self-conscious aims beyond the immediate in order to allow a natural process of self-enlightenment.

Whether such an individual is a billionaire plutocrat who lives for money and glory, or a wastrel pop star strung out on opiates, or someone oppressed by fixed ideas or servitude, is neither here nor there, in draconic terms. What matters is that one is *experiencing*. For some people, purpose is yet to be determined or realised.

The 2nd-century Greek stoic philosopher Epictetus viewed every experience as a potential lesson, a stepping-stone – and he should have known: he was once a slave of Rome, owned by a secretary to Nero. He endured great suffering but eventually became a freedman after the suicide of the emperor. His teachings are to be found in *Of Human Freedom*. Essentially, he taught that chasing desires is not to be preferred to the value of the inner life of subjective value – or what matters most to you. One's own perspective is what really matters, not the opinion of others. 'It's not what happens to you, but how you react to it that matters,' he wrote in a hymn to detachment from the madding crowd. The treasure of Epictetus is to be found in his honouring of what arises from our hearts – and this is the foundation of draconic astrology. Even in current times, of corporate and consumerist servitude, of tyrannous collective group-think and universal marketing of tinsel truths and philosophies, the individual must find her- or himself as a starting point of identifying purpose.

One must turn inwards for self-realisation. 'What is misfortune?' Epictetus asked. Answer: 'An opinion'. This philosophy detaches us from slavery to other people's values and agendas and relocates value in the individual. What do *you* think?

We talk of self-fulfilment as an aim. We speak of the desire to understand why we are born or why we seem to live lives on repeat – where, for example, one gets locked in the same kind of relationships, or one is confronted by similar sorts of problem in work, over and over again. As if life is lived on a loop of frustration. Draconic astrology presupposes that raised awareness of the self – which involves dispassionate self-examination – empowers you to discern unconscious patterns of thinking and behaving which may give rise to these loops. How other people react to us may be a feature of how we react to them in an endless dance of mirrored self-projection. Through self-consciousness (or shining a light on ourselves) we begin to see how we may be able to regulate our behavioural reflexes to bring about changes that launch us on the road to fulfilment (or less frustration), no matter how long this may take.

Soul, the draconic meaning of a life and...how a royal's angst is universal

The Spanish philosopher George Santayana gave us the great aphorism, much repeated: 'Those who cannot remember the past are condemned to repeat it.' What I have written just above is a variation on this truth. I would put it this way for our purposes: 'Those who do not self-examine get stuck in time and situations.' We individuate to release ourselves from parents or cultural restrictions, and then we must individuate again to discover what our spirit requires for fulfilment.

This is where draconic can be invaluable in breaking the loops of restriction or repetition that bind us.

The person who comes to ask the question of her or his life purpose is – by simply asking it in the first place – opening a door that cannot be shut. Self-curiosity is irresistible, but *this* self-curiosity seeks meaningful change. Something in what we call loosely the 'soul' is stirring. Something in us wants to wake up.

It is my observation, and one illustrated in this book, that the person who comes to me for a draconic analysis most probably has already an inkling of the answers to come. The astrologer Pam Crane in *The Draconic Chart* writes: 'People need little reminding of the ideals and intentions that lie closest to their hearts.'

The knowledge people seek from a draconic astrologer resides already within them. It is not the job of the draconic astrologer to act the guru and lay down a road to a destination as if teaching a lesson – some clients may seek this, but they are asking a question quite different from that being discussed here. Such people may wish to be tied and led which relocates impetus and responsibility from self to an outsider (the astrologer). The peril then is that the life becomes a sort of performance with a script written by someone else because the inner part of that person has yet to be tapped. This is not what draconic astrology is about. Draconic aims to give the soul a (louder) voice – and we need not fall out over the definition of soul. It is whatever you think it is, whatever your faith, belief system or speculation. Soul?

The question of soul

As an experiment for this book, I went to social media and posted a message requesting people to send me their definition of 'soul'. Here is a sample of contributions (those credited gave permission for their names to be used):

'Essence. It's what makes me, me.'

It's our individual fragment of the Universe or the Source therefore the part of us that is ageless and learned. It encapsulates our journey...'

'To me, the "soul" is what drives us onwards through life – whether we're willing or not. It's that "what's next?" feeling that seems to be an invisible draw to the next connection, the next thought, the next book. Like being on a quest but not knowing what you're looking for. And possibly a guiding light to get us through difficult times.'
(Margaret Cahill, director of The Wessex Astrologer)

'It's a sort of optical illusion resulting from the mind-body split.'
(Duncan Fallowell, author of *Satyrday, To Noto, or London to Sicily in a Ford* and other titles)

'I have come to the belief that our soul gives us the opportunity to physically express collective consciousness over many lifetimes in whatever way we are drawn to do so. It's never made sense to me that we have one life and that's it. I also believe an osmosis continually takes place between our soul's expression and collective consciousness, and life changes when we realise that we are responsible for how we co-create consciousness.'
(Sue Brayne, author of *Living Fully, Dying Consciously – the Path to Spiritual Wellbeing*. White Crow Books, 2020)

'The consistent guide on the many life pilgrimages.'

Soul, the draconic meaning of a life and…how a royal's angst is universal

'It is the timeless ephemera which is added to with each lifetime. We have the power to make it light or dark. I believe when we get our soul to translucency we do not have to return.'
(KP Voge)

'Spirit is my essence…my limitless source energy…my soul is my incarnated memory attached to karma, past lives, therefore my current birth chart, my culture, conditioning and purpose in this life. My soul change… Eventually the soul becomes redundant, and our spirit/source essence remains and does not incarnate.'
(Emma Gholamhossein)

'Soul is desire.'

'A temporarily differentiated part of the Absolute – the All.'

'A projection from and a piece of the Whole of Creation (or the Larger Consciousness System), comprised of an accumulation of experiences that is evolving, refining, raising its vibration, in order to evolve, refine, raise the vibration of the Whole.'
(Lisa Benjamin Paris)

'The animating consciousness that we have of ourselves as a self while we're in physical form.'
(US Astrologer Samuel F Reynolds)

'Immaterial essence that defines individuality and its humanity.'

Quite a cornucopia of different perspectives on which I make no comment. One of the contributors talks of 'karma' as a dynamic of soul, the idea of cause and effect working through an individual's past, current and future lives. This assumes that the soul is working towards balance or equilibrium. Dane Rudhyar in his book *The Astrology of Transformation: A Multilevel Approach* connects the lunar nodes to what he calls the 'karmic way'. He writes: 'Karma simply refers to the fact that any new cycle of existence is always in some manner related to or is [part of a] sequence of a previous cycle. The new cycle inherits from the old some *unfinished business* which needs to be dealt with, but it also inherits the results of some achievements.' He further writes:

> 'More specifically, the Moon's North Node symbolises new possibilities of growth on the basis of what has been accomplished "in the past" – let us say, in "past" incarnations…On the other hand, the Moon's South Node indicates in symbolic terms the pitfalls that the inertia of the past (or subconscious memory of past failures), places in the way of personal fulfilment…'

Rudhyar struggled to define soul. But on soul's function he pronounced: 'It is to serve as a base of operation for the higher type of integration – the integration of spirit and matter – during the periods in which the mind is entirely occupied with the processes of cultural, personal and individual integration' – what otherwise might simply be called living.

Many explorers of soul have resorted to opiates to access other spiritual and psychological dimensions, a Neptunian journey which otherwise is not without its addictive perils. One such explorer is Dr Christopher M. Bache, author of *LSD and the Mind of the Universe* and at time of writing, and among other things, is professor emeritus in the Department of Philosophy and Religious Studies at Youngstown State University, USA. In this book he chronicles his 'life-changing' cosmic consciousness travels induced by 73 high-dose LSD sessions conducted over the course of 20 years. He chronicles 'a shift from individual consciousness to collective consciousness, from archetypal reality to Divine Oneness and the Diamond Luminosity that lies outside cyclic existence'. On the matter of soul he offers this:

> 'However we eventually conceptualise the makeup of the Soul, the story of the Soul is in essence a story of individual consciousness –

moving systematically back and forth between the physical universe and the surrounding meta-universe on a long journey of self-development.'

The dimension he entered is a vast and impersonal soul databank of human experience so that in one trip undertaken he understood what it was to feel 'feminine' and like a woman, once he had stepped out of his conditioned sense of being a man. The cosmos he encountered is conscious and intelligent. In one interview he was asked whether the soul chooses to return to a particular time and place, presupposing reincarnation. Dr Bache's answer: 'Yes, everyone's soul [does]. In my journey work, the universe sometimes gave me mantras to work with, and one was: "Every being is perfect and deserves my complete respect". Each one of us is a warrior. You don't get to enter time and space without making certain commitments. People may not remember doing so, it may be buried deep within us, but just to be here is a remarkable accomplishment in itself and quite a privilege.'[i]

If Bache describes a reincarnation of the soul from a depersonalised place of universal experience, US astrologer Martin Schulman brings us to a personal cycle through astrology. In his book *Karmic Astrology: The Moon's Nodes and Reincarnation* (1977), he writes: 'Although we all live under the same karmic law, we each stand on a different rung of the ladder to perfection. Each step is a different growth phase [new incarnation], the most important of which is the one we are about to take.'

Thomas Moore, a US academic, philosopher, author, Jungian psychoanalyst and all-round multi-talent, is the author of the huge bestselling book *Care of the Soul*. He admits that a rational definition of soul is not possible though he characterises it as a force that ineluctably keeps us connected to life in countless different ways. In his Introduction to *Care of the Soul* he writes:

---

i   academia.edu/4093693

> 'Tradition teaches that soul lies midway between understanding and unconsciousness, and that its instrument is neither the mind nor the body, but imagination.' He adds later: 'Observance of the soul can be deceptively simple. You take back what has been disowned. You work with what *is*, rather than what you wish were there. The poet Wallace Stevens wrote, "Perhaps the truth depends on a walk around a lake."'

My grateful thanks to Anne Whitaker for drawing my attention to the work of Thomas Moore. Anne herself has a very interesting view of the soul, drawn from a surprising source of inspiration:

> 'My own take on that shape-shifting, not entirely definable entity called "soul" has in recent years most unexpectedly been helped along by reductionist science's estimate that, if the whole cosmos is energy, matter occupies only approximately 4%; dark matter occupies 23%; and dark energy occupies 73%. The existence of the latter two categories has been inferred from complex measurements, but no-one actually *knows* what they are. We just know they exist.

> 'So – we conduct our conscious, rational, quotidian lives within the 4% energy field. That leaves our personal unconscious and our collective unconscious 96% of the energy of the entire cosmos in which to roam about, allowing our imaginative faculties as free rein as they require.

> 'As I wrote in my recent essay on the Twelfth House featured in my book *Postcards to the Future*, this is where…the seeds of the future lie, where "reality" and "imagination" overlap, where religion and myth's "sacred time" resides, which myth describes, which can be perceived as God, Goddess, the Void, Brahman, the Zero Point Field…

> 'In short, that 96% field is the playground of soul-making…'

There's also a monster-sized genre of spiritualistic literature of purported past lives (recollections of pre-natal existences) or near-death experiences (aka NDEs, where the person physically dies briefly and later reports a conscious detachment from the body and encounters with spirit entities in another dimension before resuscitation and the return of the soul to the body). Another book could be written on this topic alone, but a good example is psychologist Dr Martin Newton's *Journey of Souls: Case Studies of Life Between Lives*. He used 'a special hypnosis technique' to unearth hidden past life memories in 29 patients. 'Surprisingly,' reads the blurb, 'they all displayed a remarkable consistency in the way they answered questions about the spirit world. Perhaps, it is not surprising at all. It is simply the truth. You can take this truth to help you understand the purpose behind your life choices and learn why your soul and the souls of those you love live eternally.'

Eben Alexander's *Proof of Heaven: A Neurosurgeon's Journey into the Afterlife* is another good example of a scientist whose supposed journey into the spirit world caused him to abandon the notion that NDEs are fantasies.

To psychologist James Hillman, the soul is that 'which makes meaning possible, [deepens] events into experiences, is communicated in love, and has a religious concern.'

Many clairvoyant mediums, such as Sylvia Browne, have also authored books on past lives.

In traditional religions, the soul is set within the abstractions of creed. To Roman Catholics, soul signifies the spiritual principle in humanity. In Hinduism, Ātman – the inner self or soul – is the true self. The belief in dual or multiple souls within one person is found in certain animistic traditions while in Taoism the ideal of ten souls is the starting point in determining how the soul will reincarnate. Some schools of Buddhism speak of *bardo* as a liminal or transitional state or space between life and death, a place of potential enlightenment (or dread for the less developed) before reincarnation.

Ron L. Hubbard, creator of Scientology, came up with the idea of the Thetan as representing the immortal, creator soul/self, one that reincarnates in a universe that exists only because there is agreement on its reality. It's said that Hubbard was impressed by past-life testimonies and created the Thetan concept in consequence.

The library of the soul is a vast one, as I have already said. We need only acknowledge the ideas of the soul's place in our histories, whichever history this may be. To me it is a mysterious feature that evades any absolute or agreed-on definition.

I said draconic gives whatever we call soul a louder voice. It is also a catalyst for self-realisation, a triggering of smothered or distrusted instinct for activation.

Only the questioner can know what is true to him or her. The astrologer can identify themes and central challenges; only the client can *recognise* them. Finding one's life or soul purpose cannot be delegated but one can consult on the matter for confirmation or for some guidance (to clarify and blow away mental fog or emotional distress).

Purpose can be known from an early age: a great talent may alert a person to it (the prodigal pianist, the precocious climate activist...). It may be discovered through much adversity or great success. There is no number for the ways in which purpose may be discovered. There are no age barriers or highway codes.

But among the numberless is draconic astrology – a divinatory practical tool that helps the client uncover or recover what they actually knew all along.

Chapter Three

Draconic astrology: the basic technique

In the opening chapter, I gave an outline introduction to the draconic approach. Now we will go over the same ground but in greater detail as a basis for a practical understanding of the subject. Our aim is to identify a person's life purpose(s). In the next chapter I will guide you through my step-by-step approach to analysis including synastry of self. In this chapter, there are basic rules to learn.

First, we create the tropical birth or event chart. Ideally, birth time is known to determine which two houses are home to the South and North Nodes. But even without birth clock-time, the signs in which the South and North Node sit will be an early indicator of life purpose themes. So, it is not the end of the world if birth data are minus time. The tropical nodal axis sets life-purpose themes in the linkage of past and future.

Second, we create the draconic Moon-based chart from the original tropical chart. This we initiate by moving the North Node from its tropical position in the chart to 0° Aries. We then move the rest of the chart by the name number of degrees and minutes as exists between the natal North Node position and 0° Aries. Computer software programs will do this in an instant, but it's a good idea to understand how this is done manually.

Let's take Queen Victoria's horoscope as an example (see page 61). Remember, the formula to create the draconic chart is: subtract the longitude of the Moon's tropical North Node from the longitude of each tropical planet and point. So, in Queen Victoria's chart the distance between her natal Aries North Node and 0° Aries is 19°44'. All the other planets and points are now shifted by 19°44'. For instance, the formula for her Sun

33

is: Sun at longitude 62°07′ (2° Gemini 07′) minus 19°44′ equalling 42°23′. Her draconic Sun is now at 12° Taurus 23′.

But only the signs and degrees are shifted. Planets remain in their tropically assigned houses. If you were born with Venus in the 4th house, it remains in the 4th house in the draconic chart (though there may be a shift in house if you alter house system where a planet is near a cusp e.g., Placidus to Whole Sign). But it will in all probability now be in a new sign and in a new degree.

Other details to assimilate:

- Nodes move retrograde. There are two types of node. Mean node which always moves retrograde and is an 'average' position ignoring the lunar 'wobble' (or libration). True Node takes into account the lunar orbital wobble, so it moves direct between two and five times a month.

- It is a matter of personal choice which type of node you use. Test on your charts and decide for yourself. Pam Crane uses True, I alternate between the two but prefer True. Dane Rudhyar recommended Mean.

- The difference between True and Mean is never more than 2 degrees.

- A nodal return occurs approximately every 18.6 years.

- The draconic North Node is moved to 0° Aries irrespective of whether the subject was born in the Northern or Southern Hemisphere. Rightly or wrongly, all charts are 'Northern' – a mathematical formula encoded in most software programs instantly converts Southern charts into Northern even though seasonally the Southern vernal equinox occurs on 22 or 23 September. I am aware that a number of astrologers of the Southern Hemisphere resent this 'flipping' of the charts, but this is not the place to debate it. For astrological purposes all springs commence on 20 or 21 March.

Draconic transits

Because computer software programs are routinely used to cast charts in moments, it is optional whether you want to understand the mathematics of draconic calculations. So, you can skip this bit even if my advice to student and professional astrologers is that you should always have an understanding of how results are achieved.

The draconic system has its own zodiac and transits. The 12 zodiac signs are used, but the speed of each transiting planet and point through signs is determined by the pace of the Moon's nodes. (As we have seen above, the Moon's nodes take about 18.6 years to go full circle in a horoscope.)

Accordingly, a draconic planet can spend up to a little more than 18.6 months in each sign (Pluto having the longest transits, the Moon the shortest), no matter the length of the tropical transit period. For example, Pluto's transit of tropical Capricorn is from 27 November 2008 to 21 January 2024. In that period, draconic Pluto starts at 18° Aquarius and ends at 10° Capricorn, falling not that far short of a nodal return, having traversed all the signs in between.

Retrogrades are not usually a consideration in draconic astrology (this may alter with increasing use of the technique). But draconic transiting planets do move backwards from time to time, even if this is not always discernible in some online ephemerides. To be certain, I would recommend *The Draconic Ephemeris: 1950-2050 At Noon* by Morgan C. Benton which (for instance) shows the draconic outer planet micro-retrogrades if you look carefully at the minutes. He has adopted the excellent habit of shading areas in tables where the tropical version of the planet is in retrograde even when the draconic planet is moving direct. There are other matters on calculations addressed in his short preface.

Benton explains the draconic calculation of a planet using the True North Node. For each day, the degree of the Moon's North Node is looked up in the tropical zodiac, expressed as a decimal number from 0 to 360. If the degree of the North Node is greater than the planet's degree, the following formula is used:

Draconic degree = tropical degree + 360 − degree of the node

If the degree of the North Node is less than the planet's degree:

Draconic degree = tropical degree − degree of the node

To take one of Benton's examples for the latter. At noon on 1 January 1950, the North Node was at 12.4814° tropical, about 12°29′ Aries. The Sun was at 280.51439° tropical, 10°31′ Capricorn. The nodal degree is less than the Sun's so there's a simple subtraction:

280.51439 − 12.4814 = 268.03299 (draco Sun is at about 28°2′ Sagittarius)

Other examples of calculation are given. In addition to the principal 10 planets, Benton's ephemeris also includes Chiron, Ceres and Juno. Doubtless in time other Trans-Neptunian objects (asteroids and dwarf planets such as Haumea, Makemake, and Gonggong) will be added to draconic ephemerides.

We shall see shortly how draconic transits impact on tropical planets or points by aspect and likewise how tropical planets and points resonate with the draconic.

Draconic interpretation: the spiritual route map

When we go through the horoscopes ahead, you'll see quickly how the draconic chart differs from the tropical in terms of treatment and interpretation. Observations are almost all based on my own client and celebrity chart work so this area must be treated as a work-in-progress given the thinness of historical antecedents.

The most important rule to remember is that the draconic chart is not an alternative to the tropical – a point that bears repeating. It is a supplemental specialist chart, a magnification of one area of the tropical chart, namely the nodal axis. Its area of interest is spiritual development, the direction of life travel, the identification of soul themes, major life challenges or opportunities. I have seen certain practitioners of political astrology treat the draconic chart as the principal when the tropical chart fails to deliver an election forecast that conforms to the astrologer's prejudices. This is not what the draconic chart is about.

Certainly, forecasts can be made draconically, and I have devoted a long chapter to this topic ahead. But the central purpose of draconic is to discover or uncover underlying meaning and significance, whether the subject is a person or an event or a relationship. We are looking in the draconic chart for what I call the 'headline news' of a life that sits behind what may be alluded to in the tropical. To this end I do not encourage the micro-analysis of the draconic chart: to do so is to build up an alternative to the tropical 'story' and risk misunderstanding the draconic significance.

The draconic story is not a parallel universe into which you enter if the tropical one is not to your liking. Rather, draconic adds new themes, new challenges, new perspectives that are intended to point to ways of learning from an experience or a life or situation.

In a sense, the draconic chart suggests a new destination point towards which one can grow in understanding which may not be apparent in the tropical chart.

To take myself as an example. My tropical Sun is in Gemini. My draconic Sun is in Libra. It's tempting to say, 'Oh, I have always felt more Libra than Gemini therefore from now on I identify with Libra.' I see this kind of comment quite a lot on online astrology community pages. In reality, I have never felt especially Libran (given the complexity of a horoscope), though I recognise many of the traits in me of Gemini. The Libran solar theme is a hint, though, of the type of life challenges I can expect to deal with and which I would be wise to work on for self-improvement or self-fulfilment – such as *liking* more my fellow humankind, making more of an effort to work with people in joint enterprises, negotiating, compromising; winning people over despite certain isolationist personal impulses: all Libran themes.

Social cooperation has indeed been a major problem of my life, a major challenge, especially in younger years. Underlining the point, my Venus (Libra ruler) is exactly opposite Saturn, an aspect of social struggle and possible alienation. More often than not, a chart repeats a major life theme in different ways. Draconic Libra does not mean that I cease to be a Sun Gemini, but I'll be a much more effective Gemini if I can absorb the wisdom of the Scales.

The draconic chart sets out the potential to grow and comprehend beyond the parameters of the tropical chart, even though problems and obstacles may be indicated: sometimes these impediments are central to one's draconic purpose. To describe a person's 'potential' in the draconic chart is not to say that a person is guaranteed certain outcomes or that potential will be lived up to, as we shall see. The person has to want to self-understand and grow, to have curiosity about the matter of life purpose, also to recognise the themes in the draconic chart, if spiritual progress is to be made.

Matters to be considered in draconic interpretation

Draconic interpretation involves an analysis of the tropical and draconic charts followed by a comparison of the two in synastry, a technique I have called the synastry of self (SOS). Flexibility is a hallmark of draconic in that the rules of the astrological system *you* use can usually be applied additionally or alternatively, with one or two suggested exceptions as I indicate below. For instance, a traditional (or classical) astrologer may wish to factor in such considerations as sect in evaluating the strength of a planet, using only the seven visible planets with traditional rulerships in a Whole Signs chart, and so forth. Personally, I am happy with modern approaches to astrology which may not please everybody – but feel free to apply whatever principles work for you. It is my observation that all astrology systems 'work' once understood if not mastered.

I am not a sidereal practitioner so can only address the tropical – but I see no reason why a siderealist cannot adapt draconic to their practice.

Main matters to be considered include in order (and this list is not exclusive of all matters):

- **The structure of the two charts i.e., house modalities, sign modalities and elements.** For instance, the tropical chart may be highly cardinal, indicative of high self-initiative, leadership, entrepreneurial skills, etc. The draconic chart may differ and show high mutability, indicative of strong communication gifts, a capability for objectivity, resourcefulness and flexibility. This is an early suggestion that the person's cardinal strengths may be tested with situations requiring adaptability. So far as the elemental balance is concerned, this too may vary between tropical and draconic charts: the former may have a majority in fire while the latter water. Passion is a central theme here that will benefit from a greater recognition of water's sensitivity, artistry, imaginativeness or latent skill in picking up on unsaid data. It may be the case that the individual with high passion may face a life in which there's a pronounced theme of finding fruitful compromises if other people's perspectives are to be respected. With house modalities it is in my view inappropriate in draconic analysis to attribute strengths and weaknesses to angular, succedent and cadent houses. Rather like the Moon's nodes, chart houses are zones of activity or themes of equal value: angular with start-ups; succedent with management and stability; cadent with learning and communication.

- **The lunar phase of birth.** A very useful starter in draconic analysis because it sets an overall life theme so often mirrored in other areas of the chart. For example, the New Moon type will have an Aries quality even if the chart is heavily earth with Capricorn rising. There will be a raised immediacy about the individual or a tendency to be involved in new projects and ventures. Fresh perspectives are preferred though earth will still be expressed in practicality or resilience. At the other end of the Moon's cycle, the Balsamic type has a Piscean quality, an 'old soul' energy with an instinct to find self-preservation in periodic withdrawal from the world, even if a noisy Sun Leo leader of fashion. Such a combination orients the individual to search for meaning in all that is embraced, to be very alert to trends and future-watching. It cannot be a coincidence that the majority of my clients are lunar Balsamics in search of life-purpose clarification.

- **Chart shape.** This is an important consideration, and I would recommend Wanda Sellar's *Chart Shapes: The Code to Interpretation* (The Wessex Astrologer), or the works of Marc Edmund Jones and Robert Jansky, if you've neglected this feature of the horoscope. Sellar advises that only the 10 principal planets (which includes Pluto) are factored into the assigned shape, excluding nodes, points, dwarf planets and asteroids. The shape itself – whether a Bowl, Bucket, Wedge etc. – tells something of the personality and life themes including strengths and likely challenges. And though the tropical shape stays the same in the draconic chart, the probable shift in signs may prove to be highly significant. For instance, a person may have a Bucket-shaped chart i.e., nine planets in one hemisphere and one planet as the 'handle' sitting midway in the opposite hemisphere at about 90° either way from the boundary planets. This raises the value of the handle planet because it is considered a pivot – life directions in general will be mediated by this celestial in an attempt to restore balance to the life, which seems lopsided by the cluster of planets in one half of the chart. Let's say that this handle planet is Mars in tropical Cancer, regarded as the sign of Mars' fall and a potential indicator of struggles to find independence or express anger. But what if in the draconic chart, Mars is now in Scorpio? This is a much stronger position, it's a chart 'promotion' (see below), because Mars co-rules the sign. This is a signal of encouragement to the individual that strength can be found in sticking to her/his points of view and not be deflected by other people – such an approach will help many endeavours as represented by the many planets in the opposite hemisphere. This is also an example of how the draconic chart urges us to raise our game in life.

- **Delineation.** Once you have assessed chart structure, lunar phase and so forth, both tropical and draconic charts are examined in the usual way, taking into consideration such obvious factors as planetary sign and house placements, proximity of planets to angular points and other aspects, aspect patterns, etc., to determine suggested personality and life themes. Pay especial attention to tropical and draconic chart rulers, the Sun and Moon placements, a planet of raised importance (such as its place in a chart shape or whether it is at the apex of a t-square or is the focal point of a Kite), dignity (see below) and other matters.

- **Promotions and demotions of planets in the draconic chart as part of delineation.** This is my terminology for what in traditional astrology is known as 'essential dignity' which measures the strengths and weaknesses of planets and points according to sign and degree. I must emphasise that this is an optional consideration – if it means nothing to you, learn it or ignore it. But I find it very useful, as in the example given just above. I do not apply all the rules of essential dignity. I generally do not recognise 'accidental dignity' – again, these are personal choices so use whatever works for you and your clients. But dignity degree can be useful. If draconic Saturn sits, say, in 21° Libra or Mars sits in 28° Capricorn – degrees of exaltation for these planets – these heighten positive energies and raise the 'profile' of the given planet. Dignity is a large subject and it's best that you see how it can be applied later in the book. But to summarise: a 'promotion' of a planet (where it is in dignity or exaltation) in the draconic chart is a strong indication of success according to various factors such as the sign in which the planet now sits; a 'demotion' (where a planet is in fall or detriment) is an indication of especial challenge, but not necessarily of failure. To take the above example of Mars in Scorpio: what if this appeared in the tropical chart and then Mars moved into draconic Cancer? This tells that the individual already possesses immense fortitude (Scorpio) but will likely encounter problems linked to dependency (Cancer) – the challenge will be to retain fortitude while maintaining a reasonable measure of independence in possibly complex family or other situations. Factors such as Mars' aspects will also have to be considered.

- **Tropical and draconic synastry of self.** This is the penultimate stage of the process. Having considered the nature of each of the charts and how they may vary, a biwheel comparison chart is drawn up. This in all likelihood will show new interaspects (aspects formed between the charts). Tropical Midheaven may now be conjunct draconic Venus in Taurus: this would align life direction with material value and moral or spiritual values: career may require the individual to hold firmly to an ethical line to an advanced extent in their work. It is part of their life purpose to stay true to what is held most dear as a quality or rubric. Tropical Jupiter may now be opposed by draconic Moon: this suggests that the whole draconic chart will have a series of opposites to its tropical version (because the tropical North Node is about 180° away from draconic 0° Aries, affecting all the other planets to the same extent). Finding emotional, psychological and other balances will be a major theme of a life that attracts extremes or plays on extreme traits in the individual. The invitation to the individual with such a chart is to actively consider other people's feelings and perspectives against a reflex to have things all their own way. Self-awareness may help to moderate. In the case of the Jupiter-Moon opposition, depending on sign and house, the challenge will be to invest one's higher purposes with emotional authenticity – life is not a game to be played with, not a series of theoretical dreams without consequences. Self-editing may also be a feature of this aspect since the temptation to over-express emotion may blight the life if not recognised as counterproductive.

- **Synthesis.** Probably the most challenging part of the entire analysis. Not only do you now have different perspectives of the self through tropical and draconic synastry analyses, each expressing a panoply of energies, but you have the synastry perspective. In practice, you'll find that certain themes recur throughout all three stages and that the synastry aspects enable you either to tie together certain themes already identified or to focus on powerfully indicated themes, through inter-conjunctions, -squares and -oppositions (-sextiles and -trines may also be used). Rather than try to anticipate every variation in this respect, it is best to follow me through the chart examples that follow in the next chapter, to get a sense of the draconic approach.

Tropical and draconic orbs

My advice is that you apply orbs that work for you. I allow as much as a 10° orb for the natal luminaries and 8° for other natal planets – however, the tighter the orb, the more powerful the aspect. Remember that the draconic chart is as much a birth chart as the tropical, so usual natal orbs apply, even in the synastry chart of the two.

In the case of draconic transits, as applying to or separating from a tropical planet or point, I apply a strict 1° orb either side, as with tropical transits. But some astrologers reduce the orb of transits to 30′ either side.

Aspects

I prefer to work with the conjunction, square and opposition in draconic astrology. The conjunction is the most potent and telling in my experience, especially when a tropical planet conjoins the draconic North Node (and therefore opposes the South Node). Sextiles and trines are also recognised, but usually these suggest secondary considerations of support rather than major themes. Though I recognise minor aspects such as the sesquiquadrate or quincunx in birth charts (tropical or draconic) I ignore them in draconic synastry. It's the big picture we seek. But this is an area ripe for further work.

The Moon's nodal axis

The axis really belongs to the delineation process but deserves its own category given that it is integral to draconic. We have already seen what the South and North Nodes each denotes. There is a considerable other literature on the subject, and in your own exploration, you'll find a rich variety of different perspectives. Ultimately it is for each astrologer to reach their own conclusions on the symbolism of the nodes by reading up on the subject and finding correlations in chart work.

In this book, the nodal axis represents the soul journey, whatever soul means to you and whatever the nature of the journey. The axis presupposes a constant quest in the soul to grow and perfect. And to this end, it seeks to show the life purposes that offer opportunity for equilibrium and self-fulfilment. The soul – even if unacknowledged – works through the nature of the individual through impulse, knowledge, inspiration, frustration and challenge. The nodal axis offers signposts to purpose but its work is not definitive: only the individual can recognise what is true to him or her. It is the presumption of this book that the nodal axis only tells what is already known to the individual, consciously or otherwise. The nodal axis may trigger a process of personal recognition through astrological analysis. If a given purpose is not recognised by the individual, it has no validity. The axis is not a substitute for a person's judgement.

In this section, I offer my summaries of tropical nodal themes (repeating many of the points made already but presented in capsule form) followed by short distillations of the South and North Nodes working together by sign and house in the tropical chart. These 'cookbook' distillations embody a prelude to the life purpose perspective before the draconic chart analysis – and I offer them not as formulae but as starting point suggestions.

- **South Node.** Symbolises our 'default' settings. It represents the talents and reflexive traits we are born with, along with inclinations that may arise in early personal development in this life, and from the culture, heritage and family, or from past lives (whether known or not). The South Node is not necessarily a zone of negativity or a 'malefic'. It is a symbol of what we are and what we may have been. It is the starting point from which further personal growth is possible. The soul abhors repetition and cyclic inertia just as space abhors a vacuum. The soul is drawn to those new life circumstances which have the power to build on what is familiar and known.

- **North Node.** Symbolises our growth settings. Commonly called the 'destiny point', this node represents the route to self-fulfilment or personal growth. The North Node's themes arise as a 'corrective' to, or development from, the South Node's areas of experience or familiarity. These themes may manifest in the life as a talent or driving preoccupation (as opposed to a clinical fixation) and/or through adversity or other challenge. The node may be regarded as a destination point in the evolution of the individual, reached by recognition of life purposes arising from ingrained talents and instincts.

The tropical nodal axis is where we start in finding life purpose. The draconic chart itself opens up the subject so that in effect we find multiple life purposes that may cover not just matters of career but also challenges related to emotional development, health, finance and other life areas.

Michael Lutin, former astrologer to *Vanity Fair* magazine, has characterised the nodal axis in an amusing way. He called the South Node the 'bottle' to the North Node's Alcoholic Anonymous meeting. The South Node has its comforts, but progress won't be made there sticking to old ways or habits and assumptions. The AA 'meeting' place of the North Node is the place for confronting what may be holding you back, and assures you progress once you have embarked on a new life pattern. The North Node will stretch your capacities and may not be easy, yet to embrace its message is to refresh the soul journey.

The tropical nodal axis by sign and house: suggested capsule distillations

Abbreviations: South Node (SN). North Node (NN)

SN in Aries (1st), NN in Libra (7th)

The urge to act alone is complicated by events requiring joint or cooperative action. Outcomes improve through compromise, negotiation and diplomacy.

NN in Aries (7th), SN in Libra (1st)

Joint enterprises require a sharing of experiences, yet it is also important to preserve personal independence within relationships. Boundaries may be tested.

SN in Taurus (2nd), NN in Scorpio (8th)

Material security is sought before other considerations even if little satisfaction is found. Life presents you with opportunities to face fundamental risks and apparent losses on the road to discovering that there's much to be gained from acceptance that life can never be static.

NN in Taurus (8th), SN in Scorpio (2nd)

The search for stability may be frustrated by a turbulent nature driven by unfocused anger and a craving for constant, disruptive change. The practicalities of home and self-responsibility, and a respect for stabilising value and values, help to bring balance to a life through routines and returns on hard, consistent work.

SN in Gemini (3rd), NN in Sagittarius (9th)

Expressive and naturally communicative, with a tendency to dilettantism and toying with ideas and fads, life situations will arise which encourage specialism and commitment to higher learning or a faith. The mind wishes to embrace through knowledge.

NN in Gemini (9th), SN in Sagittarius (3rd)

High-mindedness may lead to dogmatism or holier-than-thou attitudes when what will get you to a better place is both a less personal identification with ideas and a more playful curiosity that has objectivity.

SN in Cancer (4th), NN in Capricorn (10th)

Emotional attachments and subjective judgements must yield to more objectivity, at least in certain matters, such as career or public responsibilities. There's a big world out there beyond the micro-realms of family or cherished sensitivities.

NN in Cancer (10th), SN in Capricorn (4th)

A natural tendency to place order or structure over emotional realities can lead to much pain – often inflicted on others through a lack of empathy. The life lesson is to grow a heart.

SN in Leo (5th), NN in Aquarius (11th)

Immense talent and energies can be dedicated to a personal passion, but life will draw you into collective activity where broader, impersonal or humanitarian causes or objectives benefit from your drive.

NN in Leo (11th), SN in Aquarius (5th)

You're happy to work in teams but may find that you're suppressing a natural talent that is hidden in collective actions. In this life, no matter your circumstances, allow your star quality to shine. Time to step up.

SN in Virgo (6th), NN in Pisces (12th)

Too often priorities are warped by excessive preoccupation with detail and practicalities. Rigour is good but what is now needed is also a higher perspective, one that sees the bigger picture. Trusting the flow of life can be more effective than micro-managing.

NN in Virgo in 12th, SN in Pisces

Unachievable ideals or indifference to the realities of day-to-day life obstruct progress. Life now requires applying great ideas and principles to the tests of rigour and critique. Feet must be placed on the ground.

Once you have identified the themes of the tropical nodal axis, these can be applied to the tropical-draconic synastry biwheel chart where the nodal axis may have shifted to different houses: this new position helps to identify the life area that may be particularly relevant for the application of the tropical nodal axis themes. So, if for example, tropical SN is in Virgo (or 6th house)/ NN is in Pisces (or 12th house), and the draconic nodal axis now falls in the 2nd/8th houses of the biwheel, with NN in the 2nd, the need to raise the mind may be relevant to financial matters or anything to do with values.

Bear in mind that draconic houses are symbolically the same as those of the tropical.

The draconic signs and planets: higher meanings and purposes

In this section an attempt is made to distinguish the draconic meaning of each of the signs and planets from their tropical equivalents. Our starting point may be paradoxical in that the signs and planets signify the same generic themes in either zodiac, but in the draconic chart, we seek the potential of the 'higher' or universal expression of each sign and planet.

I was encouraged to give greater thought to this topic while re-reading an excellent essay on draconic astrology by Patricia Godden – in fact I published it in *The Astrological Journal* in 2017. It is titled 'Draconic Astrology: The Soul's Impulses' and can be read at astrologicalassociation.com by members of the Astrological Association. Scientist-turned-astrologer Patricia has generously granted me permission to use the essay on draconic themes, arising from a series of her meditations on each sign and planet. The republished section below is not the whole essay, I should add. Patricia asks me to emphasise that what follows are brief summaries of much longer assessments and are part of a much more substantial work-in-progress.

I am happy to endorse these esoteric meditations as prompts for further exploration. How all this works in practice is demonstrated afterwards.

Key phrases from meditations on signs in the draconic zodiac
By Patricia Godden

Attempting to work out what the soul is striving to do in a lifetime is a deep and profound aspiration. One way to understand the subtle and intangible nature of the soul and its objectives is through meditation. Meditating on the draconic level of the planets and signs of the draconic zodiac provided insights into how they may be interpreted. Some of the meditations were simple, others were more involved. The following are key phases from the meditations. In some cases, the draconic meanings of the planets and signs were a deeper level of the tropical interpretations. In other cases, draconic meditations were in total contrast to tropical meanings. The comments below attempt to explain this. The word 'Source' is used for that energy that has created all life.

Key phrases from meditations on signs in the draconic zodiac

Draconic Aries

The pure impulse to reach the Creator. Single-pointed direction to the Source of life.

Comment: This is a deeper focus for the direct approach characteristic of tropical Aries.

Draconic Taurus

There is no possession and no ownership because everything is of Source. The draconic level of Taurus is associated with the beauty and light of Source coming to Earth.

Comment: The first part of this meditation concerning the non-possessive nature of Taurus at the draconic level is different from the security derived from ownership and tangible assets associated with tropical Taurus. However, that part of tropical Taurus that is sensuous and loves beauty, particularly the beauty of nature, resonates with some of the attributes of draconic Taurus.

Draconic Gemini

This meditation indicated an emanation from the mind of Source with its infinite intellect and knowledge. This mind was absolute stillness.

Comment: This is one of the greatest differences between the draconic and tropical zodiacs. At the tropical level, Gemini is concerned with gathering many pieces of information necessitating communication, connecting things, and busy-ness. At the draconic level, there is complete stillness. This may be because at the level of the infinite mind, all information is already connected so there is no need for communication. Infinite mind is all information, knowledge and wisdom

Draconic Cancer

Spiritual light from Source feeds and sustains all life. All life is always cared for.

Comment: This is similar to the caring and nurturing qualities of tropical Cancer but applied to all levels of life.

Draconic Leo

I am in everything. I am everything. I am the Life in every cell. Spiritual Sun. Pure White Light.

Comment: Whereas tropical Leo is associated with recognition of individuality, draconic Leo relates to acknowledgement of the true self: the spirit in a human body.

Draconic Virgo

Source was pouring golden light onto the world, teaching it, correcting it. Earth is held in the golden light of Source. Earth is adapting and moving to the perfection of Source as even that evolves.

Comment: The perfection sought by tropical Virgo is a human manifestation of the soul striving towards the ever-evolving perfection of Source.

Draconic Libra

The centre understands that which is around it because all is one. I am in Source and It is in me.

Comment: Tropical Libra is associated with finding peace through harmonising different factions. At the draconic level, this quality is extended to a much deeper level, that of knowing what each party experiences, which can affect the choice of actions taken.

Draconic Scorpio

Transformation and alchemy are parts of the mysteries of life, but the real mystery is what drives these changes. Draconic Scorpio is the drive to know the mysteries of life, to understand alchemy and Source.

Comment: This is a deeper level of those facets of tropical Scorpio that seek transformation and regeneration.

Draconic Sagittarius

The forehead of a beautiful white horse touched the forehead of Source – 'third eye' to 'third eye'. Infinite wisdom flowed from Source. There was clarity of truth.

Comment: Physical and mental freedom so loved by tropical Sagittarius expands into striving for infinite truth and wisdom at the draconic level.

Draconic Capricorn

Each world acts as a portal into other worlds. All dimensions of all worlds fit together like a multi-dimensional jigsaw. Source knows the order, direction and structure of everything, and how it all fits together. It is directing earthly life through the soul.

Comment: The structure and organisation of physical life associated with tropical Capricorn is extended in the draconic zodiac to include the structure and organisation of all levels of life.

Draconic Aquarius

A cube opens to form a cross. Light comes out of the centre of the cross. The light is the truth of Source. The light and truth of Source is beyond human comprehension but an impulse attempts to help people understand it.

Comment: Tropical Aquarius strives to find truth through originality and independence. This is taken to a deeper level in the draconic zodiac.

Draconic Pisces

There is expansion into all of the known universe and then into many other universes and many levels of life. There is awareness of the oneness of all life, which then expands beyond it.

Comment: Draconic Pisces extends the transcendental qualities of tropical Pisces to encompass all levels of life, known and unknown.

Key phrases from meditations on the planets in the draconic zodiac

Draconic Sun

The spirit of the Sun is interacting with the beings of the planets. All is light. All is one. All is life.

Comment: This is similar to spirit being associated with the tropical Sun. However, it feels much deeper in the draconic zodiac.

Draconic Moon

Draconic Moon indicates that part of that totality of spirit and all possible experiences that the soul has chosen to undergo in this lifetime. All other experiences are for other lives.

Comment: The tropical interpretation of the Moon includes how a person reacts and factors to do with security. It can also indicate past soul experiences. Draconic Moon indicates the part of spirit that the soul has chosen to experience now, in this life.

Draconic Mercury

Draconic Mercury is associated with the mind of Source. This infinite mind knows what is happening everywhere and all the time. It is all knowledge and all knowing.

Comment: Tropical Mercury indicates the mind, how a person thinks and communicates. The principles of draconic Mercury are similar but elevated beyond conscious thought and the physical level of life suggesting that the soul is striving to surpass the limitations of the human intellect.

Draconic Venus

The infinite love coming from Source is too much for people currently on Earth to deal with. Venus reduces that all-encompassing love to what a human can cope with in an incarnation.

Comment: At the tropical level, Venus signifies beauty, what a person values and what brings pleasure. It also shows how and what a person loves. The draconic level of Venus indicates that part of the total love of Source that the soul is working on in the current life.

Draconic Mars

Draconic Mars is associated with the courage, strength and power of Source. All is one power. It is self-less. There is no individuality. Consideration is from an all-is-one perspective.

Comment: There are similarities between tropical and draconic Mars regarding courage and strength. However, at the draconic level, this is for the good of all rather than for pursuing personal desires and urges associated with tropical Mars.

Draconic Jupiter

Consciousness went up and up until it was close to the Sun, which is spirit. Here everything was very still: the stillness of inner truth. It was like nothingness that was everything. This was profound.

Comment: Tropical Jupiter relates to opportunities, expansion, self-improvement and trust in life. At the draconic level, this planet shows how the soul is striving for infinite wisdom and truth.

Draconic Saturn

There were two images for draconic Saturn. Both relate to karma. In the first one, a jewel opened to form a rose. Karma went into the centre of the rose and the solution to the karma emerged. In the second image, the soul went into a circle of radiant beings and there realised how to resolve previous karma. There was no judgement apart from how the soul judged itself.

Comment: Tropical Saturn relates to restrictions and limitations that teach a person what he or she most needs to learn. The above description of draconic Saturn suggests that the soul chooses what it needs to work on in this lifetime.

Draconic Uranus

A picture summarising draconic Uranus would be of a coloured star that represents physical life. Within it is a silver star, which is the soul. Within that is a white star that represents the truth, purity, power, infinite love and wisdom of Source. These factors are so fine and powerful that they are beyond what humans can process. Draconic Uranus is the transformer, stepping down the absolute qualities of spirit to what humans can deal with.

Comment: At the tropical level, Uranus indicates sudden and unexpected events, originality and humanitarian ideals, all of which bring a person closer to his or her inner truth. The position of draconic Uranus indicates that part of the absolute truth of Source that the soul wants to approach in the current life.

Draconic Neptune

Meditating on draconic Neptune was like looking at something through a sheet of glass. The gaze could fall on the glass and look at the illusion and confusion of the reflection or look through the glass towards infinity and Source.

Comment: Tropical Neptune is linked with illusion, imagination, impermanence and transcending boundaries. Draconic Neptune indicates the soul striving to see through the illusion of physical life and transcend this limitation to become one with the infinite and eternal Source.

Draconic Pluto

The spirit of power, which is unconditional love applied with infinite wisdom, and the power of Spirit. There was a feeling of dynamic stillness, that of maintaining perfection as it evolves.

Comment: Tropical Pluto is associated with change and transformation, beginnings and endings. These can be traumatic at the physical level of manifestation. At the draconic level, there is absolute stillness within evolving perfection. Tropical Pluto can relate to power. Draconic Pluto indicates how the soul is trying to reach the power associated with the love and wisdom of Source.

Draconic Chiron

A radiant being was cradling something like a very big seed pod. This is the purity of the soul as it buds off spirit to come into a human body to gather experience in the physical plane of life. Draconic Chiron indicates the perfection and purity of spirit and how the love emanating from this helps the soul through the experiences of life. It is the love that heals.

Comment: Draconic Chiron indicates the fine essence stemming from Source that drives the soul to heal unresolved human issues, which are associated with the position of tropical Chiron.

Chapter Four

The three-step approach to draconic analysis: case studies of notable people and celebrities

We have gone through the basic rules of draconic astrology and addressed the question of soul and its part in fate or life purpose. In this section, we'll observe these rules in action, applied to the charts of notable or historical people and celebrities. We have at least the benefit of hindsight to test astrological observation against actual outcomes.

Analysis involves a three-step approach which I have discovered for myself is thorough, layered and accurate. The question of life purpose is not a glib one that can be answered in a couple of pat sentences, as if the draconic chart were a fortune cookie. The question is profound in its importance, sacred if a religious belief is the predication of life, so the analysis must be equal in weight to the challenge and reality. Lives can be messy and complicated, or epic in scale of experience. A draconic analysis sets out purposes at different levels, adding nuance, step-by-step. Ultimately, as I indicated earlier, it is for the subject of the horoscope to resonate with the analysis, to recognise its truth (or not) through memory and experience.

The three steps of analysis are straightforward enough. Step 1 involves the tropical birth (or event) chart. Step 2 the draconic version of the tropical birth or event chart. Step 3 brings together the tropical and draconic charts in a synastry biwheel for an examination of interaspects, leading to a number of statements about life purpose(s). Step 3 is the synastry of self analysis already explained.

Step 1 tends to set basic life themes pertinent to purposes, such as the signs and houses of the nodal axis. Among other things, note especially planets that are conjunct either one of the nodes: these bring their themes to questions of fate and destiny. Step 2's draconic analysis will usually show planets and points in different signs and degrees, depending on the distance between the natal North Node position and the vernal equinox point. In the previous chapter I identified the key things to look out for, such as planetary promotions and demotions (or dignities) between the two charts. Step 2 will tend to show how the individual best conducts their life, or which strategies to adopt, in the quest for fulfilment. Step 3 is a synthesis of sorts, often confirming themes thrown up by Steps 1 and 2, but also emphasising other matters with shifts in house positions and interaspects. The result is a 'layered' analysis which juxtaposes basic life challenges and purposes with those that draw on higher energies or consciousness.

The best way to understand these abstract rules is to study charts, to practise.

I'd like to return to two people analysed in Dennis Elwell's late 1970s' *Astrological Journal* essay: Queen Victoria and Karl Marx.

Queen Victoria: the challenge of independence

Step 1: Victoria's topical natal chart. It's a surprisingly 'young soul' chart, full of vibrant energy and forthrightness, and bears little resemblance to many of the stultifying characteristics we associate with 19th century Britain in her name, the co-called Victorian Era.

The princess was born under a rising and impulsive New Moon in Gemini with Venus and Mars in Aries and Midheaven in Aquarius. The chart is highly mutable and airy with a high cadent score (telling us of a powerful need to communicate and self-express) even if many planets are close to the angles: no surprise, then, that throughout her life from the

The three-step approach to draconic analysis

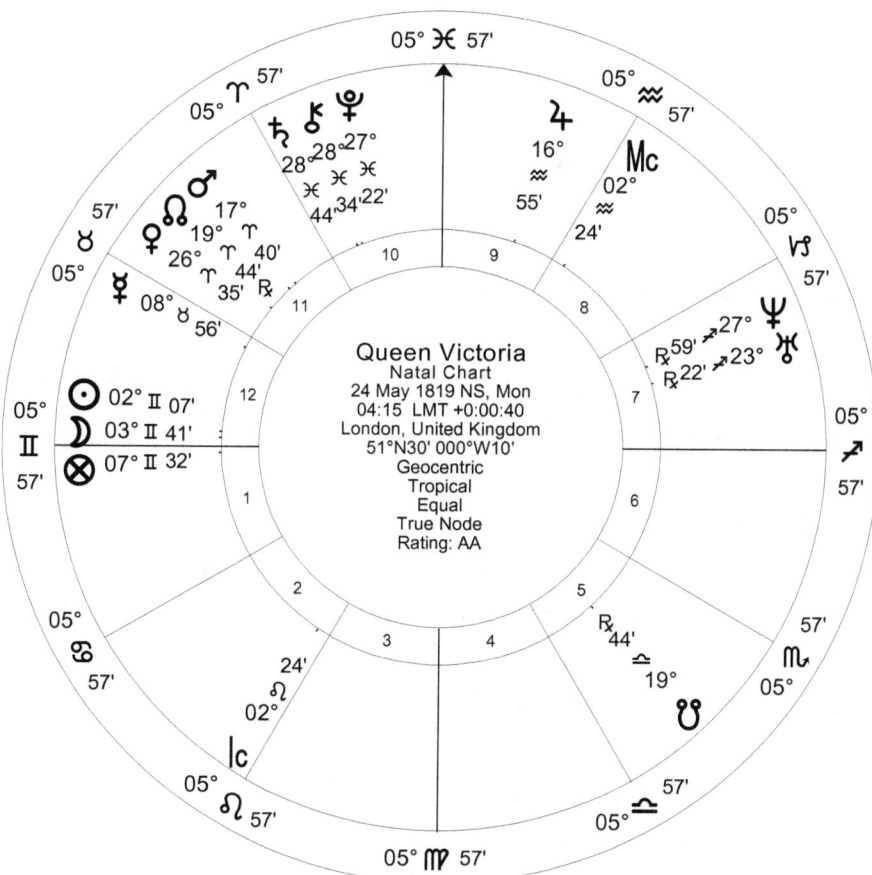

age of 13 to up to 10 days before her death in 1901 aged 81, she maintained private journals, now collected in 141 volumes and running to 43,000 pages.

These diaries were so frank in their original form that Princess Beatrice, Victoria's youngest daughter and literary executor, expurgated them of anything deemed scandalous or transgressive to the royal family. A great many of her letters were also destroyed.

All that cadent and Gemini energy found an outlet in an interior world of record.

The nodal axis cuts across the 5th and 11th houses with – as we have seen already – North Node in Aries in the 11th house. This sets the theme of finding or preserving personal identity in the house of collectives – and the keeping of diaries may be viewed as one manifestation of an independent perspective, a psychic place solely her own.

As constitutional Queen under the thumb of Parliament she was notoriously difficult to 'manage': she broke with traditions, often resisting the wishes of her Prime Ministers. And after the death of her consort Albert, she withdrew from public life for 10 years. Her later-life platonic but intimate friendship with her Indian Secretary Mohammed Abdul Karim scandalised her court and realm just as much as her earlier bond with personal attendant John Brown had triggered envy, suspicion and gossip.

Her South Node in the 5th and in Libra suggests that an essential component of growth in this incarnation is the transition from 'two' of the couple to 'one' of the self, from the intimacy or support of partnership to finding oneself as a singleton. The early death of Albert, a terrible blow to her, was a rebirth moment when she was given the opportunity to find her strength and reset her needs.

Her tropical chart establishes independence against the 'group' or society as a major element of her life purpose. As if to accentuate this point, note that the chart shape is a Bowl with Uranus – planet of rebelliousness, independence, innovation – the lead planet in the 7th, zone of partnership. Whatever life lesson had to be learnt most probably would arise from an unexpected occurrence or fracture in partnership(s).

In another sense, Uranus brought her close, nonconformist friendships with male friends such as Mr Brown and Abdul Karim.

Step 2: Victoria's draconic natal chart. All planets and points are shifted by 19°44′ because this is the distance between Victoria's natal North Node and 0° Aries. But of course, planets remain in their tropically assigned houses.

The three-step approach to draconic analysis

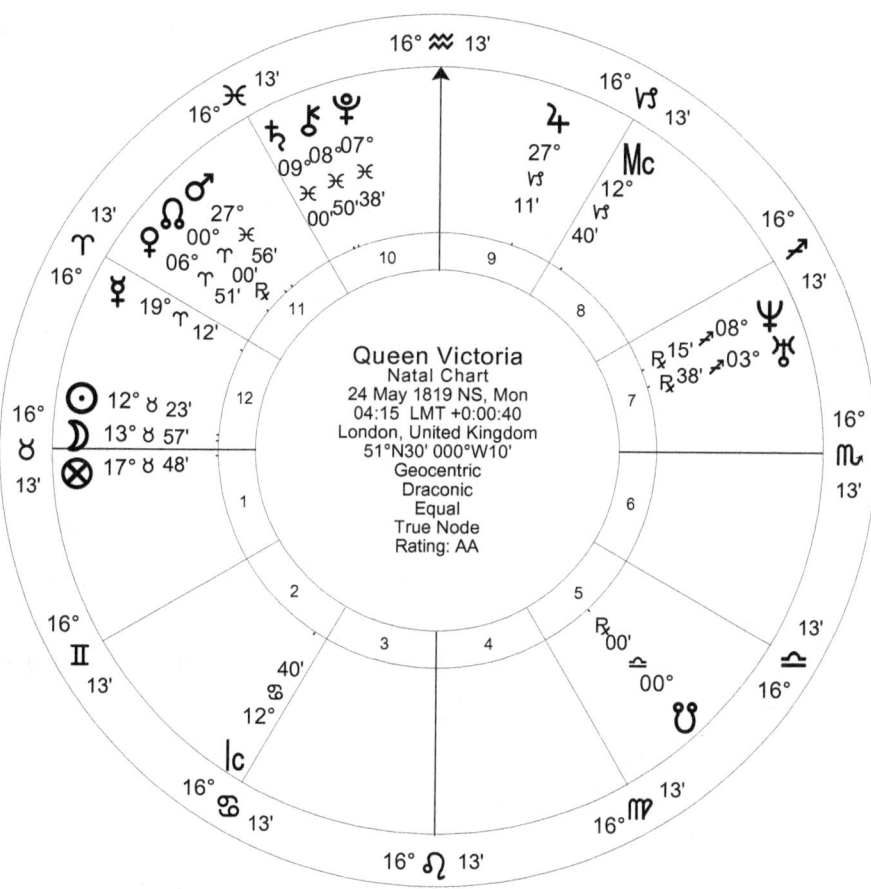

This chart of higher purposes is a lot less mutable. Fixed and cardinal energies now rule which suggests that in order to find greater self-fulfilment, she will need to be both her own boss and resolute. Whereas the tropical chart has a free-spirit quality, the draconic feels more tied and dutiful. The Midheaven has shifted from Aquarius to Capricorn, sign of conformity, authority and governance (and monarchy). Jupiter also in Capricorn, sign of its fall, is therefore a demotion from tropical Aquarius: while Jupiter is expansively shapeless in nature to find its strength, Capricorn shapes and restricts to find its strength.

Even if this were the chart of an ordinary person, we would say: 'It is part of your life purpose to find your strength against limitations or traditions.'

Tropical air is abundant. Draconic air is absent, though cadent energy remains high. The absence of an element is one of the chart's focal points. It is as if the chart is saying: 'You cannot speak what you think, it is better that you do not.' The chart could also be saying: 'Work on how you communicate, find ways to get across your truths to the world; it won't be easy!'. As we have seen, the Queen buried her real message to the world in diaries.

Tropical Gemini energy is now Taurean at the rising point in Taurus. As Queen, Victoria had purposes beyond personal ambition or impulse. She represented her nation, its empire, its peoples. Her MC in Capricorn ties her interests to those of the state in a bond of duty and symbolism; Taurus rising plays to the nature of her persona in the state. We associate Taurus with value and moral values, with prosperity and stability – leitmotifs of the Victorian Era. Charles Dickens' *A Christmas Carol*, published in 1843, is almost pure schmaltz these days, thanks to family movie reboots. But its original thrust was a huge attack on Victorian materialism. Oscar Wilde also mocked Victorian hypocrisy, such as in *The Importance of Being Earnest*, where marriage is characterised as a business deal in the minds of many, not a love match. It is a comic satire about false values.

The Taurus New Moon is the harbinger of a new age of material growth and social propriety dressed up as moral values. Victoria's draconic chart sets out her purpose as representing the times over which she reigned, even as other life purposes are served by her incessant writings and stand-offs with the parliamentary executive.

How can these two charts be reconciled? Let's look at the tropical-draconic biwheel.

Step 3: Victoria's tropical-draconic synastry of self biwheel chart. The synastry chart emphasises key themes already identified but gives them priority and shape.

The draconic nodal axis is shifted to the 4th and 10th houses in the Equal system, with North Node in Aries in the 10th, zone of monarchy or public responsibilities and duties. The node is not alone. Four draconic planets and three tropical are also in the 10th. This is a clear indication that it is part of her soul purpose to retain a strong personal independence in

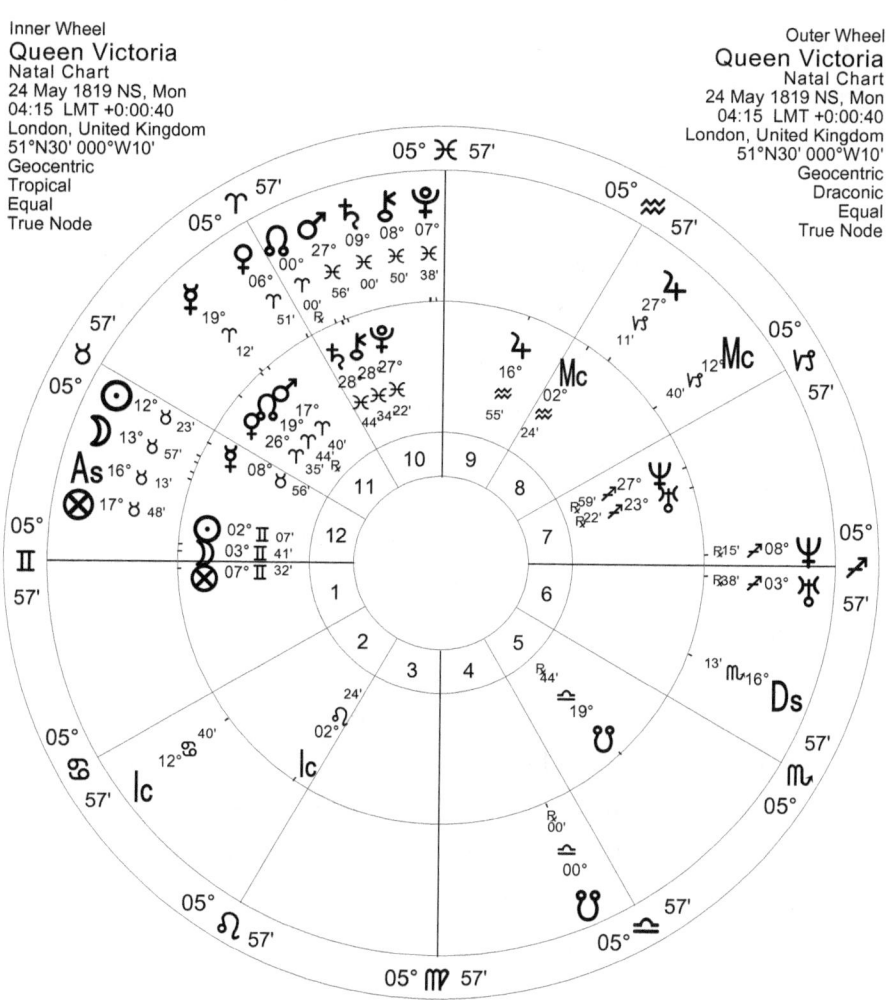

whatever major role is assigned her in life. Tropical Saturn in Pisces cuts through the axis along with Chiron and Pluto, suggesting that the Aries theme must also work with Piscean flavours of consideration of others and self-sacrifice: a huge challenge given Aries' need to have it all its own way, on its own terms.

While the tropical New Moon rising is in late-stage 12th-house Gemini, the draconic version takes us deeper into the 12th house in Taurus, emphasising that part of her lot in life is to be an actor behind-the-scenes, a borderless exemplar of Taurean values in a chart zone of veils, isolation and sorrow. This draco New Moon draws in tropical Mercury by conjunction, resonant of draconic Mercury's conjunction with tropical North Node and Mars in the 11th house in Aries: these are powerful messages of a mercurial nature, of the need to find her voice no matter the pressure to conform.

Significantly, draconic Jupiter in Capricorn strengthens Saturn's energy by conjunction with tropical MC in Aquarius in the 8th house of self-empowerment, reiterating that living and working within severe restriction or responsibilities is a vital component of success.

Draconic Uranus on the Descendant opposes Victoria's tropical New Moon, drawing in themes of work and relationship on the cusp between the 6th and 7th houses. Uranus' position here is an alert of sudden life changes and ruptures, of possible openings into unconventional bonds with others. No matter how painful these may be, inner growth and maturity lie within these experiences as potential.

The biwheel has a symphonic quality in that various different messages work in harmony to identify how one experience or challenge may serve to help other experiences or challenges towards self-fulfilment. Was Queen Victoria ever self-fulfilled? We cannot answer that question definitively given that so much of her life was governed by expectation, protocol and hypocrisy. But we see at least the draconic energies that informed her life which tie well with what we know of her.

Karl Marx: the purpose of creating heaven on Earth

As a counterpoint to Victoria – exemplar of hereditary entitlement and royal privilege – Karl Marx is a stark one. Born a year before the Queen in 1818, the philosopher, journalist and socialist revolutionary Marx advanced critical theories designed to replace capitalism with socialism in pursuit of a society where the people have a share in the things they produce. His major works *The Communist Manifesto* (co-written with Friedrich Engels) and *Das Kapital* identify class conflict and the exploitation of labour as the drivers of capitalist society. Marx's central concerns were the 'use value', 'labour value' and 'exchange value' of commodities.

Ideas of material value and ethical values lie at the core of the Marxist perspective.

In *Kapital*, Marx writes of a typical capitalist [my italics]: 'He is only capital personified. His soul is the soul of capital. But capital has one single life impulse, the tendency to create *value* and *surplus-value*, to make its constant factor, the means of production, absorb the greatest possible amount of surplus-labour. Capital is dead labour, that, vampire-like, only lives by sucking living labour, and lives the more, the more labour it sucks.'

Step 1: Karl Marx's tropical chart. Astrologically, Taurus is the sign of value and values, among other things. Material value has to do with worth in terms of money or exchange. In another sense, values are the ethical principles that help decide what is right or wrong. Value and values are measures of sorts, of ideas and corporeal and incorporeal things. We ought not to be surprised to learn that Marx is an über-Taurean with a New Moon (i.e., Sun and Moon) and a dignified Venus in the Bull. And if you're interested in fixed stars, Marx's Sun is conjunct Menkar (aka Menkab), which, though Saturn-like and rather severe, is sympathetic to the misfortunes of people in 'bad situations'.[ii]

---

ii   Hazel, Elizabeth, *Little Book of Fixed Stars: Expanded Second Edition* (with star commentaries by Michael Munkasey).

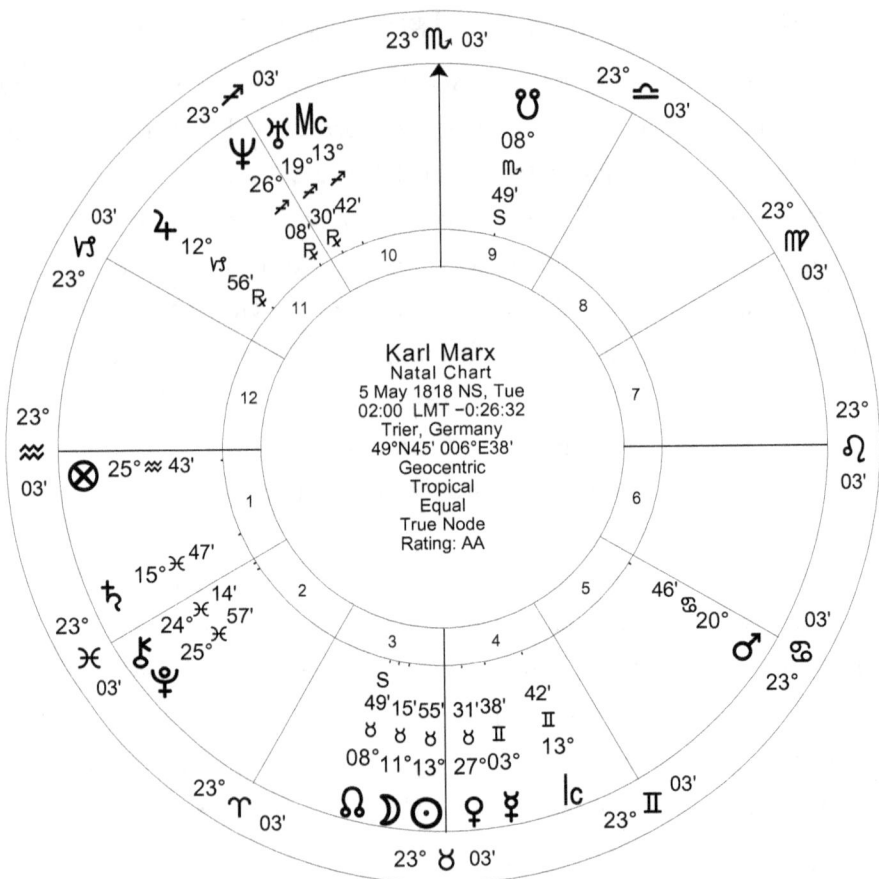

There are indications of the nature of Marx's life purposes in his tropical birth chart. It has a Locomotive shape with chart ruler Uranus leading the way, planet of revolt, conjunct Midheaven in Sagittarius, sign of philosophy, in the 10th house of career. More to the point, North Node is also in Taurus conjunct the New Moon in the 3rd house, bringing themes of value to the destiny point in the zone of writing: Marx also worked for newspapers. South Node therefore sits in the 9th house in Scorpio, describing Marx as perhaps an afflicted but profound thinker whose purpose in this incarnation is to a find practical applications for his ideas.

His Taurus Moon is last-stage Balsamic, perfect for the materialist sage who spent many years in the reading rooms of the British Museum working alone on *Kapital*. One might say he was born to forge a whole new measure of value. The Marx chart is fixed in the main with a majority elemental earth representation. Good starting points for a man who would move against the grain of society. But cardinal energy is low, which is surprising given the bold and pioneering nature of his work.

Step 2: Karl Marx's draconic birth chart. Cardinal energy is now by far the majority sign modality: the higher purpose chart points to the need to initiate boldly to achieve self-fulfilment. The boldness message is made clear by the shift from planetary Taurus to draconic Aries: New Moon, Venus and Mercury are in the draconic Ram starting, of course, with the North Node at the vernal equinox point.

It is fitting that the tropical Saturn-themed fixed star Menkar is now reflected in Saturn's new status as chart ruler, because draconic Capricorn rises. 1st-house Saturn is also promoted from Pisces to draconic Aquarius which the planet rules in old astrology. This 'lift' in Saturn's status tells me that the Aquarian themes of societal collectives, humanitarian ideas and/or revolutionary influence play a big part in the life purpose.

Another promotion is Jupiter's. In its fall in tropical Capricorn, it is now dignified in draconic Sagittarius, a superb placement for the advancement of philosophical ideas: added to which, Jupiter sits in the 11th house, the zone of Aquarius and collectives, resonating with Aquarius Saturn's rigour by sextile.

Neptune, Uranus and MC move from tropical Sagittarius to draconic Scorpio. This does not take away the philosophical theme of the Archer, but rather adds the delving, researching fight of the Scorpion to radiate ideas. This is underlined by the promotion of Mars: in its tropical fall in Cancer, it is raised to draconic Gemini (in the 5th) as ruler of Marx's draconic New Moon: these are strong indications that Marx must expect to have to face much resistance to his work (as he did), and that his medium of message will be the written word (Gemini). This 5th-house placement is

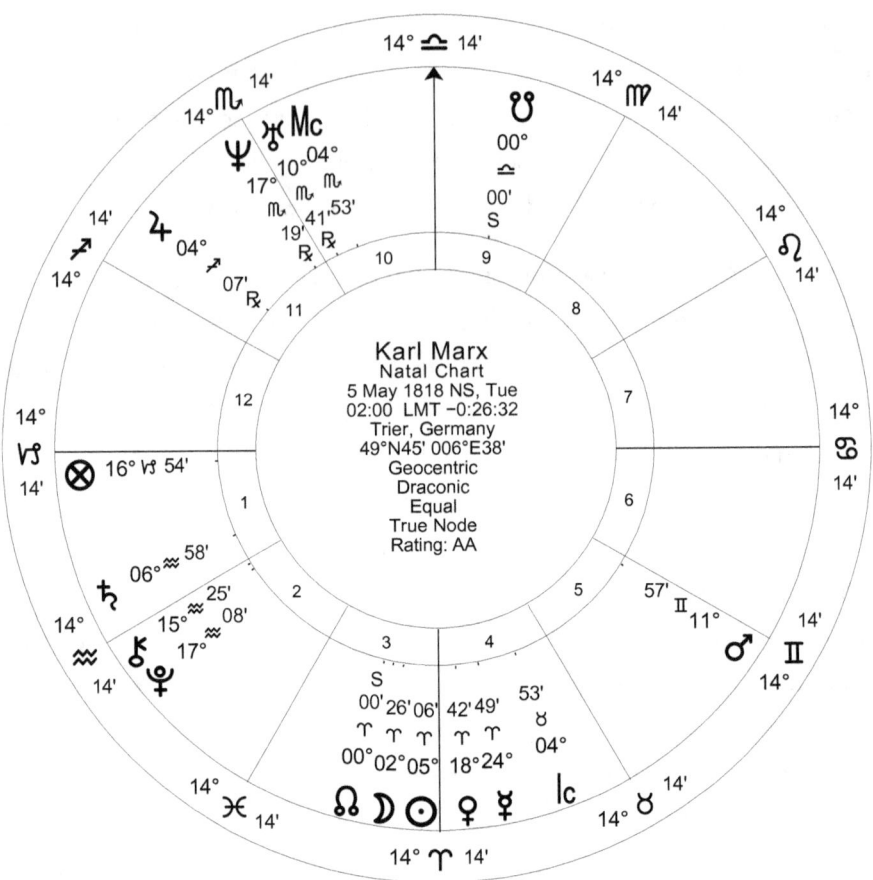

the traditional chart zone of the Sun, taking us to Marx's Sun which sits in Gemini's zone of the 3rd house, forming a constructive sextile to Mars. A harbinger of success.

Step 3: Karl Marx's tropical-draconic synastry of self biwheel chart. We have already identified important themes in Marx's tropical and draconic charts. The synastry wheel adds priority, definition and clarity to these.

The most significant revelation is the shift of Marx's draconic Aries planets to the 2nd house. This is the astrological equivalent of italics, making more sense of what is to be found in the two charts when taken individually. The tropical chart underscores Taurus and value. The draconic

The three-step approach to draconic analysis

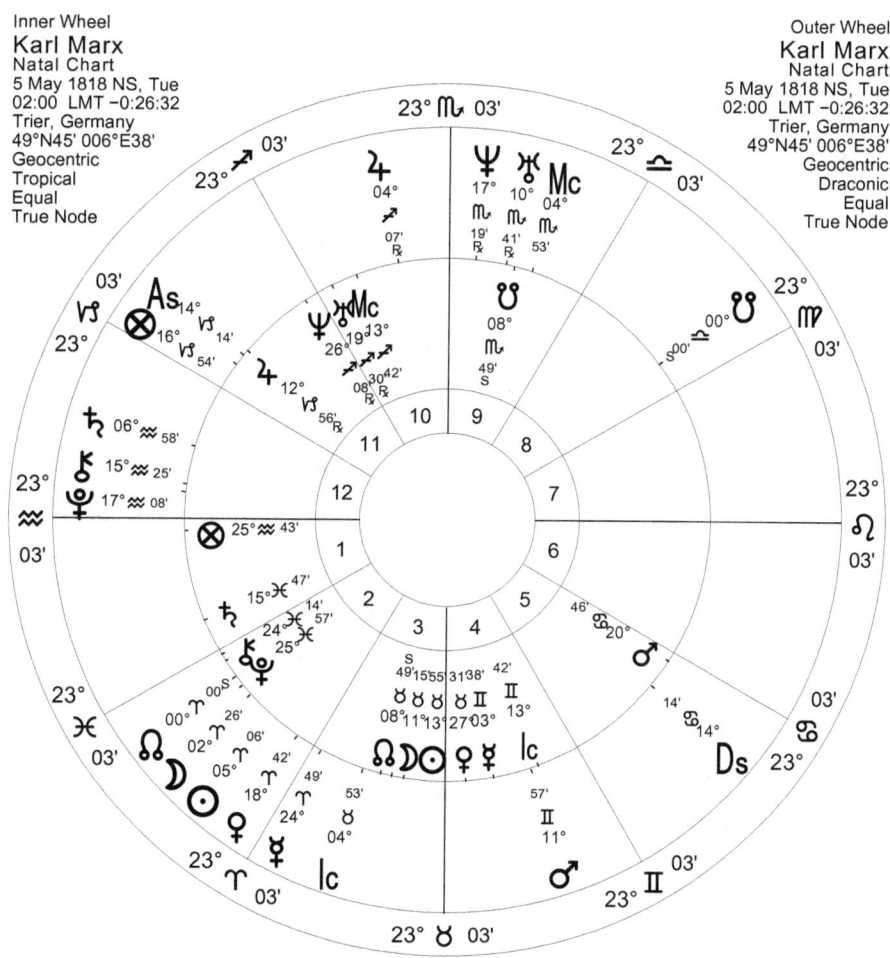

underscores Aries and initiative. The synastry chart clarifies where the cardinal energy should be applied, to the zone of value and values (the 2nd).

And what is Marx's role precisely? Draconic Ascendant (conjunct Part of Fortune) sits on tropical Jupiter in Capricorn: the personality is identified as a philosopher or 'guru' (his name would become an 'ism', Marxism) in the 11th house of collective ideals. Draconic dignified Jupiter in Sagittarius sits high in the chart in the 10th house opposite tropical dignified Mercury in Gemini in the 4th, an excellent aspect for intellectual and philosophical studies. The 4th-10th axis also draws in notions of the relationship between the people and state power: the Gemini-Sagittarius polarity directs intellectual energy into literary expression – and the opposition aspect itself involving these two planets tends to challenge traditional ideas and trigger controversies.

The draconic nodal axis cuts through tropical Pluto in Pisces in the 2nd, a feature of transformative effect, echoed by draconic Pluto rising in Aquarius. The life will not leave the world as it was found – at least in its most extreme manifestation. The tropical nodal axis draws in draconic MC/Uranus at the South Node while North Node draws in tropical New Moon and draconic IC: a complex combination of energies linking life direction and purposes with past and future. A practitioner of reincarnation astrology might interpret this as a past life beset by the irreconcilable obstacles of status or tradition (MC is square Saturn): in this incarnation, the soul seeks to reconfigure society for the removal of such obstacles to justice or success. Another way of viewing it (from a non-reincarnation perspective) is that the soul has a heightened awareness of injustices that arise from classical, elitist philosophies (9th-house tropical South Node) and is inclined to work against such anachronisms. In a purely soul sense, the individual desires to establish a 'heaven' on Earth (Taurus, 2nd-house), a utopian place where everyone has proper value by a code of equitable values.

The essential soul purpose is the removal of inequity.

There's much else in this chart to examine, but I have identified the 'headline news' of the charts. Bear in mind that in the draconic sense, we are not concerned with any moral, economic or political assessment of Marxism, socialism or communism. Our sole interest is the soul's intent or potential. The consequences of an individual's effect on the world is another matter.

Hedy Lamarr: a genius talent from nowhere

A major Austro-American Hollywood actress of the 1930-50s who for a while rivalled Garbo and Dietrich – she was described in her prime as 'the most beautiful woman in the world' – Lamarr starred in such hit movies as *Samson and Delilah* and *White Cargo*. Such was her acclaimed beauty that her face inspired the look of two cartoon beauties, Snow White and Catwoman. Ostensibly she was born to be 'just' an iconic silver screen goddess. Almost from the beginning she showed an interest in acting and dancing, and at age 12 won a Vienna beauty pageant. Her passage to dream factory stardom involved little struggle, with MGM head Louis B Mayer soon putting her on a $500-a-week contract after she impressed him on board a New York-bound ocean liner.

Yet another talent emerged early in life, one for science. On walks with her father he engaged her mind with descriptions of how cars or the printing press worked. Though she would have no formal science education, she soon turned her mind to inventing new mechanisms and products. Sometime boyfriend Howard Hughes – then one of the richest men in the world, a business magnate, aviator and philanthropist – soon recognised her genius and allowed her to work with his scientists. She designed him a new wing shape to make his planes more aerodynamic.

During World War 2, she created a 'frequency hopping' signal that set radio-controlled torpedoes off course and could not be jammed. Her technologies helped pioneer today's WiFi, GPS and Bluetooth communications systems. Later in life she received awards for her inventions, becoming the first woman to receive the Invention Convention's Bulbie Gnass Spirit of Achievement Award in 1997, given to individuals whose creative lifetime achievements in the arts, sciences, business, or invention fields have significantly contributed to society.

Chasing the Dragons: An Introduction to Draconic Astrology

Step 1: Hedy Lamarr's tropical chart. Dual talents as movie star and science geek surface in the Seesaw shape of Lamarr's chart, with two opposing clusters of celestials either side of the chart; two highly developed sides to the life. Focal points in a polarity are the Moon-Neptune conjunction in Leo in the 1st house opposite the Jupiter-Uranus conjunction in Aquarius around the 8th-house cusp. The conjunctions either side allow a wider orb to be applied as each planet pulls in the other.

The Leo planets in her persona chart zone speak theatre, glamour, illusion (as in movies) and emotional reflex. Moon rules this chart with Cancer rising; a Moon born for stardom to its nth degree. The Aquarius

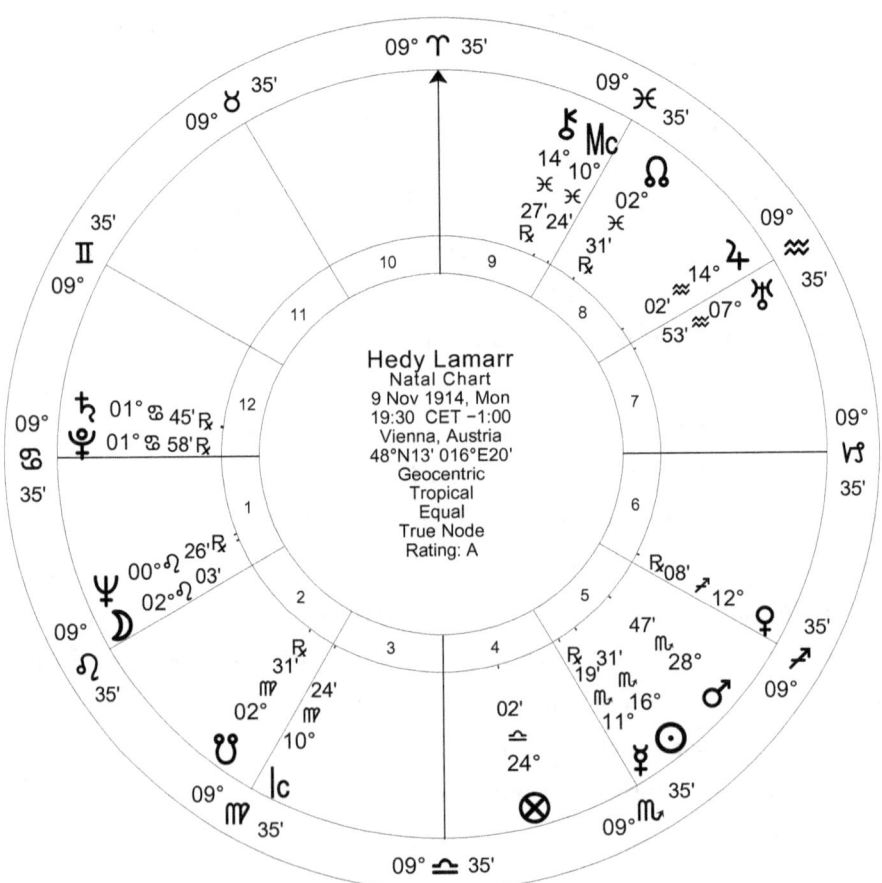

planets take us into science with Uranus in its dignity. Ordinarily we think of oppositions as indicative of a need to find a synthesis of two contrasting energies, a meeting point or even compromise. I have found in draconic astrology that the opposition may also tell of two distinct 'departments' in the life that need not be reconciled, only compartmentalised.

Water is by far the majority element of the tropical chart, with no earth. This is surprising given what we now know of her skills in science which requires practical understanding. But we do know that she was subject to inspirational ideas and left it to others to sort out the details. An abundance of water leads us to instinct and emotion, to artistry, yet Lamarr also possessed a rational high intelligence. Water is associated with memory in its lunar expression, and the Moon rules Lamarr's chart. Was her natal intellect fed by past-life memories?

The nodal axis falls across Virgo-Pisces, with North Node in the latter in the 8th. The modern ruler of Pisces is Neptune and accommodates the movie career. The old ruler is Jupiter, accommodating science, because of its proximity to Uranus and position in Aquarius. Take your pick. In another sense the nodal axis picks up an innate preoccupation with mechanical causation – Lamarr was forever tinkering with machinery – and asks her to further this preoccupation into something of broader use, perhaps to serve humanity in some way. Her radio-hopping technology arose from her frustration that as a Hollywood star she was doing nothing to help the War effort against the Nazis. Pisces, as we have seen already elsewhere, operates best in a place without borders, where domains are no longer sacred: it is a curious fact that Lamarr's genius for science was in-built, and that she played with ideas and technologies, mixing disciplines, until she reached eureka moments. It is indeed tempting to think that her science instinct was but a past life 'memory' brought back to do something really useful.

Pluto-Saturn rising, exactly conjunct, in Cancer in the 12th, bring a tremendous focus on micro-matters – and this conjunction has a bearing on her Scorpio Sun through modern rulership in the 5th house, zone of Leo. Lamarr's drivers are to express and to investigate.

As for her Venus – it's in fiery, easily bored Sagittarius, disposited by an independent and hot/cold-blowing Aquarius Jupiter. The wonder is that she married *only* six times.

Step 2: Hedy Lamarr's draconic chart. There is a dramatic elemental shift to fire with Leo rising, Sagittarius Sun now chart ruler. Sagittarius is the last of the fire signs, mythically the most learned of this element, and we associate the Archer with philosophy and scholarly knowledge. Such a combination encourages Lamarr to yield to her passions rooted in

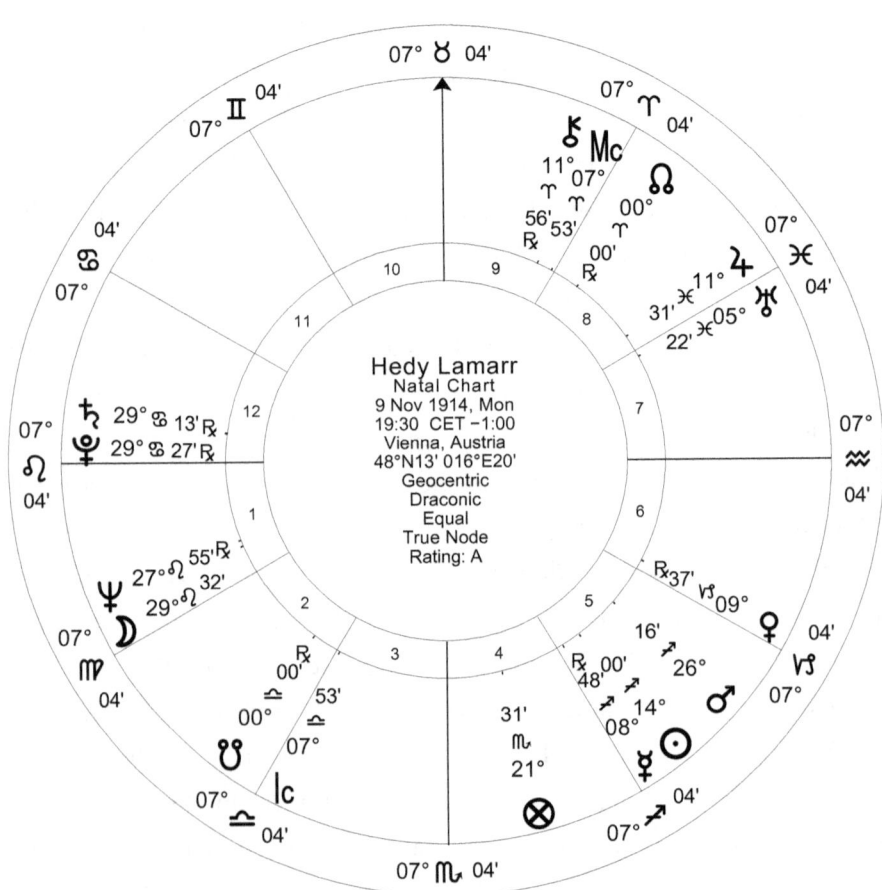

knowledge, urged on by a Grand Trine in fire drawing in Pluto (and Saturn just out of sign) and MC/Chiron. A vast pool of potential awaits to be utilised in this chart.

The Leo Ascendant embraces all that needs to be expressed in the Lamarr Sun, theatrical and scientific. Moon and Neptune stay in Leo, she is a destined movie star. But Uranus and Jupiter have slipped out of Aquarius and into Pisces, mixed blessings. Jupiter is in its old dignity, therefore promoted. Uranus has lost its dignity, therefore is demoted, and finds itself in a sign that does not care for borders or definitions: this is also the sign of giving to others and of self-sacrifice. While Lamarr was acclaimed for her inventions, she never made a cent from them. Her frequency hopping patent expired in the 1960s before her ideas were implemented, developed for wireless communication systems 'that allow more users to communicate simultaneously with less signal interference.'[iii] She could have made billions of dollars. She was effectively robbed, but the world was the beneficiary. That's Pisces in action.

Where Pisces sits in the tropical chart, Aries now replaces in the draconic, including the Midheaven in Sagittarius' zone of the 9th house. It is part of her life purpose to pioneer, break new ground, from a place of mystery or diffusion (Pisces).

No one has yet adequately explained how she became a world class inventor with no science education.

Step 3: Hedy Lamarr's tropical-draconic synastry of self chart. Draconic Uranus in the transformative 8th house conjoins tropical North Node while draconic Moon-Neptune form a dissociate conjunction with tropical South Node: an articulate expression of what we know of Lamarr's amazing life.

Science through Uranus is merged with her destiny point in Pisces. Whether from a past life or simply a natural talent in this life, she is born with theatrical and mesmeric gifts – but the dissociate nature of

---

[iii] Smithsonianmag.com

Chasing the Dragons: An Introduction to Draconic Astrology

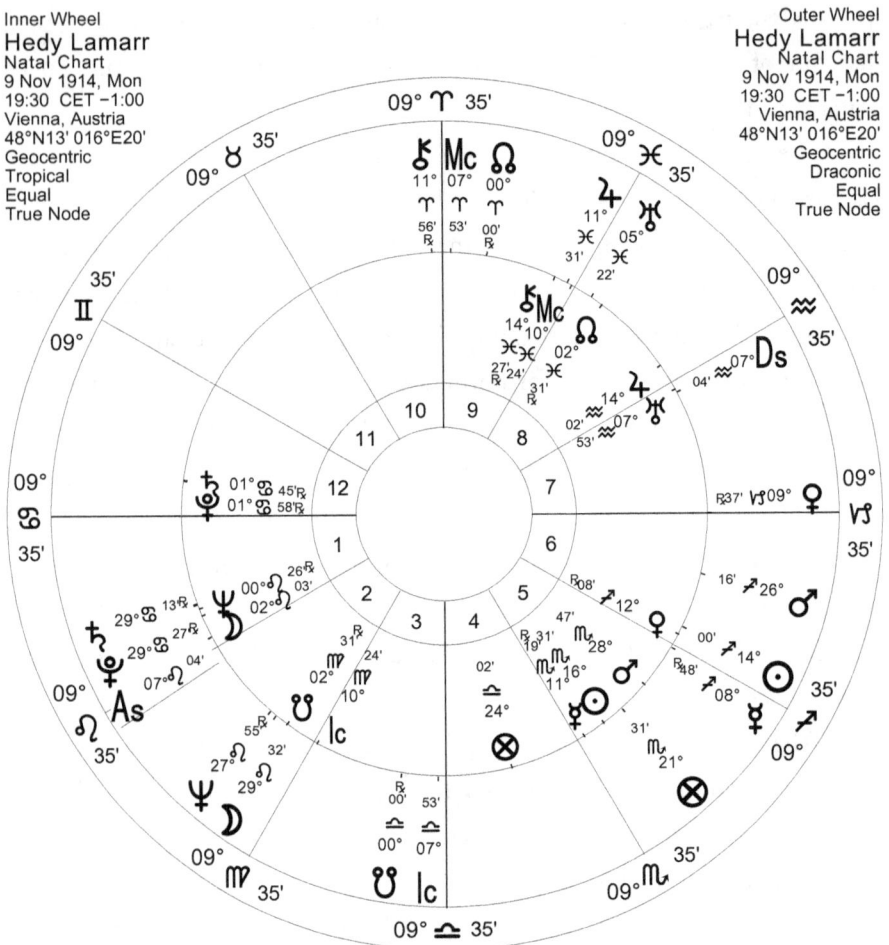

the conjunction of Moon-Neptune with the South Node (Leo-Virgo) is a hint that her commitment to all that's entertainment or illusion will not be total. There will be dissatisfaction as Virgo's search for granular reality chafes against Leo's razzle-dazzle. As Lamarr herself once said: 'Any girl can look *glamorous*. All she has to do is stand still and look stupid.' A lack of challenging movie roles led to boredom: it was essential to her evolution that she did so as her extraordinary intellect for science gained greater expression.

Note that the draco nodal axis sits across the 3rd/9th houses with Aries North Node in the house traditionally associated with Sagittarius and higher knowledge. Draconic Jupiter, ruler of Sagittarius, echoes this by conjunction with tropical MC in Pisces.

Draco Descendant is exactly conjunct tropical Uranus: a classic aspect for multiples marriages (six as we have seen in Lamarr's case) and odd or astonishing relationships with eccentrics, geeks and fellow pioneers. Her frequency hopping invention was developed with the avant-garde composer George Antheil. They first met when she sought his advice on enhancing her upper torso and he recommended glandular extracts (one of his books is titled *The Glandbook for the Questing Male*). Their conversation later turned to torpedoes. And Howard Hughes, her old swain with the planes, became notorious in his later years as a recluse holed up in a hotel penthouse suite, storing his urine in countless jars.

It was part of her life purpose to work in partnerships with brilliant but perhaps troubled or peculiar souls.

Yet draconic Ascendant is conjunct tropical Moon-Neptune in the 1st house in Leo, a reminder that it was also her lot to shine theatrically.

Greta Thunberg: precocious climate activist and her inner struggles

Swedish environmentalist Greta Thunberg rose to prominence at the age of 15 when she led school strikes over what she felt was a lack of political action in response to climate change. She demonstrated outside the Swedish Parliament holding up a banner that read: 'School strike for climate'. Soon, her example caught the public imagination and by 2018 Friday school strikes by young students were a weekly occurrence in many nations.

She is held in such high esteem internationally that she is a favoured speaker at UN or governmental climate conferences. To minimise her carbon footprint, in 2019 she sailed to New York from Plymouth to attend one such conference. The so-called 'Greta effect' is a mark of her influence on the world stage and on people of all ages.

What has helped in part to widen her popularity is her fluency in English. And she has a gift for the ringing phrase or response. Before COP26 in Glasgow in 2021, she mocked world leaders as mere noise dispensers of 'blah, blah, blah' in their hopeless efforts to mitigate climate change. She also has a resourceful and barbed wit as US President Donald Trump discovered when in 2019, he mocked her accolade as '*Time* magazine's Person of the Year'. In a post on Twitter, he jibed that she should work on her 'anger management issues' and 'go to an old-fashioned movie with a friend'. He added 'Chill Greta, chill!' in the tweet, which began with him branding her *Time* award as 'so ridiculous'.

Eleven months later, Thunberg found the perfect moment for revenge. As defeated Trump raged on Twitter, making baseless allegations of voter fraud in the 2020 presidential election, she tweeted in response to his 'STOP THE COUNT' rant: 'So ridiculous. Donald must work on his Anger Management problem, then go to a good old-fashioned movie with a friend! Chill Donald, Chill!'.

Touché.

Her extraordinary example has inspired many books, including biographies. And her own title *No One is Too Small to Make a Difference* – a collection of her eloquent speeches before the UN, EU and World Economic Forum – is an international bestseller: in November 2019, Thunberg was named author of the year by Waterstones.

Step 1: Greta Thunberg's tropical birth chart. We do not have a time of birth, so the chart is shown for midday and is absent of houses. We do not know where the planets should sit in the wheel, so the chart starts at Aries. In draconic astrology lack of birth time makes little or no difference as the nodal axis is slow moving. The Moon is in Capricorn all day of birth.

The three-step approach to draconic analysis

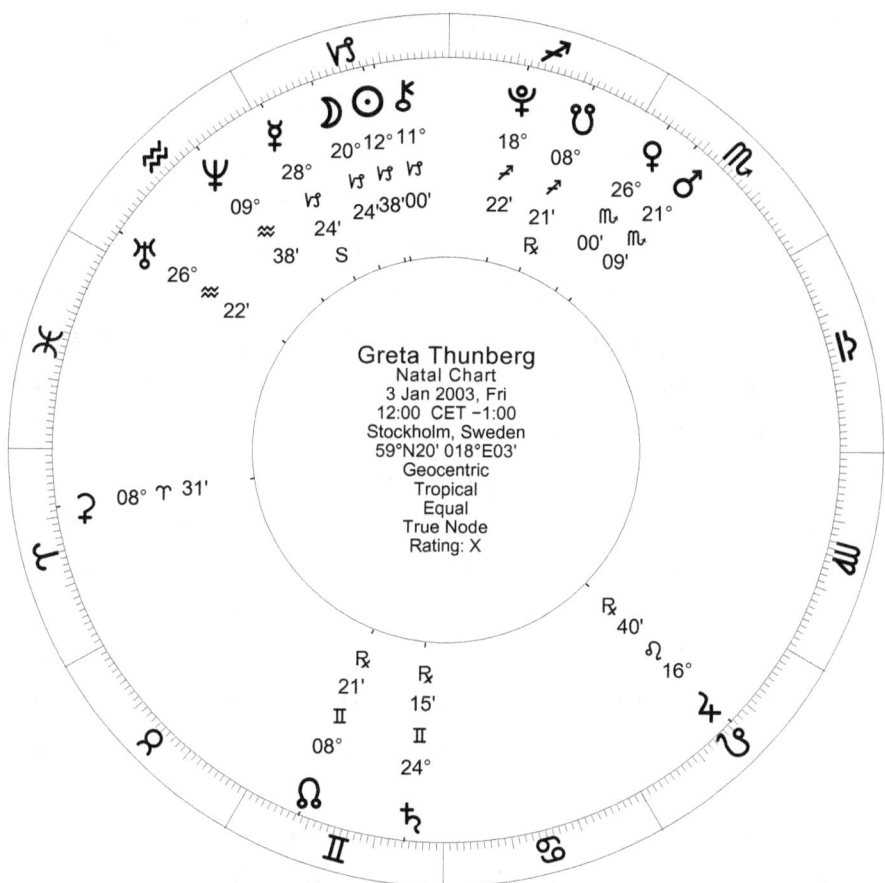

North Node in Gemini establishes Thunberg as a communicator – it is her destiny to send a message to the world, although precisely what that message might be is not at all clear in the tropical chart. It can only be said that the nodal axis starts in Sagittarius, that she has come into this world possessed of awareness and high learning but is now set the task of adapting her message to an audience and relaying lessons to a wide range of people (Gemini).

The South Node is out-of-orb conjunct Pluto, but I shall recognise the aspect. Pluto is associated with heavy and profound experiences, sometimes with depression, rage, secrets and abuse. Linked to the South Node, in past-life terms, you might say that Thunberg brings a karma of trauma which may serve as a basis for deep insight into other people. Thunberg has spoken publicly of how she first began to become aware of environmental abuses at around the age of 8 or 9, and this led to depression and an eating disorder at age 11, consistent with a Pluto/South Node conjunction. Pluto's transformative effects are often presaged by crisis. In Thunberg's case, the depression is a measure of the depth of her calling because what triggered it was the incomprehensible behaviour of her fellow human beings. The clash between what she saw and what she expected of people triggered crisis and then a wake-up call to her destiny.

Natal New Moon in Capricorn is cardinal and galvanising, immediate, fast-acting, bold, and rooted in principle. There is no time to lose with this Moon. The closer she was born to midnight of 3 January, the more pressing is this Moon's need to start out. Note, however, that Moon (emotion) dislikes Capricorn (isolation), so Thunberg's early-life crisis is consistent. Uranus is strong in Aquarius – the rebel, the awakener – and Saturn (which rules her Sun, Moon and Mercury) sits in Gemini, placement of the serious, uncompromising message.

The chart shape is irregular in that it falls somewhere between a Bucket and Seesaw: eight of the 10 major planets form a tight cluster across just four signs with both boundary planets in dignity, Mars in Scorpio and Uranus in Aquarius, with two handle planets, Jupiter and Saturn. I am inclined to see this as a focused Bucket given the tight arrangement of planets and the weight of the two handles, raising the value of communication and passionate driver (Jupiter in Leo). If nothing else, the shape reminds me of a battering ram, appropriate given Thunberg's effect on the world.

The chart is cardinal/fixed – initiatory and determined – quite earthy but low in air and fire which does not seem to equate with her amazing communication skills or passion. It will be interesting to see what her draconic chart says.

The three-step approach to draconic analysis

I have added Ceres in Aries to the chart, asteroid of 'mother earth' in current thinking. It sits exactly sextile/trine her South and North Nodes, a suitable alignment given what we know of Thunberg's environmental causes.

Step 2: Greta Thunberg's draconic birth chart. The Capricorn cardinal energy of the tropical chart is replaced by a fixed Scorpio vibration, an alert that a central part of Thunberg's life purpose involves a resolution or determination to fight. She must stick to her guns, in a manner of speaking. A large number of planetary demotions in the dignities describe many tricky challenges on the soul's journey.

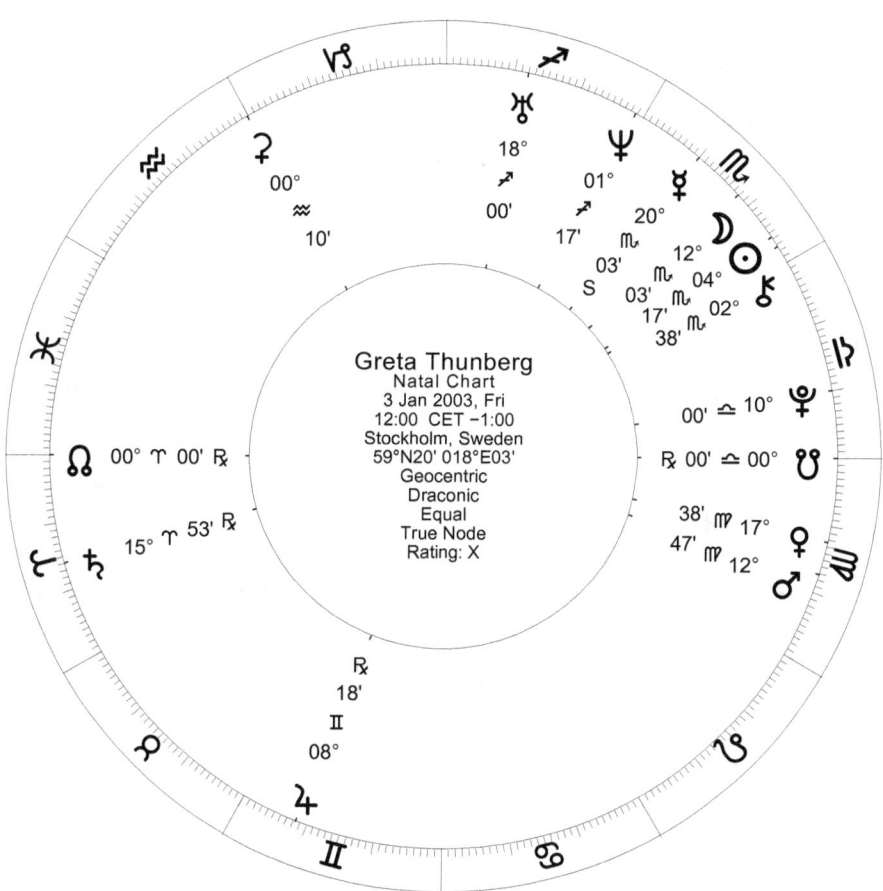

With reference to the two co-rulers of the Scorpio stellium: Mars is demoted to Virgo (neutral) and Pluto to Libra (also neutral). This suggests that part of soul purpose is to learn how to explore multiple ways to fight her cause: Mars' place in draconic Virgo especially takes her in a literary or at least writer's direction where attention to analytics is crucial. The fight will be hard work for sure, though you don't need astrology to appreciate that.

Air remains an under-represented element which does suggest Thunberg has reason to work hard on communicating her truths. In 2019 she did reveal that she is on the autism spectrum and that this condition may have contributed to her viewing the world in 'stark terms'. She now regards the condition as a 'superpower' because it has given her immense awareness of global problems.

The two handle planets Jupiter and Saturn are also demoted, the first to Gemini (detriment), the second to Aries (fall). Once again, these demotions are no sign of eventual failure in the slightest, only that the pathway is beset with challenges, not least to find patience and fortitude with steady Saturn in fractious Aries, and high-minded Jupiter in scatter-brain or populist Gemini.

Uranus, too, is demoted from Aquarius to draconic Sagittarius: she will need to work on changing mindsets to gain greater traction for long-term good rather than through eruptive events or demos: it is arguable that she is already doing this.

Step 3: Greta Thunberg's tropical-draconic synastry of self chart. The most striking feature here is that draconic Jupiter is exactly conjunct tropical North Node in Gemini: an old head (Jupiter) on young shoulders (Gemini, sign of youth). Jupiter in this aspect greatly blesses the soul purpose with enlightenment; it is a driving one, and we should not be surprised that she has enjoyed rapid success at such an early age. Jupiter expands range in many ways, in terms of knowledge, popularity and terrain.

The three-step approach to draconic analysis

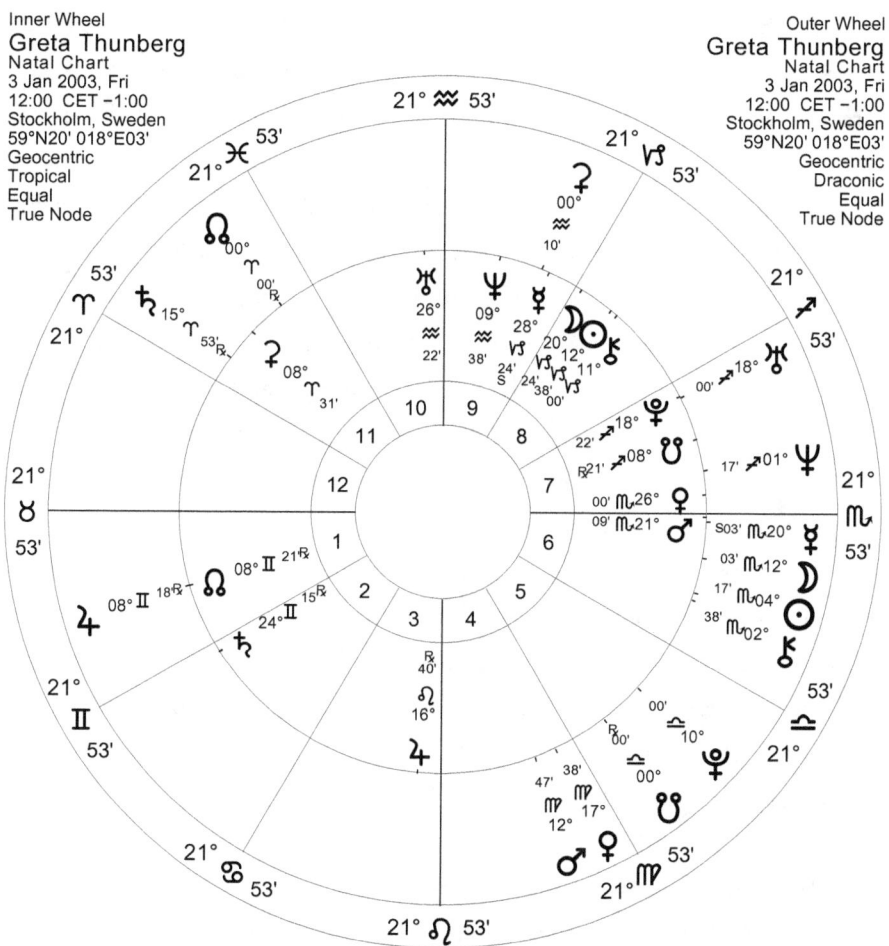

This potentially bestows a 'guru' status on the native, something that people the world over seem to acknowledge/recognise in her, even climate change deniers.

The soul purpose will not be easy to pursue with Jupiter in its detriment in Gemini. Purpose can be derailed by egotism, pursuit of personal honours or glory, by exaggerated or unrealistic expectations or playing to the gallery. Considerable work will have to be devoted to viewing life proportionately.

On the other side of the chart, tropical Pluto sits very widely conjunct the South Node, as we have seen. Now there is an addition to the aspect. Draconic Uranus is exactly conjunct tropical Pluto in the 7th house: a combination that brings together independence and fanatical tendencies (*in extremis*): a reforming zeal that breaks with old ways of life and pushes new models for a better life. Behaviour may be provocative because the soul wishes to draw attention to iniquities, but outcomes could be mixed, varying from controversy to outright conflict. Lifelong popularity cannot be assured because of the tendency to test norms and say the unsayable. This aspect is sufficiently wide of the opposition tropical North Node-draconic Jupiter conjunction to be treated more as a potential risk area than an inevitable sign of extremism.

More strongly opposed to tropical-draconic Pluto-Uranus is tropical Saturn in the 2nd house in Gemini. In terms of Pluto, this is all about the 'dark side' of life and exposure to it from an early age. We are reminded of Thunberg's depression and horror at what humankind is doing to the planet. As for Uranus opposed by Saturn, this produces a rebellious and outspoken individual, one usually set against authority and capable of confrontation. Moderation of these traits so that people are not left appalled or insulted is the advised strategy.

Dwarf planet Ceres (symbolic of Mother Earth themes) is also significantly aspected. Its draconic version is dissociate conjunct tropical Mercury in the 9th house, in the early minutes of Aquarius, indicative of a new age of technology and ways of working with nature. Mercury is the messenger of these changes, and Thunberg is part of this. Tropical Ceres in Aries is opposed by draco Pluto in Libra (11th to 5th houses): the meaning of this is not entirely clear but we can say that themes of environmental 'nurturing' are linked to hidden things and power. In one sense, Thunberg can expect to encounter powerful forces opposed to her work; in another sense, she possesses tremendous power to effect change, but it will be necessary to moderate or strike balances to win powerful people over.

There's much more to see in this chart, but the main points are made. The synastry chart captures a great deal of what we know of Thunberg. Her aim to wake the world up to climate change and to encourage world leaders to act is clear. Less clear to the public (perhaps) but evident in the chart are tensions within her that need to be reconciled for more effective action. Life purpose is not just about her environmental aims; it is also about gaining better self-control to be effective; working on very powerful inner energies and reflexes which if left unreconstructed can sabotage even the best of endeavours.

Her soul has taken on a huge task. There is every reason to think she is helping to change the world for the better. It's all in the trying.

Oprah Winfrey: Mega-rich, mega-influential – a spiritual figure?

Winfrey is one of the wealthiest self-made people in the United States today and rated the richest African-American of the 20th century. According to *Forbes* she was the only black billionaire in the world between 2004 and 2006. She became the first black female billionaire in 2003 and she remains a leading philanthropist.

She has made her estimated $3 billion fortune from her media and business empire built from her hugely popular TV talk show series, *The Oprah Winfrey Show*, which ran for 25 years until 2011. She has starred in movies such as *The Color Purple* (winning three film award nominations), turns books into bestsellers with her endorsements...and we could go on and on about her achievements which are legion and on a monumental scale. She still interviews celebrities from time to time: her TV conversation with the Duke and Duchess of Sussex (aka Meghan and Harry) in 2021 rocked the UK royal family and created headlines across the world with the couple's allegations of racism in the House of Windsor.

Winfrey fully uses her celebrity to promote the interests of groups she deems persecuted or under-represented, and she has been acclaimed for pushing animal rights. She is regarded by many millions of people as a spiritual leader and is sympathetic to the work of paranormal practitioners. She has a fusion approach to faith, seemingly mixing different New Age and Christian ideas into her own brand of belief: she once said, 'God is a feeling experience and not a believing experience. If your religion is a believing experience...then that's not truly God'. When in 2008 Winfrey's book club endorsed spiritual teacher Eckhart Tolle's *A New Earth: Awakening to Your Life's Purpose*, the book sold many more millions of copies.

She has shown great courage in tackling racism and other social evils, facing much criticism and death threats. With so many different accomplishments to her name, can draconic astrology distil essential life purposes?

Step 1. Oprah Winfrey's tropical birth chart. Given Winfrey's extraordinary business acumen and gift for making serious, plutocratic money, it's appropriate to find the financial zones of the 2nd and 8th the busiest of her six house axes.

In the 2nd, her Aquarius Venus is cazimi, that is, exactly conjunct the Sun bar eight minutes (the required cazimi orb must be under 17 minutes) and this aspect traditionally is a sign of potential great success and glory. We say Venus is in the 'heart of the Sun' and benefits from solar radiance.

Traditional and modern astrologers differ in their understanding of Venus. Mods associate the planet with love and money (Libra and Taurus, the signs it rules); trads with relationship, beauty, persuasion, etc: nothing to do with money. Deborah Houlding, in her book *The Houses: Temples of the Sky*, scolds modern astrologers for imbuing Venus with financial themes when no ancient source supports this mythic link. Mods tend to associate houses with signs and with ruling planets (Venus with Taurus with 2nd, for instance) and this is my position. Over and over again, in the charts of my

The three-step approach to draconic analysis

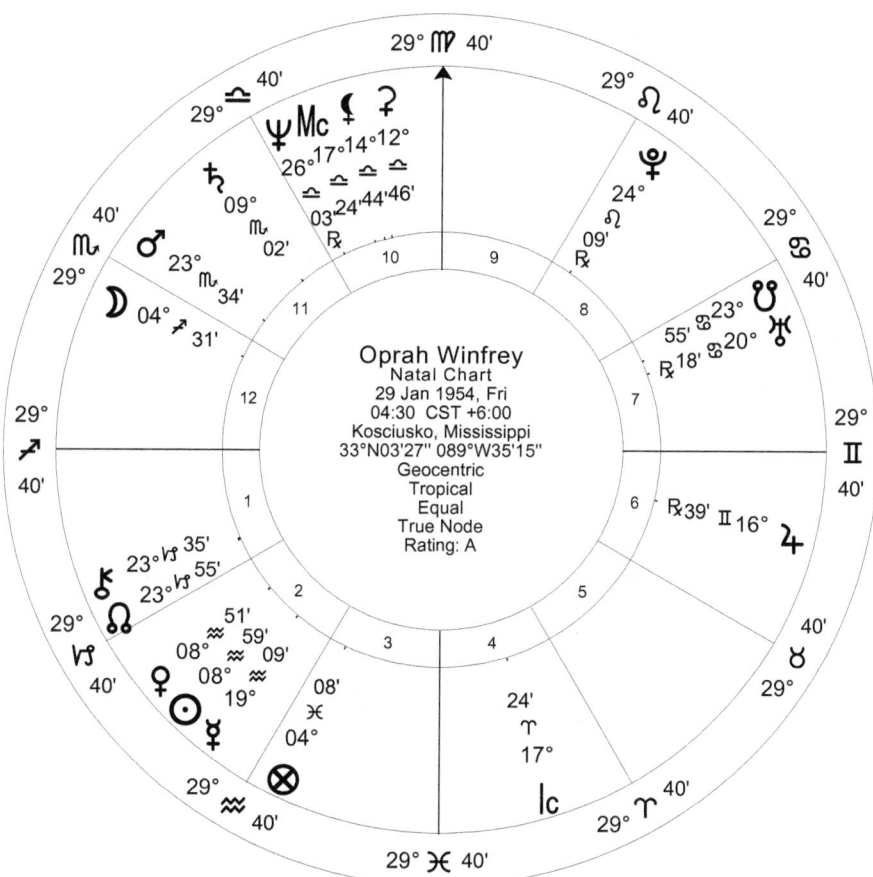

clients, Venus speaks not just of relationship and the gifts of negotiation or seduction, but also of value or money and values – in other words, Venus betokens the things held dear by the native.

Look at billionaire Howard Hughes' birth chart and you'll find Venus on top of his North Node. Elon Musk – *Forbes*' Richest Man in History with a $300 billion fortune at time of writing – has Venus trine North Node. Mark Zuckerberg, co-founder of Facebook (or Meta as it's now known as), with an estimated $120 billion stash, has Venus in Taurus trine Jupiter in Capricorn.

Mercury too is in Winfrey's 2nd-house Aquarius, planet of mind and mercantile topics. Mercury is part of a Grand Trine in air, which you'd expect of someone who has made a fortune from talking, promoting a confession culture and publishing. Note that the air element is in the majority in her chart. A 2nd-house Aquarius will be making money from pioneering business, doing things in an individual or idiosyncratic way, and will be involved in many different types of work and business.

Winfrey's nodal axis is complicated: South Node Cancer (conjunct Uranus), North Node Capricorn (conjunct Chiron), 7th to 1st respectively. The soul is set for rebellion and challenge; the world is viewed as a place of anachronism if not inertia. The future can be so different, so much better than what has passed or is passing. Uranus inclines the nature to the promise of the future. The South Node is immersed in matters of heritage, dependency (within relationships especially) and family expectations. The North Node seeks a structured basis for personal growth through career but one fed by compassion and memory, given Chiron's proximity. The destiny is to create a hard-headed and structured manifestation of inner energies (Capricorn) built from the personality (1st).

The nodal axis is part of a cardinal t-square whose apex is Neptune in Libra in the 10th house, weakly conjunct MC in Libra. Among other things, this Neptune infuses ambition and career with a desire to make bonds of peace and understanding. There will be a driven idealism, a parallel dream world, that aims for a utopia, even if there's a rational concession that this is flawed Earth not perfect Heaven. Winfrey's ecumenical spirituality is bound up with life purpose. Neptune in its best expression also seeks to promote values of benevolence, and we see this in Winfrey's philanthropy: for instance, in 2020 The Oprah Winfrey Charitable Foundation, with assets of US$172 million, donated US$10 million to Covid-19 relief efforts.

The MC's tropical ruler is Venus in the 2nd, which ties up career with finance and with benevolence. Mercury also in the 2nd disposits Winfrey's Jupiter in Gemini in the 6th, the zone of work and caring, and Jupiter rules Winfrey's Moon in Sagittarius in the 12th, the zone of Neptune. This Third

Quarter Moon is mature about activism and responsibility which in the 12th takes on a strongly spiritual dimension as potential.

Jupiter has raised importance in Winfrey's chart. It rules through Sagittarius rising, and it leads the Locomotive chart shape. Her impact on the world is through enlightenment, wealth, big business, religion and other Jovian associations. But in Gemini (Jupiter's detriment) there are problems – Winfrey's faced much adversity on her road to success, such as early-life rape and neglect. The 6th house – associated with health and wellbeing – is also the domain of how we deal with personal crisis, sickness and reversals of fortune. Though Jupiter here is debilitated (a factor which may symbolise early-life problems, though Jupiter is nonetheless supported by sextiles and trines), it is still the planet of growth, so that it may be said that Winfrey has used her own suffering to advance her message to the world (as indicated by Gemini).

Step 2. Oprah Winfrey's draconic birth chart. Cardinal energy is now dominant in place of tropical fixity. It is her destiny to win through proactivity, to initiate and be her own boss, though the tropical message of resolution is required. Aries is the sign of the self-made. Winfrey has plainly lived up to her potential in this respect. Fire also rules, passions are monetised.

Pisces rises, elevating the spiritual status in her life as we saw in the short biography. Modern chart ruler Neptune moves into Capricorn, linking the spiritual with career. Locomotive lead planet Jupiter shifts to Leo, ruling MC. Pluto is promoted to Scorpio in the 8th, a potent zone as planet, sign and house are associated. This speaks of transformative effect on others, of a great instinct to confront and understand negative experiences and of financial talent. Saturn, too, is promoted to Capricorn, excellent for career, and Mars remains strong in its exaltation in Capricorn.

We have seen already how draconic Aries so often is to be found in the charts of highly dynamic or pioneering people. In Winfrey's case,

Chasing the Dragons: An Introduction to Draconic Astrology

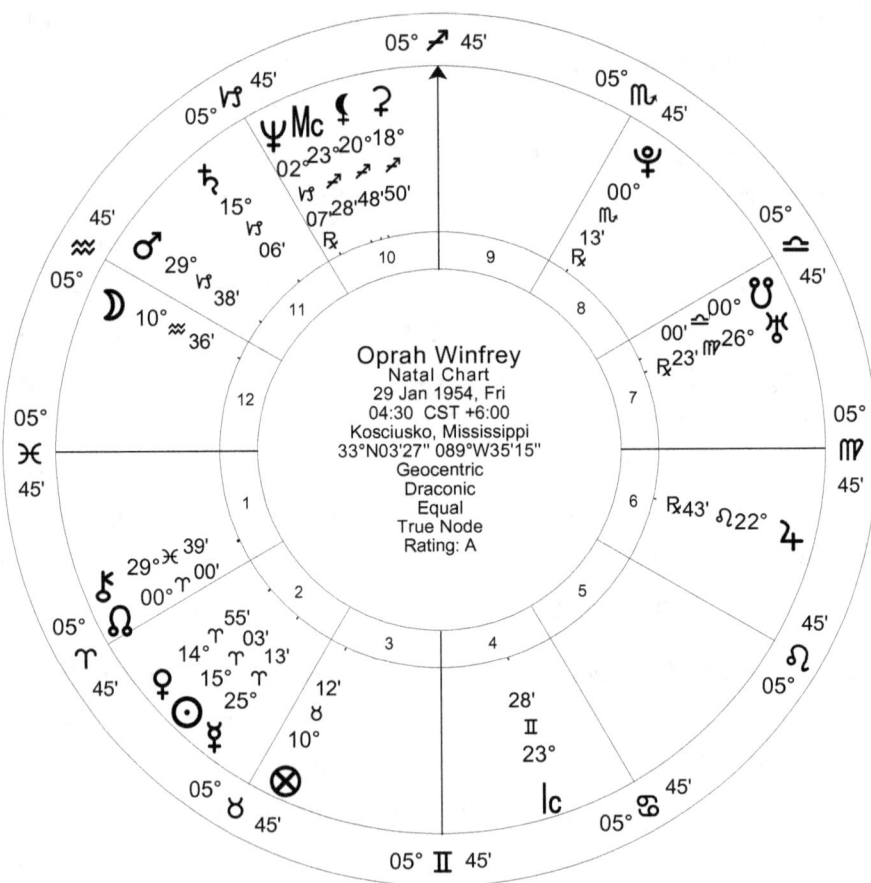

her three tropical Aquarius planets are now in draconic Aries in the 2nd: finance is connected to pioneering example. Chiron and Uranus no longer share a sign with the Moon's nodes: Uranian fervour is best focused on the remedial effect of Virgo while Chiron slips into Pisces, the sign of soulful resolution of pain in its best effect.

The three-step approach to draconic analysis

Step 3: Oprah Winfrey's tropical-draconic synastry of self chart. This chart is especially busy, and I'll only highlight the major messages. The importance of Winfrey's spiritual purpose is evident with draconic Neptune rising in Capricorn, cutting across the Ascendant point to loosely conjoin draconic MC rising in Sagittarius, a bridge between a career of enlightenment or large-scale dissemination and soul/faith interests. Draconic MC is further supported by a sextile to tropical Neptune.

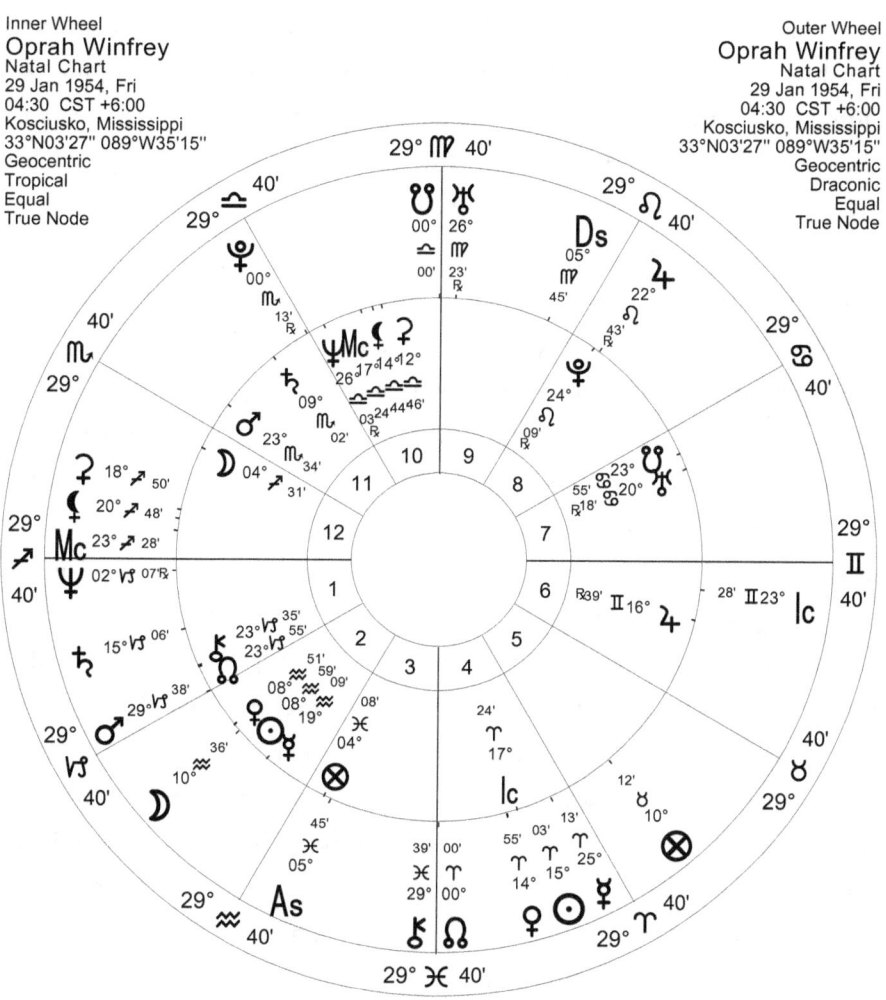

Draconic Venus-Sun-Mercury in Aries in the 4th house, prefaced by Aries North Node, in opposition to the tropical Libra celestials, implicating tropical IC/MC, describe a zone of potential conflict and past abuse. (Notice how close draconic Sun [Winfrey] is to tropical IC, the familial/heritage point.) Such an abundance of Aries energy may point to the problems of family. But that same energy helps the individual to self-identify and acquire the fight to break away – and exalted ruler draconic Mars, and tropical Mars in dignity, signal the power to do this.

One of the bedrocks of Winfrey's emotional power and popular reach is her personal history which she has shared with so many others who have suffered similarly. Draconic Uranus in Virgo right at the top of the chart close to South Node establishes her life role to pioneer new life approaches intended to promote greater wellbeing.

The success of her personality as a brand is suggested by draconic Ascendant conjunct her tropical Part of Fortune in the 3rd of communications. In Pisces, a universal or spiritual purpose is indicated, taking us back to ruler Neptune rising. Draconic Moon in Aquarius in the 2nd conjunct tropical Sun/Venus bestows tremendous charisma and determination as subconscious and conscious energies fuse into a force of nature, often a larger-than-life person. Because the Moon represents the past and possible other incarnations, the merging of solar and lunar energies might suggest a soul of great experience intent on making a huge difference to the world – it is a separating conjunction, symbolic of a new era or cycle. That all of this occurs in the 2nd house is a blessing on finance, incidentally.

The overall 'sextile' nature of the synastry chart – because the distance between tropical and draconic North Nodes is just over 60 degrees, likewise between other points and planets – is a powerful indicator of success, if the individual finds the strength built into the chart.

Distance converted simply into aspect often helps to determine quickly just how challenging the fulfilment of life purposes may be.

The three-step approach to draconic analysis

In Winfrey's chart we witness a symphony of themes that involve personal evolution and worldly aims – inner growth intimately a part of the outer.

Nelson Mandela: overthrowing the status quo

Mandela suffered 27 years in jail before becoming President of South Africa in 1994, the nation's first black head of state. A lawyer by training and of royal heritage, he was a leading anti-Apartheid campaigner who campaigned from the early 1940s as a member and later leader of the African National Congress. In power he dismantled the racist civil structure of South Africa yet also worked for reconciliation, understanding that the country had no future if it remained divided between black and white. He pronounced that 'courageous people do not fear forgiving, for the sake of peace'.

His presidency did not diminish his charisma or values, and he is one of the few major leaders who left power even more respected nationally and internationally than when he gained it. To South Africans he was 'the father of the nation', and globally an icon of democracy, likened to Mahatma Gandhi and Martin Luther king Jr as a civil rights leader, as close to being a 'secular saint' as is possible. Detractors accused him of terrorism in his fight against the Apartheid state. But once he was in a position to act on his principles of justice and racial equality, he remained true to them all the while living frugally and donating half of his presidential salary to poor children. In 1993 he was awarded the Nobel Peace Prize, part of which prize money he gave away to help street children. He died aged 95 in 2013.

Step 1: Nelson Mandela's tropical birth chart. (*Please note that Central European Daylight Time used for Mandela's chart substitutes for South Africa Standard Time [unavailable in Solar Fire]. Both time zones are two hours ahead of Coordinated Universal Time.*) Mandela's chart is straightforward in establishing life or spiritual purposes. His nodal axis falls across his Ascendant-Descendant axis. Venus on the latter is closely conjunct South

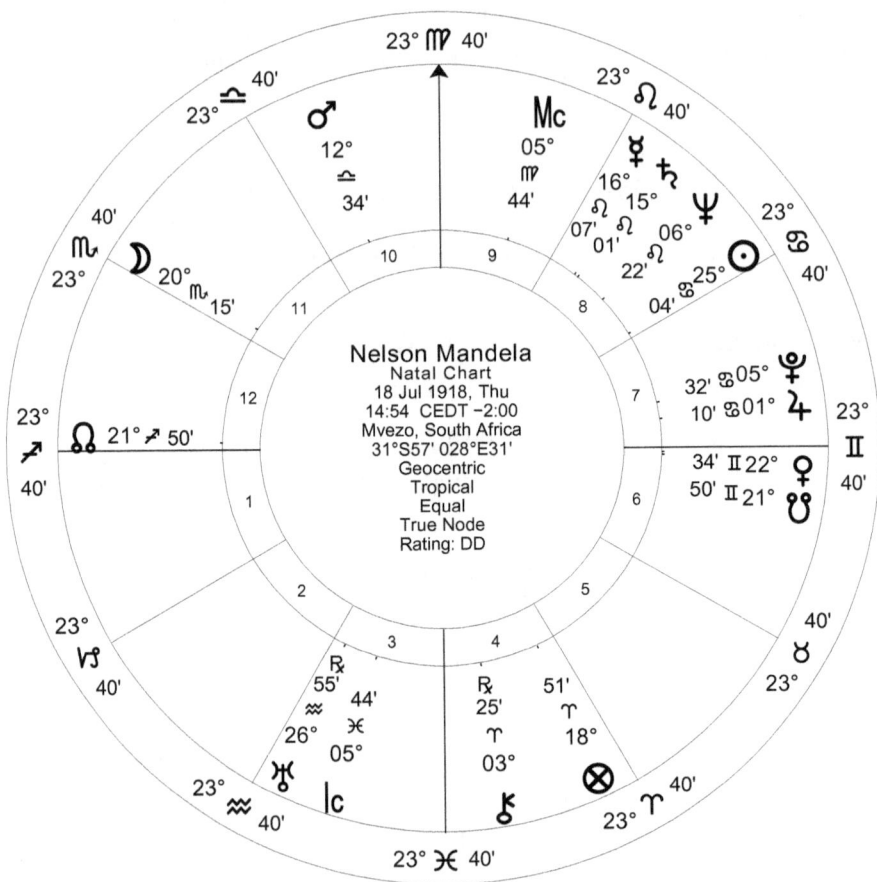

Node, associated with a privileged birth, charisma, much charm and popularity. This combination ingrains the soul with social and societal familiarity, bestowing sophistication and ease in relationships – all of which apply to Mandela. These traits will smooth his way in life.

But his destiny of North Node in Sagittarius, personalised on his Ascendant point, sets him challenging aims – it is the sign in its best expression of justice, internationalism, equality. Enhanced by chart ruler Jupiter exalted in Cancer (Mandela's Sun sign) in the 7th, one of the zones of Venus, this is an excellent place to promote harmony between two discrete groups (in the mundane or worldly sense of Apartheid). Jupiter's conjunction with Pluto brings powerful convictions to ideals: Pluto's sign of Scorpio is on the 12th-house cusp of universalism (plainly *not* 'self-undoing' in this context).

The move away from Venus towards Ascendant opposition suggests problematic relationships and the need for a realisation that acting independently will be part of life challenge and purpose. He married three times, his most famous wife being the fiery Winnie Mandela ('I think I married trouble' he once said of her) and divorced twice due to his political career/activism and adulteries. Throughout his life he complained of loneliness, leaving aside protracted imprisonment.

The sign of major trouble in his career direction is Mars in its detriment in Libra (the sign of the 7th house) in the 10th house: the sign's inclination to include chafes against the planet's resolution to exclude or to act in a way that is incompatible with cooperation.

The Equal 8th house is very busy, predominantly Leo but including the Cancer Sun. Tremendous self-identification with an empowerment theme will be asked of the individual in a chart zone associated among other things with crisis and fear of loss.

The chart shape is a Bucket with Uranus as the handle, dignified in its own sign in the 3rd house. Buckets often describe a dominant if not overbearing life purpose; Uranus in the 3rd as planet of revolt blesses rhetoric and rebellion underpins the rest of the chart. He was born to overthrow what he perceived as unjust, and the fixity of Aquarius implies struggle (Uranus square Moon in the 11th, zone of Aquarius).

His First Quarter Moon in Sagittarius will demand major risks be taken, often found in leaders, because there is so much to prove. In the 12th house, this is a hard position, because the 12th rules confined places such as jails.

Chasing the Dragons: An Introduction to Draconic Astrology

Step 2: Nelson Mandela's draconic birth chart. Cardinal energy is elevated, but fixity remains in the majority: he will need to be a leading actor with resolution to fulfil a life purpose. He will have to take the initiative.

North Node and Ascendant sit together in early Aries, a 'battle cry' combination. Aries is the warrior: this chart tells graphically of a fight to be embarked on. Chart ruler Mars is promoted to Capricorn in its exaltation, a blessing for the fight in the world of politics and governance (10th house). Tropical Sagittarius rising speaks of justice, yet it will have to be fought for through draconic Aries.

Draconic Sun is quincunx North Node and Ascendant: a heavy hint that the individual faces inner disconnections. He will need to

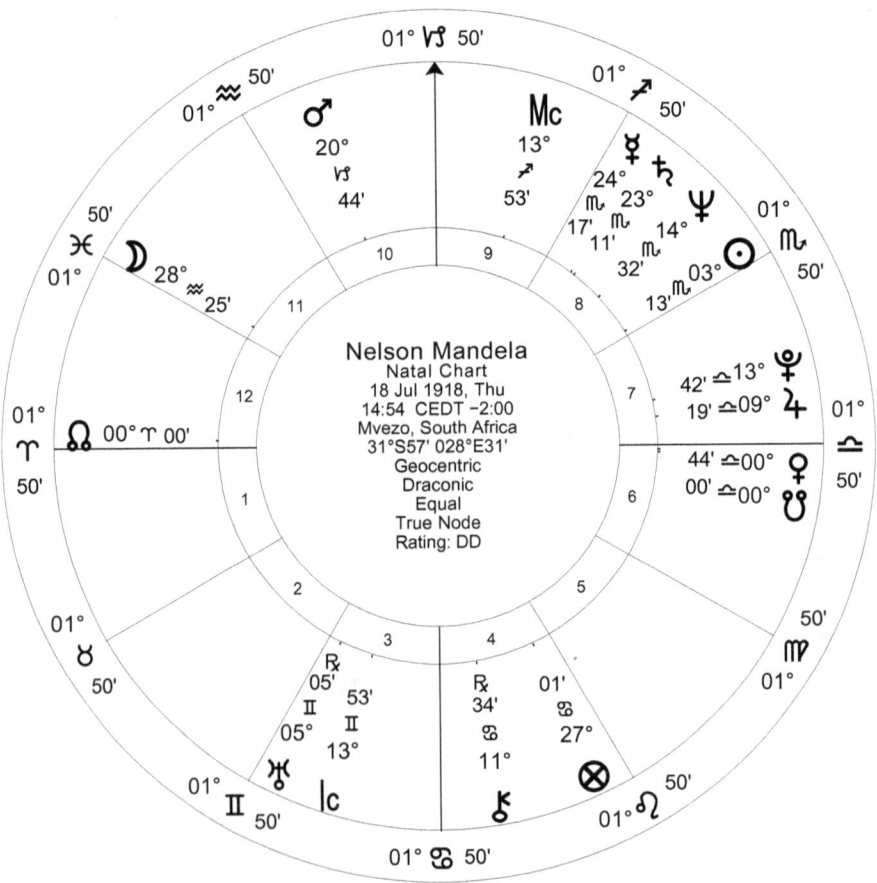

98

compartmentalise activities, beliefs and motivations of a contradictory nature, perhaps against his own impulses. Mandela was an activist labelled a terrorist, but he would later say that the ANC's armed struggle 'was forced on us by the government', such as the 1960 Sharpeville Massacre when police opened fire on a crowd of black people, killing 69 and wounding 180.

Venus opposite is promoted to Libra, enhancing charisma and appeal to the outer world. But the fight may be at the expense of Venus' rule, the realm of relationships, given Libra is on the 7th-house cusp. On a purely personal note, it is known that Mandela womanised and may have fathered children outside of his three marriages: expansive Jupiter is loosely conjunct Venus in the 7th.

The 8th house is now all draconic Scorpio, the house of the sign, an excellent association for self-empowerment, a life-or-death fight or struggle. Nothing in the 8th house can stay the same because its modern theme is 'transformation' which, despite the objections of certain traditional astrologers, is a pertinent application to this zone.

Uranus' move into Gemini in its own zone of the 3rd elevates Mandela's articulacy: as a lawyer he was precise in his use of language, eloquent and stirring with a gift for memorable phrasing. At his 1962 incitement trial he declared: 'I am a black man in a white man's court'.

Jupiter's and Pluto's move into Libra in the 7th italicises the theme of 'working together', two sides coming together.

Step 3: Nelson Mandela's tropical-draconic synastry of self chart. Draconic North Node and Ascendant move to the 4th house conjunct tropical Chiron: homeland and pain go together here, South Africa and apartheid: in Aries (and in the very early degrees) a new world is envisaged.

Other 4th-house modern associations are evident. Draconic Saturn in Scorpio sits on tropical Moon (planet of the 4th-house zone) in the 11th, descriptive of the fight against collectives which will involve isolation.

Chasing the Dragons: An Introduction to Draconic Astrology

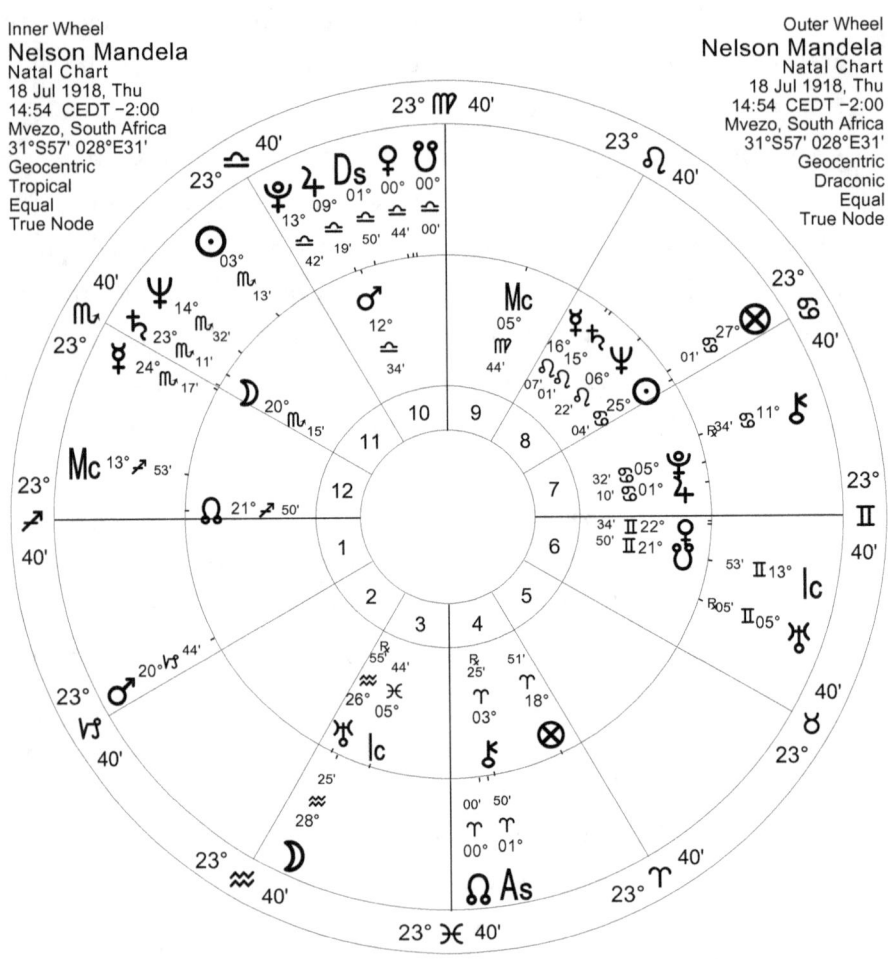

Draconic Moon is conjunct tropical Uranus in Aquarius (sign of the 11th) in the 3rd speaks of 'freedom from...'

Libra brought to the busy 10th is most appropriate given the unifying role Mandela played as president despite much contention: tropical Mars conjunct all the draconic planets and points warns of this. Echoing this, draconic Mars in the 1st in Capricorn opposes tropical Sun: he may 'become' the state, but the state is also against him, at different periods of his life. Tropical Sun's conjunction with draconic Part of Fortune in Cancer in the 8th foretells victory in the matter of homeland and change.

The three-step approach to draconic analysis

Leaving aside what we know of Mandela, it is plainly his life purpose to 'transform' homeland and empower his heritage and to do this by struggle and activism. It is curious that the house of Aries, the 5th, is empty given Mandela's history. But it's telling of the way fate cast him in the role of civil rights fighter against the state: circumstances served as the trigger, not innate aggression or criminality. Draconic Mars in Capricorn (government) rules this 5th zone, just as does Mars in Libra in the 10th (zone of Capricorn): his enemy is the state, at least until he is victorious.

Britney Spears: the fight against patriarchy and limitation

The American singer-songwriter, actress and dancer is one of the most successful and iconic performers in pop music history. She began as a child star, and at age 12 in 1993 she joined TV series *The Mickey Mouse Club*, becoming a 'Mouseketeer' along with the likes of Justin Timberlake whom she would later date for a short while. In the late 1990s she became the 'Princess of Pop' as a teen sensation. She has sold 150 million albums across the world as of 2020. And her studio albums *…Baby One More Time* and *Oops! I did It Again…* are among the bestselling albums of all time. Among her nearly 50 single releases, 2004's 'Toxic' is Spears' most streamed single in the US with 448 million streams as of June 2020.

However, her mental health became a media issue in 2007 when she was pictured shaving her hair off with clippers and attacking a paparazzo's car with an umbrella. Further odd behaviour was witnessed during a custody battle over her sons with ex-husband Kevin Federline, and in 2008 she was committed to a psychiatric ward at the Ronald Reagan UCLA Medical Center. Subsequently, a court placed her under a conservatorship (a form of court-appointed guardianship) co-led by her father Jamie Spears, giving him and a lawyer almost complete control over her personal life, career and assets. Such an order is usually made where a person is deemed lacking in capacity to manage their own affairs. This arrangement endured for nearly 14 years despite repeated legal attempts by Spears to free herself. She was supported by her fans' vociferous #FreeBritney campaign and by such fellow stars as Timberlake and Cher. Madonna likened Spears' conservatorship to slavery.

A claim in court documents filed by her father that Spears suffers from dementia has yet to be substantiated by medical evidence. It was commented on that in the first few months under the conservatorship, Spears embarked on the 'Circus' world tour which grossed US$132 million – requiring stamina and commitment that do not sit well with the notion that she has dementia or other mental problems.

In November 2021, a US judge ended the conservatorship amid media questions about its appropriateness. Spears was depicted in the media as a victim who finally broke free of the sexism and misogyny of the 'patriarchal' legal system, setting a precedent for others attempting to liberate themselves from conservatorships. On Instagram, Spears posted a message to her 37 million followers after the termination of the conservatorship: 'I think I'm gonna cry…[it is] the best day ever…' On the website *Spiked*, Chief Political Writer Brendan O'Neill wrote: '[Spears'] newfound freedom could well represent…a revolt against the legally imposed restrictions on her life.'

Not just still a pop icon, she is now perceived as a celebrity idol of personal liberation, especially in the sexism struggle.

Jamie Spears denies all allegations that he was responsible for the restrictions imposed on his daughter and at time of writing has demanded that they be investigated.

Step 1: Britney Spears' tropical birth chart. As in Mandela's, chart ruler Venus is conjunct South Node. Planets close to the nodes are always of great significance. We may speculate as to the immense charm that is Spears' default trait, but the thing to note is that Venus in Capricorn is disposited by Saturn while Spears' exalted Saturn in Libra is disposited by Venus – in other words, we have a mutual reception by square. With Venus

The three-step approach to draconic analysis

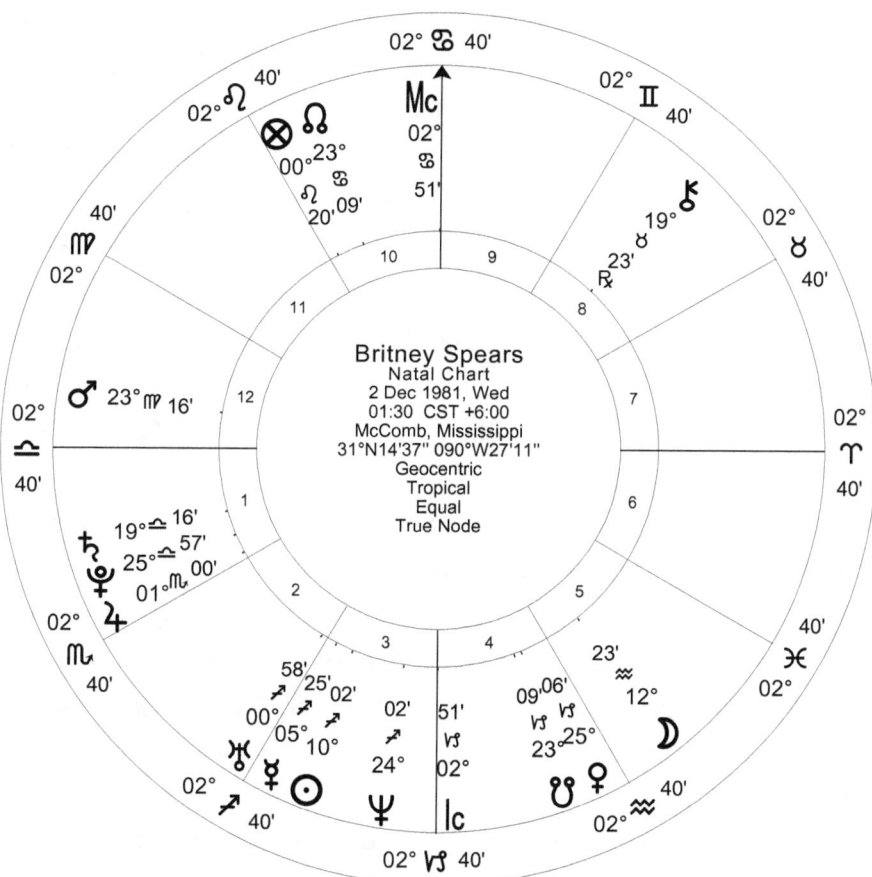

in the 4th house, this square alerts to a potential problem in matters to do with family (4th), father (Saturn), authority (Saturn again) and relationship within the family (Venus). The mutual reception should mitigate the square to some extent, smooth its edges, but the square is complicated by Saturn's conjunction with Pluto: Pluto adds restriction and obstacle, its position in Libra leans toward relationships as an area to watch for restrictive or power controls on the person (1st house).

Pluto rules the 2nd house with Scorpio on the cusp, zone of income and assets: another area to watch for control issues.

Reincarnationists might very well deduce that Spears enters this life to address matters of Saturn and Venus: restriction within relationship, limitations on life pleasures and freedoms imposed by authority.

The nodal axis encompasses Capricorn South Node to Cancer North Node in the 10th, as does the IC/MC axis, also in the Equal 10th. Once again, Saturn themes apply which can embrace matters of personal freedom and authority. The nodal direction of travel is away from authority's potential restrictions towards Cancer's greater humanity and sensitivity (in this context), but this is a zodiac sign of dependency questions. We see that one life purpose has to do with a fight – Mars in Virgo in the 12th is exactly sextile/trine the nodes.

Cancer is associated with the 4th house, so matters to do with home environment are a major theme already in the tropical chart. Its ruler the Moon (sextile Sun in Sagittarius) is in Aquarius in the 5th, sign of personal independence in the house of the individual's creative passions.

The Bowl chart shape puts Mars in the lead, another suggestion of a destiny of 'fight', though Mars' sharp edge is not at its best in the nebulous or barrier-melting 12th house which in another form can represent places of isolation or confinement. Impetus may be interrupted by chaotic situations or thinking. Mars is disposited by Mercury, which is in its detriment in Sagittarius, an impediment but not one irredeemably so.

Her chart is highly cardinal, she is born to take the lead. Her Crescent Moon is knowing and full of expectation but can be faced with problems of how to act or activate.

If you include fixed stars in your practice, Antares is exactly conjunct Spears' Sun[iv]. Antares, a massive reddish celestial associated with Scorpio (not Sagittarius), has the quality of the sign's old ruler Mars and

---

iv According to Michael Munkasey in *Little Book of Fixed Stars: Expanded Second Edition* by Elizabeth Hazel. Other sources vary on Antares' precise position in Sagittarius, but all would put the star in conjunction with her Sun.

The three-step approach to draconic analysis

astrologically prepares the individual for military strategy and battle. It has a fearsome (even a 'Toxic') reputation in mythology.

Step 2: Britney Spears' draconic birth chart. The most striking feature of this chart is that it captures the creative strength of Spears in a much more emphatic way than the tropical. Sun, Mercury and Uranus are in Leo, sign of the vivacious theatricality we associate with Spears at her best. Draconic Sun is in its strength, a star that cannot be ignored. This is part of life purpose, to display and perform, but as we have seen in other charts, a spiritual journey is often also wrapped up with emotional challenges.

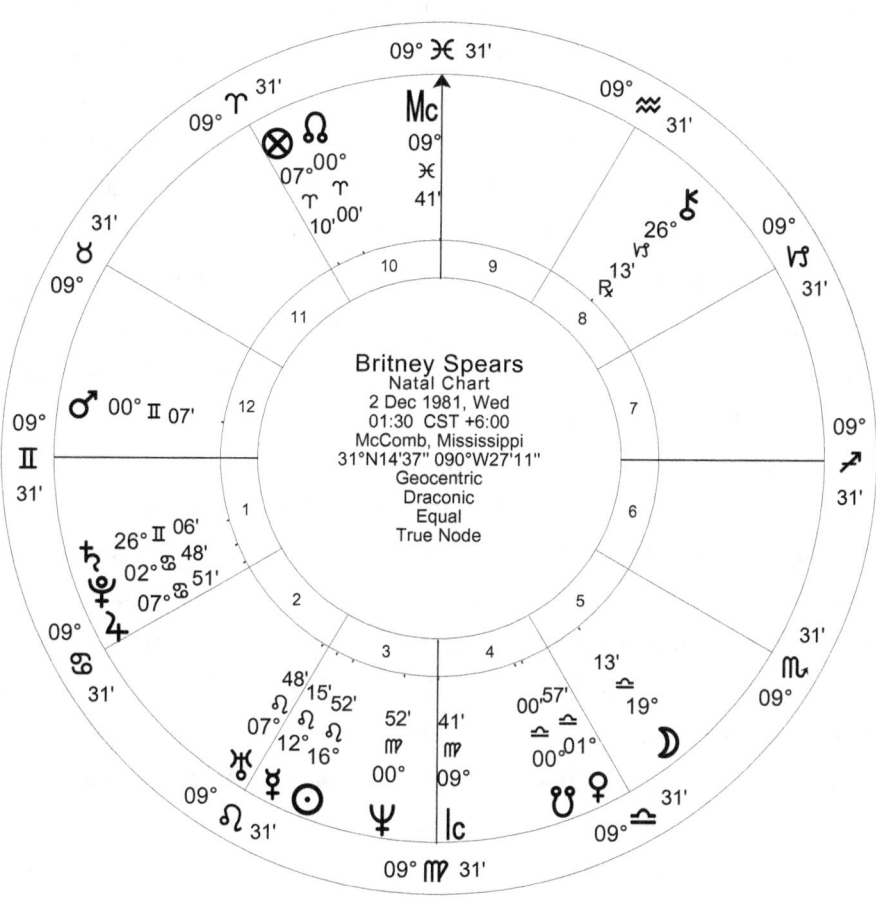

Venus is in its dignity in Libra, a promotion of significance. This alerts us to the 'relationship' issue in Spears' life and the problems we saw in the tropical chart. The transition from tropical Capricorn to Libra is the passage from restriction to a shared pleasure, to equality – this is a Spears challenge. Underscoring this is the Moon in draconic Libra, orienting the nature in its highest form towards finding harmony in relationship and with the world in general.

North Node in Aries in the 10th also tells us that it is a destiny point to take command of life direction: node ruler Mars is now in Gemini disposited by Mercury, promoted to the neutral sign of Leo. Mercury rules the draconic chart through Gemini rising: though the planet is in an applying conjunction to the Sun and combust – thought of as debilitating in traditional systems – I am not persuaded that this is of huge significance, given Mercury's frequent proximity to the Sun. At most, the combustion may signal a need to stay focused, just as with Mercury retrogrades.

Mars in draconic Gemini directs to adaptability and the power of words: with Sun in the 3rd house, the zone of Gemini, there is a resonance here between Spears' creativity and her power to communicate/radiate. Mars' 12th-house placement may suggest a future where she addresses issues pertaining to psychology, isolation, confinement and other meaningful themes. Her post-conservatorship life, invested now with the theme of 'confinement' of a sort, may be the springboard to a new 'career'.

Jupiter's exaltation in Cancer in the 1st resonates with the 4th house, the sign's natural home, suggesting the potential of growth through resurgent independence. Pluto now shares Cancer with Jupiter, a conjunction of power and resilience, which may be expressed in a variety of different ways. It may be part of Spears' life purpose to find her power through detachment from parts of family or through a family of her own or some other reinvention pertaining to family life.

Air is greatly promoted in the draconic chart, encouraging greater communication and dispassion as a source of strength.

The three-step approach to draconic analysis

Step 3: Britney Spears' tropical-draconic synastry of self chart. The tropical chart indicates plainly that there are issues to do with authority/father and relationship with the family. The synastry of self analysis makes this and other identified themes a lot starker.

Over in the 12th house, draconic South Node conjunct Venus rising is sufficiently close to tropical Mars in Virgo to confirm that contention must be expected in matters of relationship (in old astrology we might even say a male-female contention if we wish to continue gendering the planets as

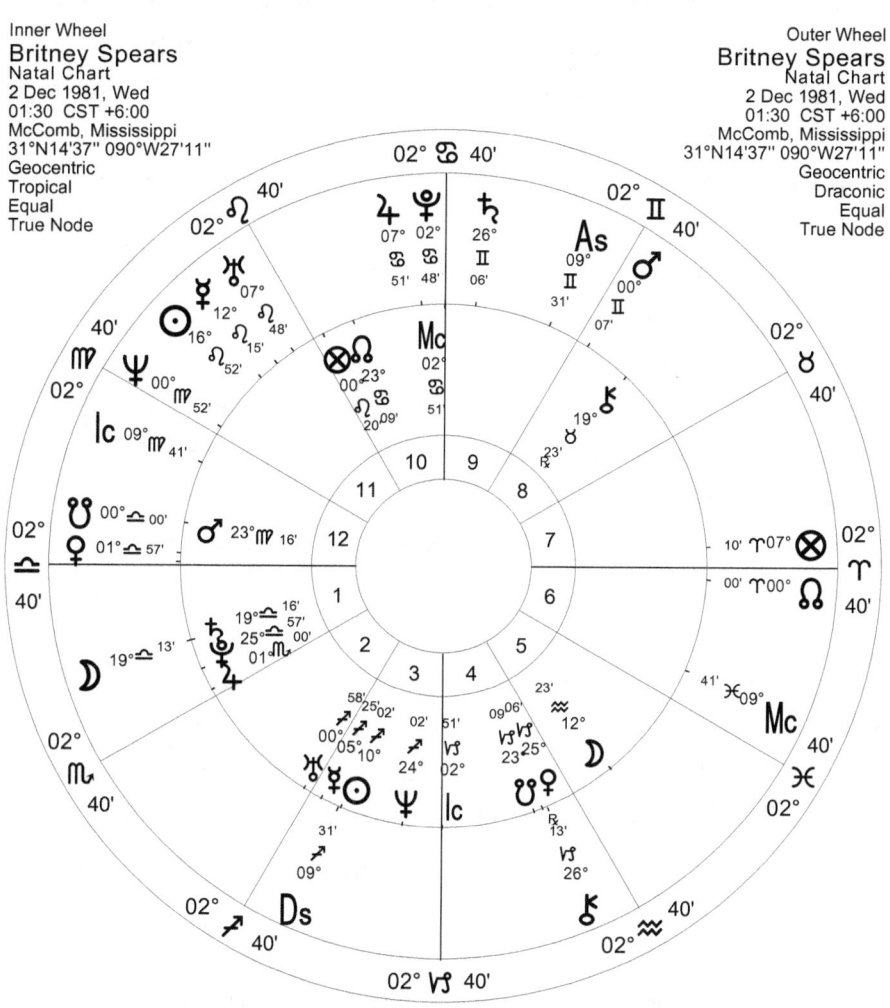

per the ancients). The out-of-sign nature of the conjunction (Libra-Virgo) takes the matter into the area of health, care and wellbeing – perhaps this denotes the healing power of resolved or addressed conflict.

But the draconic South Node-Venus-tropical Mars conjunction forms the apex of a highly problematic t-square that includes draconic Pluto-tropical MC in Cancer at the top of the chart and IC in Capricorn. The Pluto-MC conjunction bestows huge career ambition, even obsession, and accomplishment. But it also signifies the possibility of over-controlling influences within the family sphere (Cancer, square South Node-Venus). This is amplified by Pluto's opposition to the IC which is ruled by Saturn on the Equal 4th-house cusp: family/father/authority are implicated in matters of control or influence. It is a major theme of the chart, and most probably represents the problems Spears faced during her conservatorship, if not before. Or even to come.

The oppositional energies potentially find resolution through conflict with the apex planets and point (Libra-Virgo).

Draconic Pluto is disposited by draconic Moon in Libra in the 1st house – and you can see which tropical planet it conjoins exactly: Saturn. Just three minutes between them. Tropical Pluto is close by to stir things up further. This graphically symbolises the very personal nature of the problem (1st), involving the family (Moon) and authority/father (Saturn). And power (Pluto). The nature of the problem is relationship (Libra) and issues over equality.

Draconic North Node in Aries on the Descendant conjunct Part of Fortune in the 7th makes a lot clearer the life challenge Spears faces in preserving her independence within relationships. The draconic nodal axis forms a t-square with draconic Pluto in Cancer – suggesting that a great self-empowerment is available to her through family crisis and finding a healthy balance in her unions and alliances.

It's interesting to see draconic Descendant conjunct her tropical Sun in Sagittarius in the 3rd house, and draconic Mars in Gemini sextile North

Node: the two aspects are saying similar things, pointing to the need for greater freedom and staying independent.

Perhaps in a past life she was over-dependent on others, allowed others to 'consume' her (remember, tropical Venus conjunct South Node in Capricorn in the 4th). But you don't have to embark on a past-life quest. In this life alone, one sees the themes of her life played out in the charts. The former Princess of Pop she may be – and the draconic indicators reflect her stardom – but her soul requires as much as anything else air to breathe and the freedom to operate. Liberation in union.

Chapter Five

Draconic forecasting: transits and solar returns

It could be argued – against the current fashion – that astrology is mostly about forecasting. A simple delineation of a natal chart will include references to future likelihoods as character inclinations, strengths and weaknesses are identified. Vagueness, qualification or back-covering whatiffery does not turn a forecast into something else. Horary offers a direct Yes or No to questions while electionals decide on a favoured day or phase for an identified event. Secondary progressions describe emotional weather at any point of time while solar arc directions offer specificity. AstroCartography tells you where in the world you are more likely to find love, career or whatever – yes, that's a forecast of sorts, albeit one that applies natal chart patterns to geographic maps as opposed to the making of predictions. If you go through most of the techniques of astrology, forecasting in its general sense is hard to factor out because the very nature of astrology makes a nonsense of past, present and future as fixed zones. Astrology makes a Tardis of us all, a time machine that hurtles back and forth.

I say all this because a whole book could be written on the many ways in which draconic astrology can be used in forecasting – in fact, I am tempted to write it. As Pam Crane demonstrates in *The Draconic Chart*, midpoints, horary, progressions, etc may be used in draconic analysis. In this short introductory chapter, I confine matters to transits and solar returns – and we shall see how draconic transits can be used for forecasting in addition to tropical transits.

Chasing the Dragons: An Introduction to Draconic Astrology

It is a little-explored area and what follows is based entirely on my own work.

Before we get to the chart studies, remember that draconic focuses on the past as a guide to the present and future and seeks to answer the question of the significance of an 'outcome'. What is the underlying purpose of an event? What possible value might it have? Why is it happening? Draconic works on the principle that past and future are linked through experience, that outcomes are often consequences of actions or inactions. This idea is not news to tropical or sidereal astrologers, but in draconic it is presupposed that a given outcome is an opportunity to rebalance, heal, challenge or compensate.

A Moon-based system explores emotional and spiritual continuums set against surface life events.

Tropical transits and aspects can describe literal results or outcomes, and the same can be true in draconic. However, there is an implicatory feature in draconic that is not present in the parallel tropical – as if the draconic 'message' is setting out a future context in which a situation may be better understood. The precise outcome may be inferred from the context indicated in the chart. It is for the astrologer, as judge of the chart, to assess what the implication or inference may be – astrology has always acknowledged the 'judicial' role of the practitioner and it's no different in the draconic system. A chart may speak to us, yet the 'message' reaches us via interpretation of symbols and judgement.

It follows that the draconic chart should not be treated as an alternative to the tropical chart. It is a supplementary, specialist chart, adding another dimension to what is apparent in the tropical chart. On any given subject – whether a natal, mundane, synastry or other chart – I have discovered a remarkable concordance between tropical and draconic. The two work well together if the strengths and point of each are appreciated and used together to describe the bigger picture.

Draconic transits can be applied not just to draconic natal/event charts but also to tropical natal/event charts, in my experience, so long as you bear in mind the different purposes of either system.

The orb used for draconic transits is as for tropical, 1° either side. But astrologers have different views on orbs, so apply what works for you.

If this all sounds a little abstract, let's look at some charts to see how these rules are applied in practice. Given that we are looking at the charts of events that have already occurred, what I am setting out to do here is to demonstrate the symbolic potency of draconic transits when they link by aspect to tropical or draconic planets and points.

The planets involved and the aspect they form must be strongly pertinent to the event in question.

The Covid-19 pandemic

A good example of what I mean is the natal chart for the coronavirus (or Covid-19) pandemic for end of 2019, Wuhan, China. Views differ on the pandemic's 'birth' moment. I have based the selected chart on the date given by the World Health Organisation (WHO) when the Wuhan Municipal Health Commission, China, reported to the WHO a cluster of cases of pneumonia in Wuhan, Hubei Province – 'a novel coronavirus was eventually identified'[v].

The great mundane astrologer André Barbault forecast in 2011 the probability of a pandemic in 2020-21. His essay 'An Overview of Pandemics' (translated into English from French in the May-June 2020 issue of *The Astrological Journal*[vi]) cited a planetary imbalance in the tropical zodiac chart, specifically 'a quintet of slow-moving planets gathered within about 100 degrees, and which includes a Jupiter-Saturn-Pluto conjunction [in

---

v   Who.int. Look for WHO Timeline – Covid-19.
vi Astrologicalassociation.com. In members-only archive. Barbault used his Cyclic Index to evaluate risks of war and pandemics etc., as explained in this issue.

Chasing the Dragons: An Introduction to Draconic Astrology

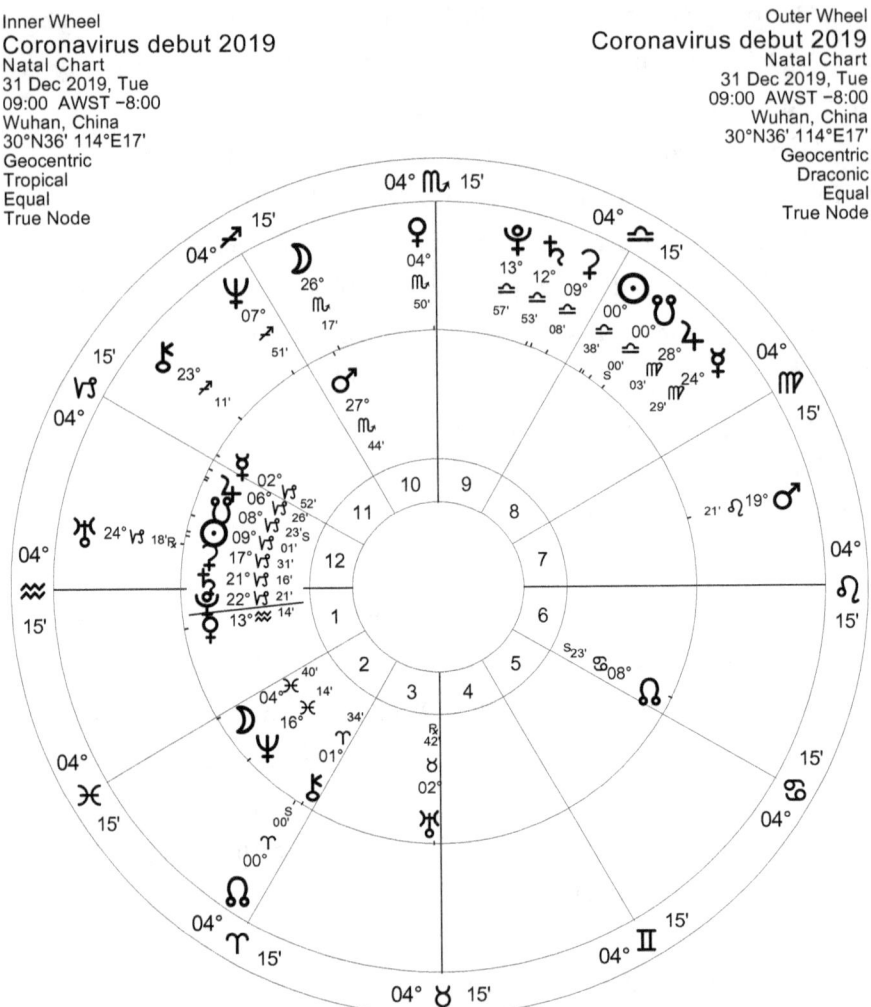

Capricorn]'. Such abnormal chart imbalances he associated with raised risks of catastrophe such as war or pandemic.

The Capricorn abundance of planetary tropical transits is plain to see in the inner wheel of the coronavirus biwheel with Saturn and Pluto set to conjoin exactly on 12 January 2020 – the conjunction cycle of these two planets alone has its own associations with disruption in mundane or world astrology.

Draconic forecasting

Before I drew up the draconic version of the tropical, I recall saying to a friend apropos the pandemic, 'Where is Uranus in all this?' Covid-19 had distinctly Uranian features. Uranus is known as 'The Great Awakener', a planet of revolution and change, that stirs us from torpor or inertia or ignorance. The pandemic hit the world at great speed, seeming to come from nowhere like the proverbial bolt from the blue, spreading about the globe in a matter of weeks, thanks mainly to international air travel. Almost in an instant, lives on a worldwide scale were altered as societies faced lockdown (a Capricorn association), the suspension of what had passed for reality for so long. Tropical Uranus' trine to the Capricorn stellium via the lower octave of fellow mind planet Mercury scarcely expressed the impact or scale of the plague.

My friend advised me, 'Why not look at the draconic chart?'

And there it is. Draconic Uranus in Capricorn conjunct the tropical stellium. It conjoined tropical Pluto as far back as August 2019 around which time (or a little before) it is thought that the coronavirus was already embedding in Wuhan or surrounding areas. Draconic Uranus' proximity to the tropical stellium – immersed in Capricorn associations – brings the energy of 'awakening' to the correlations identified by Barbault with chart imbalance. With the benefit of hindsight, we see the draconic warning sign in addition to what is already apparent in the tropical chart.

Draconic Uranus' position is a forecast of sudden upheaval or event related to Capricorn themes for the time period, but one loaded with the suggestion that there is much that must be learnt from this upheaval. What lessons must be learned is a matter of opinion, whether to do with treatment of animals in the human food chain (Wuhan's unhygienic 'live-animal markets' are among origin suspects), genetic engineering or the general responsibilities of science.

More broadly, many people in lockdown had time to reflect on their lives and to reflect not just on less stressful alternatives (such as working from home, relying more on the internet) but also on humanity's impact on global environment as pollution levels lifted temporarily with the absence of planes in the skies and cars on roads.

The tropical stellium indicated the peril to come; draconic Uranus the way forward if we stay awake.

Britney Spears again: a liberation forecast

In the last chapter we finished with Britney Spears' charts. Her conservatorship ended on 12 November 2021, a major event of release from what many people regard as an oppressive legal restraint on her freedom. The tropical forecast chart is articulate of this so let's examine it first.

This chart shows Spears' birth chart (inner wheel) and the transits for 12 November 2021 – the precise clock time is not hugely significant for our purposes, so I have set it for midday (the actual time is probably around 3:30 pm PST, but news sources are imprecise), and I have not relocated the outer chart to Los Angeles, the place of the court decision.

Tropical South Node is conjunct natal Uranus in Sagittarius, consistent with liberation from a long-term situation (South Node symbolises the past) via a judicial process (Sagittarius). The early degrees signal a new life cycle or episode. Transiting Pluto sits in conjunction between natal South Node and Venus in Capricorn in the 4th, indicating a fundamental change in the chart zone of family and relationship, ruled by Saturn (authority or father). Transiting Saturn in Aquarius appears to be out of orb conjunct natal Moon in the 5th, but actually is in a lunar conjunction cycle, having stationed direct on 11 October 2021, and first conjoined Moon on 31 March 2021, a few days after Spears applied to the LA Superior Court to have her father Jamie replaced as conservator.

Aquarius sets a theme of independence within the realm of family (Saturn-Moon conjunction): ruler natal Uranus is exactly square Moon (rebellion, detachment from past), transiting Mars in Scorpio is applying

Draconic forecasting

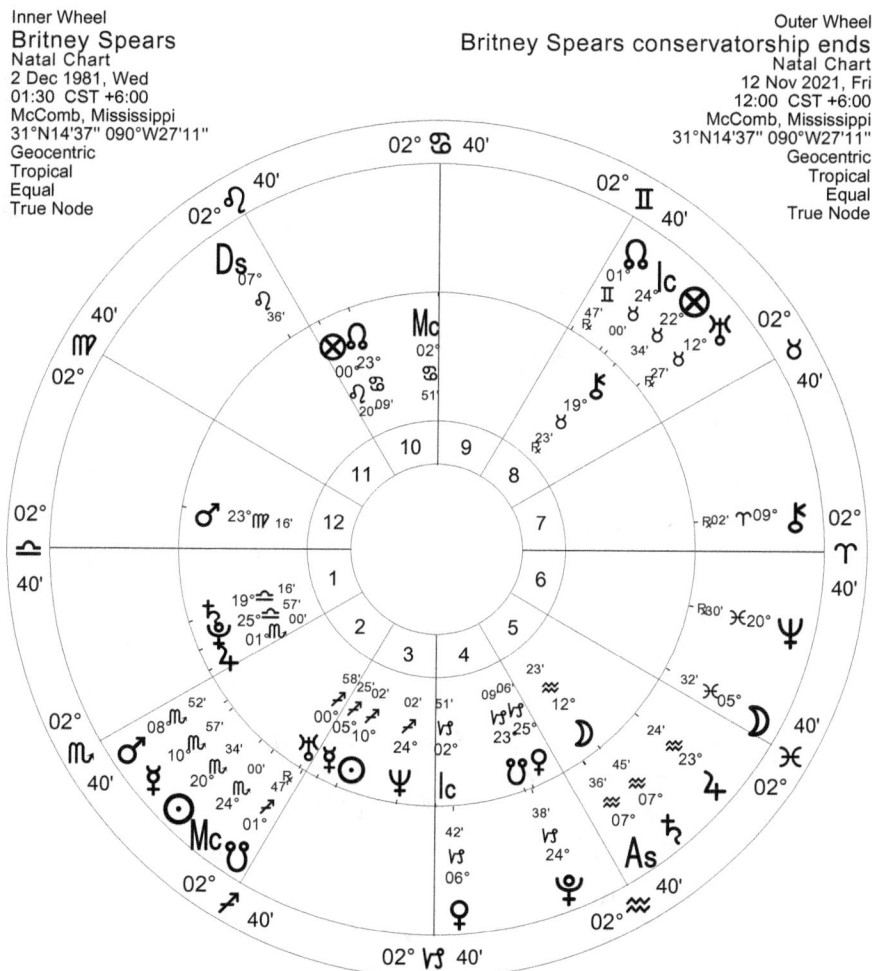

to square Moon (fight) while, as we have seen, a transiting South Node is conjunct tropical, liberating natal Uranus.

In the biwheel for Spears' tropical natal chart and draconic transits (outer wheel) for 12 November 2021 there are two interaspects of particular interest, both featuring Saturnian energies.

The first is draco Moon just entering Capricorn conjunct natal IC, the point of ancestral roots, private life and things hidden from the subject. Moon as one of the luminaries is casting light on a family matter in the

Chasing the Dragons: An Introduction to Draconic Astrology

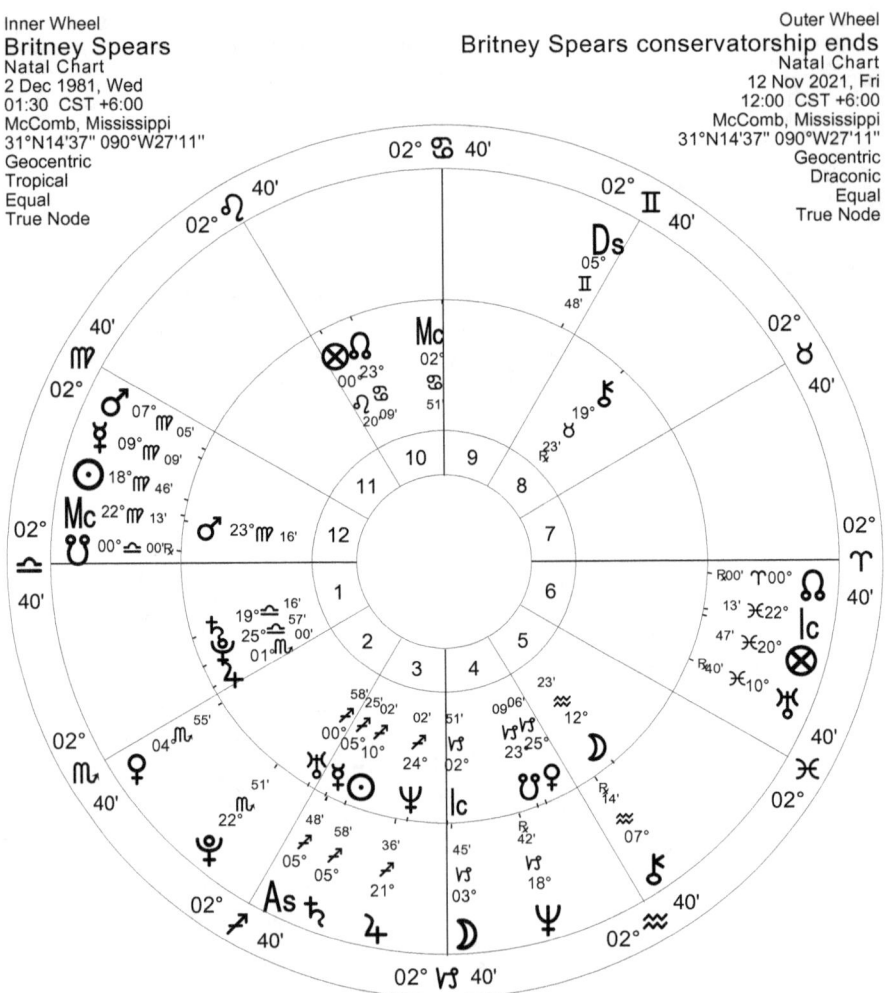

cardinal sign of Saturn (Capricorn), ruler of definition, authority and consequences. Moon also rules the opposite angular point the Midheaven in Cancer. Given the timing, this may be interpreted as a starting point for family-related matters to be set on a new path of order and arrangement.

A secondary interpretation identifies women or a woman (Moon) as playing a key part in this process – the judge who ended the conservatorship was female (Judge Brenda Penny). Draconically, this suggests a shift or release from patriarchal/legal power though not one that necessarily ends the father/daughter relationship for good. It looks more like a 'repositioning' given the nature of the opposition aspect with the future possibility of a reconciliation. The draconic nodal axis close to the Ascendant/Descendant axis in Libra-Aries respectively forms a slightly out-of-orb t-square to the Moon/IC conjunction, infusing the aspect with a relationship theme (as part of a cardinal Grand Cross if we include MC), which suggests the need to address underlying (IC) factors and motivations for a fuller understanding of the conservatorship and its termination.

The other Saturnian theme is set by draconic Saturn exactly conjunct tropical Mercury in Sagittarius in the 3rd: Mercury's detriment is counterbalanced or out-weighed by sign ruler Jupiter in its strength in Sagittarius in the 3rd. Given the timing, a judicial 'saviour' is suggested, justice is done. This is an excellent moment to reboot plans along a more ambitious, independent pathway (Sagittarius) but one that has clear parameters (3rd house).

This chart suggests a restart moment.

The wholly draconic forecast biwheel chart (i.e., draconic natal with draconic transits for 12 November 2021) lays bare the stark significance of the conservatorship termination.

Significantly, draconic transiting Uranus sits at the top of the chart in the 10th house conjunct draconic natal MC in Pisces. The most obvious meaning is major change in public profile with Uranus' twist of an 'awakening' moment. This message is not made explicit in the previous charts. And Pisces tends to work against restrictions or borders, or even conservatorships. The exactitude of the conjunction is out by just one minute, strengthening the message of independence as a major component of the planet.

Transiting draconic Mercury sits opposite Uranus/MC in Virgo in the 4th. This Mercury is particularly bold because only two days earlier, it conjoined draconic transiting Mars, now two degrees behind. In the literal

Chasing the Dragons: An Introduction to Draconic Astrology

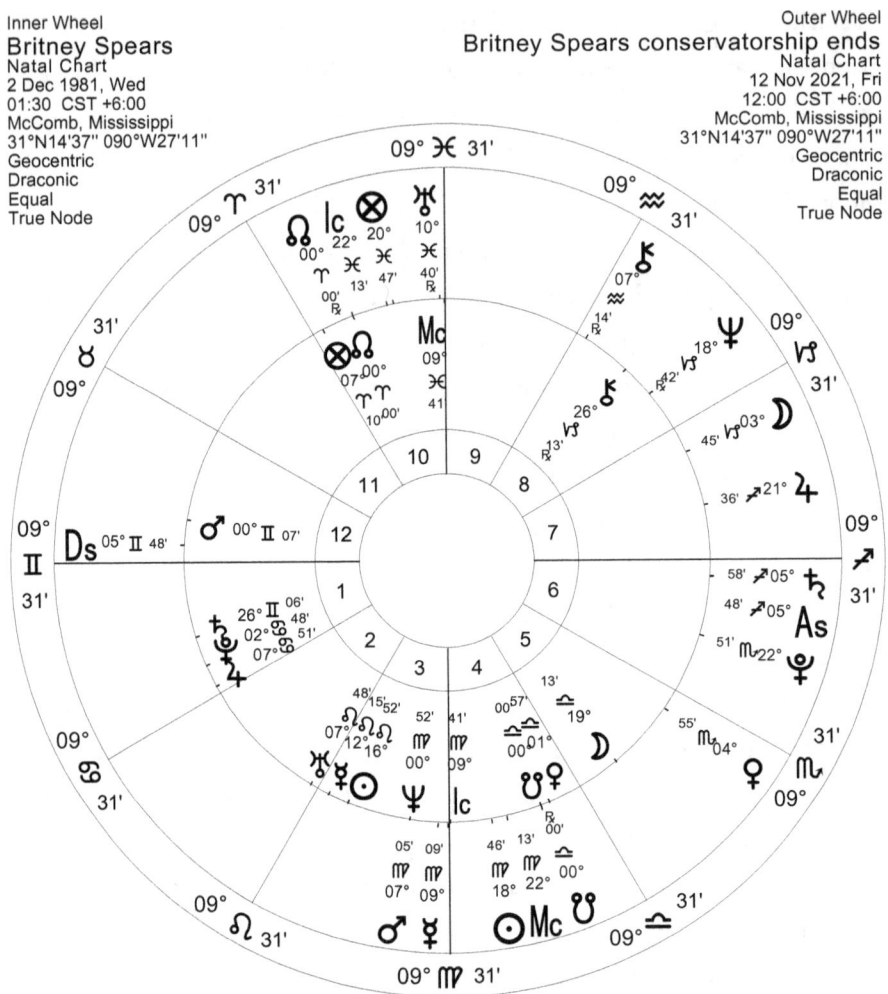

sense this is an explosive moment, as the media photos showed Spears celebrating her 12 November victory.

But the opposition suggests that the termination of the conservatorship is not without its complications and challenges. If Spears is to make the most of her new-found 'liberation', she must factor in the grounding energy of Virgo in her life; in effect to bring order to a place which in the past was chaotic at times and then latterly oppressed. Personal freedom is not to be equated with anything-goes under this aspect: it must co-exist with personal responsibility, a hands-on philosophy, with attention to details. This is the draconic message – not so much a forecast as a piece of advice.

The context of the chart presupposes a time of restriction because the timing of the event with Uranus in exact conjunction with MC marks a 'release from'.

Also worth noting is that draconic transiting Moon in Capricorn in the 7th is in tight opposition to natal Cancer Pluto in the 1st. Once again, the immediate picture is not all it may seem. The aspect literally describes a rupture or galvanic happening in a family relationship. But Pluto digs beneath the surface of things, so there's a need for further discovery or investigation to find out what may be hidden in the relationship in question. Pluto also signifies entrusted or shared money. A healing of sorts (of Spears or the relationship or both) requires more openness before resolution.

The termination of the conservatorship has a 'rebirth' feel to it; it is an opportunity to grow but only by assimilating hard or dark lessons (Pluto). The draconic approach respects freewill; there is nothing fatalistic about success or failure.

Donald Trump: Who wins the US presidential election 2020? Forecasting by draconic solar return

In the summer of 2020, a magazine asked me to predict the outcome of the US presidential election in November of that year. Generally, my approach in matters of this sort is straightforward: I analyse the transits chart against the natal chart of a candidate for the moment that the polls close, in this instance New York 9:00 pm.

The Republican 45th incumbent, Donald J. Trump, sought re-election against the Democrat candidate Joe Biden. Polls generally favoured Biden by smallish margins. But Trump had won the 2016 election against the odds in his contest with Hillary Clinton, perhaps one of the greatest election upsets in modern political history. He had held no political office before the presidency and struck many as entirely inexperienced and hopelessly compromised by past personal and business scandals. His public profile had been raised through the TV reality show *The Apprentice* in which he tested and 'fired' mini-me Trump entrepreneurs in competition for business favour. Following the 2016 result, trust in pollsters collapsed. Clinton had led all the way in the polls as Trump manically traversed the nation in the Trump Organization's Boeing 757 'Trump Force One' plane, giving incendiary speeches in different parts of the US, often on the same day. The public impression was that he seemed everywhere, dynamic, and the antithesis of a Washington insider. He successfully nicknamed Clinton – a former First Lady during husband Bill Clinton's presidency – 'crooked Hillary' on Twitter where he posted daily messages to his millions of followers, circumventing the hostile mainstream media, or 'Fake News' as he called TV channels and newspapers.

Could Trump repeat his victory in 2020, defying apparent political gravity again?

To answer the magazine's question, I first analysed Trump's natal chart with the tropical transits for 3 November 2020 in a biwheel. The North Node return sitting tightly between natal Sun and Uranus conjunct both Moons certainly suggested a new life era and an emotionally climactic moment on the day, but defeat or victory was not plainly indicated.

The most powerful aspect against Trump was the opposition of transiting Pluto (flanked by Jupiter and Saturn in Capricorn) to his Saturn: this suggested loss of power or control, or a shift to a new order of life which disrupts a person's authority, especially if it is imagined that life can be conducted on the same terms as before. Pluto seeks to bring about correction, usually through crisis or revelation. Opposed to the life structures of Saturn, Pluto was bound to cause an earthquake, I felt. This aspect alone persuaded me that Trump probably faced defeat or at least an enfeebled second presidency.

Draconic forecasting

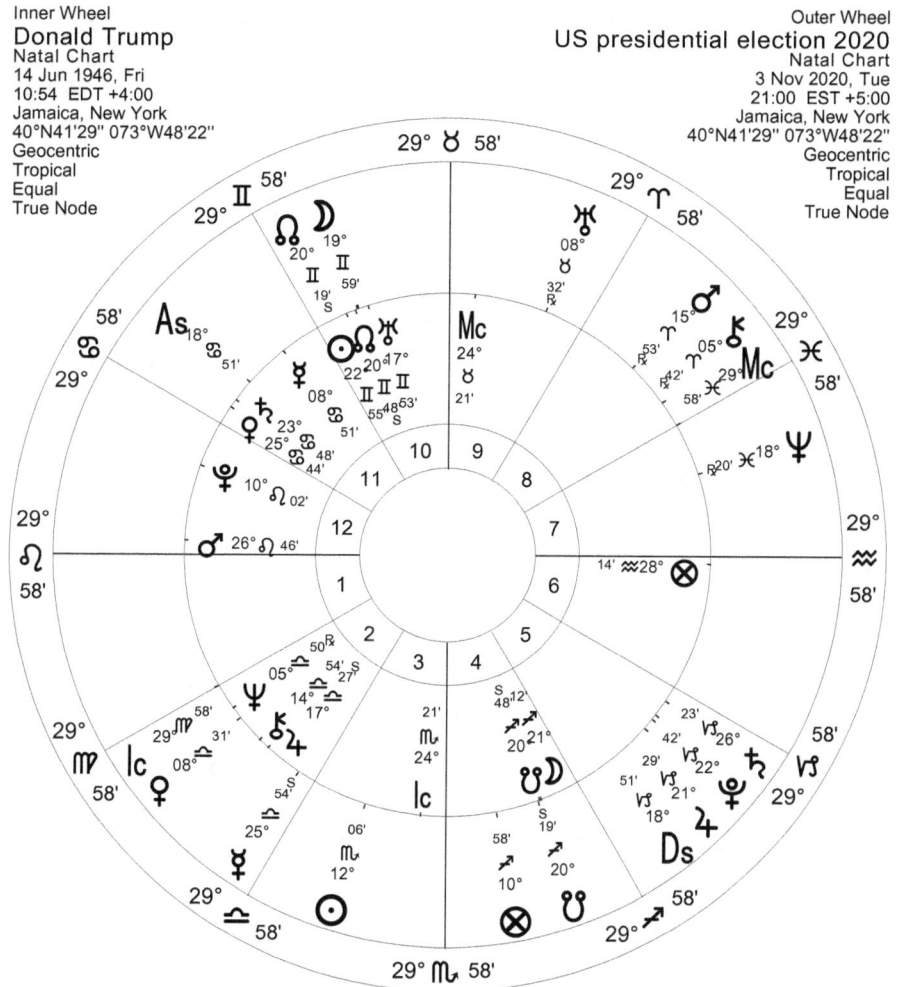

Biden's chart (not shown) for the day was more promising with transiting Sun starting to conjoin his Scorpio stellium in the 12th house via Mars strengthened by dignity but challenged by poor aspects (such as Pluto square).

I then took a less orthodox approach to the question and drew up a Trump draconic solar return for 2020.

For this, you must first draw up the *draconic* birth chart. This puts Trump's Sun in early Aries with Gemini on the Ascendant. Because the

Chasing the Dragons: An Introduction to Draconic Astrology

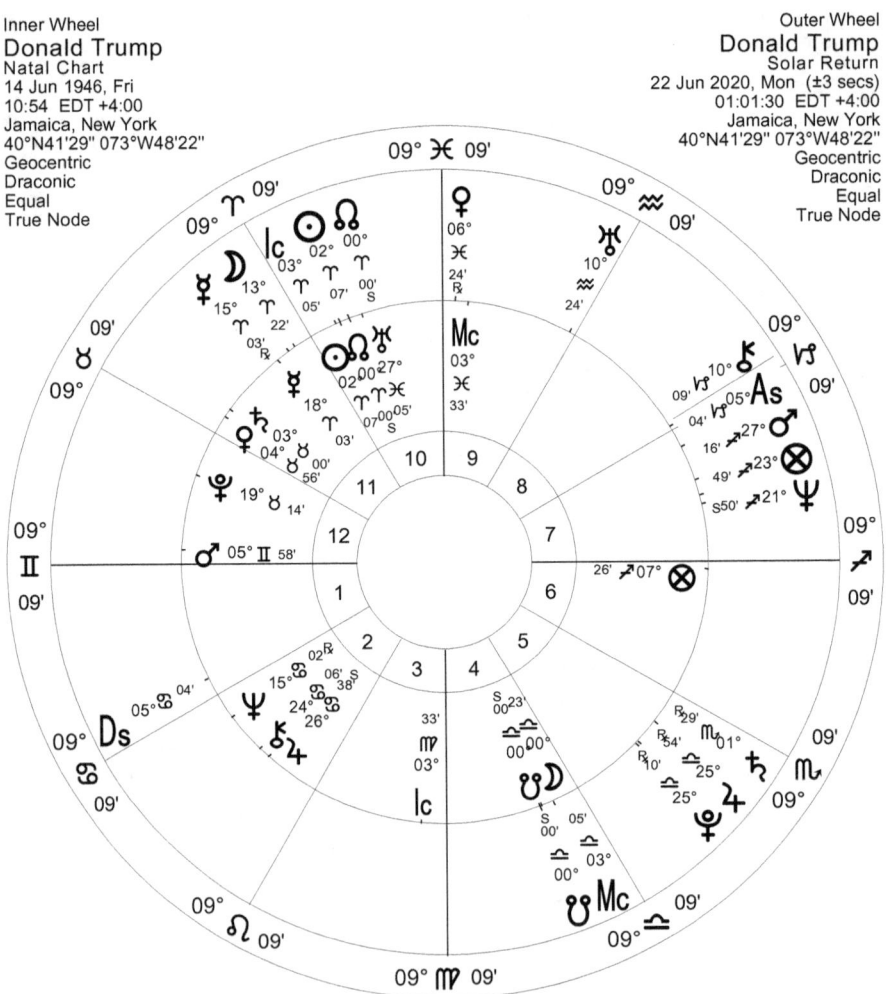

draconic Sun completes a return in about 11 months, the draconic birthday (i.e, transiting draco Sun exactly conjunct draco natal Sun) is usually different from the tropical birthday. So, the chart shows that Trump's draconic birthday was on 22 June 2020, not the 14th of his tropical chart.

The most glaring thing about this solar return is the abundance of Aries in the chart region of life direction and professional connections (10th and 11th houses) which in mundane astrology also rules executive and governmental power: eight planets and points in total.

Draconic forecasting

I said earlier in this book that in draconic, always try to look for the headline news. This feature of the solar return alone did not answer directly the question of whether Trump was likely to win: the return chart is for the year ahead and may embrace different situations. But in the context of a re-election, I inferred from the chart positions of the Aries energy that if a person is seeking more of the same, more of what has preceded the solar return year, 'more presidency', then Aries is not the sign for that. Aries is the fresh start, the new 'year', the new life or pathway.

I also factored in the fractious 7th-house SR draconic Mars' exact square to draconic birth Uranus in the 10th, a marker of instability and the risk of surprise outcomes. Transiting Venus is exalted at the top of the biwheel in Pisces, perilously close to natal MC which perhaps tells us that he'd have a lot more time on his hands for pleasure pursuits. Mr Trump is an enthusiastic golfer by all accounts.

Pope Francis I 2020 controversy: sensitivity between tropical transits and draconic natal positions

In September of 2020, I gave an online Zoom talk on draconic astrology to the Astrology Student Conference run by Frank C. Clifford's London School of Astrology and Wendy Stacey's Mayo School of Astrology. I examined the charts of Pope Francis I, and I forecast that in October 2020 the Pope was likely to clash with his followers or cardinals or say or do something of major import that would create controversy. And on 21 October 2020, the Pope (and the astrology) did not disappoint. News broke that he supported the idea that same-sex couples should be allowed to enter into civil unions. The BBC news site reported:

> '[The Pope] made the comments, which observers say are his clearest remarks yet on gay relationships, in a documentary directed by Evgeny Afineevsky. "Homosexual people have a right to be in a family," he said in the film, which premiered on Wednesday. "They

are children of God and have a right to a family. Nobody should be thrown out or made miserable over it. What we have to create is a civil union law. That way they are legally covered.'"

Consternation, from cardinals to laity, at the Pope's remarks followed inevitably, though socially liberal observers welcomed them.

To demonstrate this correlation between charts and events, let's take a closer look at Pope Francis' tropical and draconic birth charts, and then the tropical transits for 21 October 2020. The midday time was selected for convenience; precise time is not essential for our purposes here. Also, for the transits chart I have used the Mean Node for a change to emphasise a point below.

I won't give a thorough analysis of the Pope's chart, but just pick out some essential details. His tropical chart (inner wheel) is descriptive of what we know of him. The zodiac sign of church, Sagittarius, is his Sun which is conjunct North Node and dissociate conjunct ruler Jupiter in fall in Capricorn, all in the 6th house, chart domain of small animals. St Francis of Assisi is the patron saint of animals (and ecology). Jorge Mario Bergoglio – the Pope's birth name – assumed the saint's name to honour his work for the poor. A neat tie-up of associations between astrology and life.

The conjunction of Uranus and MC in the 10th in Taurus is an early indication of potential maverick or independent tendencies. The Saturn-Neptune opposition on the 9th-3rd Pisces-Virgo axis, embracing a number of life areas such as church and perspectives, also alerts to potential conflict between doctrine (Saturn) and a broader practical or pastoral spirituality (Neptune in Virgo).

Note also the so-called feminine planets, chart ruler Moon and Venus in Aquarius conjunct on the 8th-house cusp. In the draconic birth chart (middle wheel) both are promoted to Taurus, with Venus in its dignity and Moon exalted: the interest here is the planets' association with women. This can suggest among other things that part of his life purpose is to

Draconic forecasting

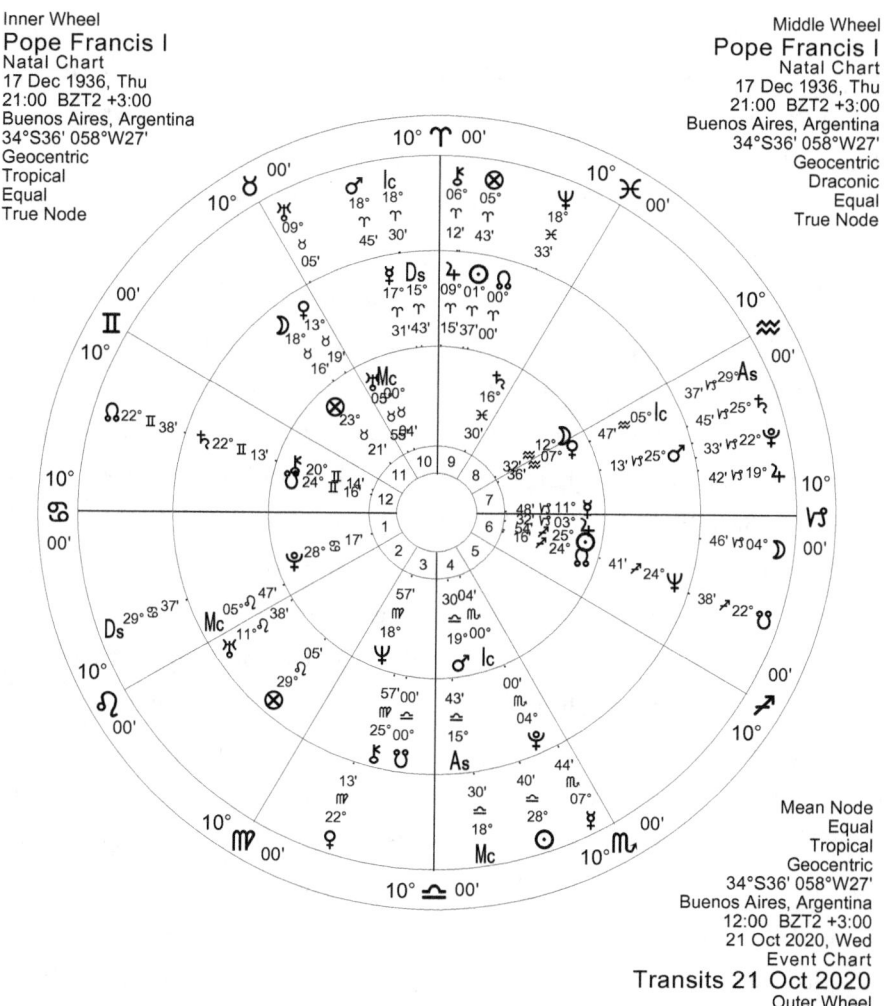

promote women's rights – and in January 2021 he did indeed change the law in the Roman Catholic Church, allowing women to administer communion and serve at the altar for the first time. Earlier, he had declared of church governance that 'women should be fully included in decision-making processes.' His reforms fall far short of admitting women into the ordained priesthood, yet his zeal against conservative ideas and practices in the Church is a consistent one and garners some appreciation as steps in the right direction against centuries-old traditions and prejudices.

The draconic chart also reassigns his tropical Sagittarius and Capricorn planets to Aries brought appropriately to the 9th and 10th houses of church and life direction/career. As we have seen elsewhere, Aries is the bold independent marching unto war of sorts. The chart identifies literally the life areas where this boldness will be required, in the realms of church and life direction.

The draconic Saturn-Neptune opposition empowers the tropical nodal axis, with tropical North Node exactly conjunct draconic Neptune in Sagittarius: this heightens idealism in the Pope, with truth and justice as cornerstones. Life or soul purpose is both to expand the positive aspects of his creed and dissolve barriers between faiths and perspectives. He has said: 'I believe in God, not in a Catholic God, there is no Catholic God.' On another occasion he stated: 'For me, ecumenism is a priority. Today, we have the ecumenism of blood. In some countries they kill Christians because they wear a cross or have a Bible, and before killing them they don't ask if they're Anglicans, Lutherans, Catholics or Orthodox. The blood is mixed.'

At the other end of this opposition in the 12th house, draconic Saturn in Gemini conjoins tropical South Node: following the astrological logic of the aspect, Gemini is the 'lower' energy of the two oppositional signs in its focus more on the message *per se* than the calibre of the thought (Sagittarius). Saturn as 'doctrine' in the sign of the mind sits in Neptune's modern realm of the 12th house, and the planet's proximity to the tropical South Node (as representing tradition or the past) indicates the Pope's challenge to migrate from rigid doctrinal approaches as a 'karmic' purpose to an elevated form of spiritual awareness, as symbolised by draconic Neptune in the 6th house (zone of the under-represented and vulnerable.)

The Pope's life challenges will not be easy: draconic Ascendant conjoins a debilitated tropical Mars in Libra in the 4th house where draconic Pluto is perilously close to tropical IC in Scorpio – stirring up all kinds of hidden perils and poisons, arguably in the Church's history. Among the many subjects of scandal that have come to light during this papacy is the Vatican Bank (Pluto) and its alleged history of money laundering: Francis has instituted a clean-up at the bank. Draconic MC is dissociate conjunct Pluto in the 1st house, underscoring this Pope's reputation for bringing about fundamental changes.

So, to the third wheel for the tropical transits of 21 October 2020. North Node conjoins exactly draconic Saturn in Gemini in the 12th. I have used the Mean Node simply to emphasise exactitude; the True Node is also conjunct Saturn but a little behind in the 21st degree. This triggering of Saturn by the destiny point draws in the entire opposition and the clashes already described, involving also tropical Chiron close to South Node as well as tropical Sun and Jupiter in the 6th. The North Node's opposition to Neptune via Saturn from the house of Neptune symbolically captures the difficulties arising between age-old ideas and more universal notions, suggesting a challenge to conservatism but not an overthrow. Oppositions work best by reach-out, not by bleach-out.

It's also worth pointing out that transiting tropical revolutionary Uranus was (1) in a conjunction cycle with tropical natal Uranus in Taurus conjunct MC in the 10th, (2) due to reconjoin later in 2020, (3) applying to square draconic Uranus/MC.

Victor Olliver: a life purpose and the forecast of a death (or transmutation)

Forecasting death is a problematic area in astrology. The nature of modern astrology eschews determinism and distrusts the forecasting of absolutes.

The major objections to forecasting death are twofold. One has to do with the nature of astrology, that it is a symbolic language: planets, aspects, etc. are open to multiple interpretations but along defined theme spectrums. For instance, Saturn is associated with generic themes of structure, order and melancholy which subdivide into the likes of timekeeping, restriction and solitariness, and further into sapphire, fathers, teeth, etc. Dennis Elwell in *Cosmic Loom* describes the symbols of astrology as 'holons', an idea adapted from Arthur Koestler's *The Ghost in the Machine*. A holon is something that is a whole yet also part of a bigger something or whole. The holon may be likened to facets of a diamond, each one of which is a side in itself as part of something multi-sided, each side catching the light independently at different angles. In interpreting an astrological holon, we have to consider a number of possibilities that are true to the symbol, such as a planet.

Given the multi-faceted character of symbols, no astrologer can ever be sure that physical death is the only outcome of a forecast. What in any case is 'death'? Terminal outcomes may be identified in a chart, but who is to say that the foreseen situation is inevitably mortal death? Perhaps a job or marriage is ending; perhaps a certain life phase is approaching its end. Not the life itself.

The second objection is ethical. To foretell death is to plant a traumatic idea in a client. It may be an idea that is subsequently worried over for years. The great likelihood is that the due date of death will be wrong. Not once, in my time as an astrologer, have I been presented with any persuasive, empirical case that astrology can consistently foretell mortal death to the day. Certain astrologers put it about that modern humankind fears death unlike the people of olden days when mass death was a constant through pestilence, poverty and war. I have news: death has always been feared. No society, at any time in history, has welcomed death or been relaxed about mortality. Bereavement is not a modern invention.

Yet the paradox is that astrology covers all life situations, including the end times. What tends to be ignored is the question: 'What does death mean to you?' Or: 'What part does death play in your belief system?' Is 'death' loss, tragedy, release, relief, activation? In general terms we all react to the news of death in different ways, often according to our relationship and history with the deceased. If mortal death is detectable in a horoscope, in my view the symbolism for it is likely to be of a subtle and personal

Draconic forecasting

nature, not necessarily or always involving planets or aspects that are traditionally associated with death.

The personal symbolism of death may be determined by relationship and life condition, by personal beliefs and/or cultural conditioning...and here I am going to offer an example from my own life of what I mean. This example may serve as basis for a greater exploration in astrology of the nature of death or just simply be a one-off.

But what if all deaths are one-offs in astrological terms?

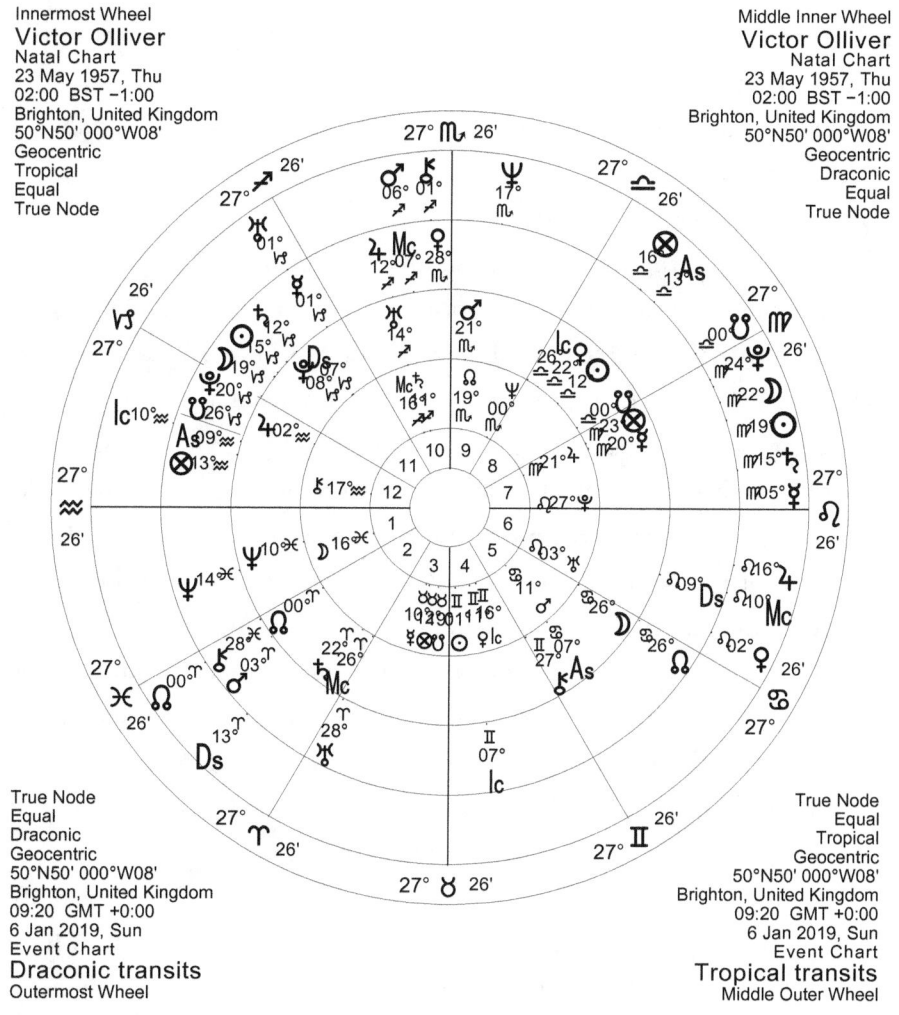

The quadriwheel could be called a 'death chart'. I prefer the label 'transmutation chart'. I'll explain why in a moment.

It is the chart for the moment my mother passed away, on 6 January 2019, under a tropical Capricorn solar eclipse – an event once associated with calamity or bad news. It was also Epiphany, commemorating the revelation of Christ to the Magi or Three Wise Men who were most probably astrologers. The captions identify each wheel, but because quadiwheels can look forbidding, here's a quick guide. The inner wheel is my tropical birth chart; the next wheel out is my draconic birth chart; the third wheel out is the tropical transits chart for 6 January 2019; the outer wheel is the draconic transits chart also for that day.

Our main focus is on two houses: the 1st house where you'll find natal Moon, draco natal Neptune and tropical transiting Neptune; and the 9th house where draco Neptune transits.

In astrology the Moon represents many things such as feelings and memories, but also the mother. Neptune is freighted with symbolism, from seas and forms of caring to optical illusions (such as movies); but it can also indicate loss by aspect. Another association is transmutation – 'the action of changing or the state of being changed into another form', to quote from a dictionary. It is a matter of belief whether the death of a person marks the passing of a life from the physical body to a spirit realm. It is my belief that this is the case, that material life transmutes to the spirit, hence my preference for the term 'transmutation chart'.

What I am seeking to show with this quadriwheel is how all the Neptunes worked together in relation to natal Moon in the months leading up to the peaceful death of my mother in her 96th year on 6 January 2019. Locked into the chart is a clue of the period in which she would pass and its impact on me. The clue was there from my birth.

To me, her death marked the end of a loving personal responsibility which was a major life theme in adult years for reasons I won't go into. Then, I became her carer in the summer of 2009 when she was diagnosed with a lymphoma (from which she recovered), just as tropical transiting Neptune conjoined my Ascendant point in late Aquarius, and draconic transiting Neptune was in an applying sextile to my Ascendant. The Ascendant conjunction was a marker of a new life phase dominated by Neptune's associations – in this time I was made redundant from my last office-based job in London, so I was ready for the next life stage. I also started a correspondence course in astrology.

Tropical natal Moon in the 1st raises lunar symbols in personal priorities, and its conjunction with draconic natal Neptune brings themes of responsibility (perhaps to an advanced extent), especially in its own sign of Pisces. Another chart indicator that home or 'mother' would be big themes in my life is the positioning of my Sun and Venus in the tropical 4th house, the traditional zone of Moon.

In the months leading up to my mother's death, from early summer 2018, tropical transiting Neptune began to conjoin my birth Moon having already made contact with draconic birth Neptune. Around this time, her physical condition went into steep decline (she had recurrent lymphoma, but we only learnt of this in the days before her passing). About two years earlier I recall writing to Frank C. Clifford in a private Facebook message that 'I bet my mum dies when Neptune hits her Moon' – meaning the conjunction.

So, this is the point or question: was the draconic birth Neptune position in Pisces a subtle hint from the moment of my birth not just of especial responsibilities to my mother but also identification of a period when those responsibilities would end with her passing, triggered by tropical transiting Neptune conjoining draconic birth Neptune and tropical birth Moon?

And what of draconic transiting Neptune in Scorpio? At the moment of her death, it was in a separating trine to my birth Moon, exact around the time my mother was admitted to hospital in December 2018 – in the 9th house, zone of 'travel' or new worlds, among other things.

This 'forecast' of death through the birth Moon and Neptunes is only possible in retrospect. One sees an inexorable pattern whose constituents are true to respective symbolism. But the holonic nature of astrological symbolism forbids certainty in forecasting.

There are other clues in the quadriwheel which retrospectively support the above. Remarkably, tropical transiting North Node is exactly conjunct my draconic birth Moon in the 5th in Cancer: this more literally maybe construed as the ending or beginning related to personal destiny and family/mother themes. In the draconic transits wheel, the solar eclipse is in Virgo in direct opposition to the Moon-Neptune conjunction, exact only a few hours earlier before death: resonant of old terminal associations under solar eclipses. Draconic transiting Saturn opposes natal Moon and tropical transiting Neptune: a release or liberation point. There are other pertinent interaspects which I'll leave you to discover.

Just to recap. I had to search within myself to understand my life priorities and how these might help me understand my charts. One sees in the quadriwheel a symphony of associations across different zodiacs all working towards hinting at or identifying periods of certain events and outcomes.

GlaxoSmithKline: Do corporate personalities have souls? A multi-billion-dollar healthcare fraud settlement

Primarily we have looked at the charts of people. Now we turn our attention to a non-person, specifically to a company which astrologically can be treated as a 'person' in the sense that it is under law a 'corporate personality' or a 'judicial person' as distinct from its board of directors, members and shareholders. This non-human person is liable for its own debts in the usual course of events.

Can such an entity have a 'soul or life purpose'? Certainly, a company will have been set up for specific purposes as defined by human beings – a non-human entity cannot have a 'soul', but a company represents the sum total of its many human souls and their collective intentions, objectives and skills. As astrologers we look to find the primary purpose(s) (described in a company prospectus) reflected in its natal chart as our starting point. If there is a match, we can proceed with some confidence not just to make forecasts but also propose spiritual or 'karmic' outcomes and events in the draconic chart – always remembering that the tropical chart is our first port of call: this should show the likelihood of a forthcoming event-type. We then look to find what may be learned in the draconic chart.

GlaxoSmithKline (GSK) is a British multi-national pharmaceutical company and one of the largest of its kind in the world. It is older than the chart data suggests, with an origin date of 1873: however, I have used the date for its last incorporation (27 December 2000) following a merger that created a much larger, reinvented company. Its business is threefold: the manufacture of prescription medicines, vaccines and consumer healthcare products: 'We deliver our long-term priorities of Innovation, Performance and Trust through each of our three businesses,' it states on its website, gsk.com. The capital letters are GSK's.

Alas, GSK has fallen short of stated integrity in recent history. Following US Department of Justice investigations into the company, on 2 July 2012 GSK put out a press release announcing that it would plead guilty to various crimes of fraud that included, among other things, promoting drugs for unapproved uses and failing to alert the US authorities to safety data about a diabetes drug. In all, 10 drugs were at the centre of the scandal. It also pleaded guilty to paying kickbacks to doctors. On this day, GSK agreed to pay the largest healthcare fraud settlement in US history: $3 billion. 'As part of the settlement, GSK agreed to be monitored by government officials for five years,' reported BBC News.

Could this event have been forecast without the benefit of hindsight? Maybe not in its specifics, but we would seek major chart indicators of a threat to GSK's existence, of deviant or criminal conduct and of financial loss. We must also bear in mind that 2 July is an announcement date: predating this, the company had been investigated for years by the US Department of Justice, the CIA and other state and federal bodies.

First, we'll look at GlaxoSmithKline's tropical/draconic biwheel.

The tropical natal inner wheel chart does not point obviously to the drugs and healthcare purposes of GlaxoSmithKline in my view. This immediately sets up an alert that there could be a disconnect between its stated aims and how it does business – as indicated when we look at the

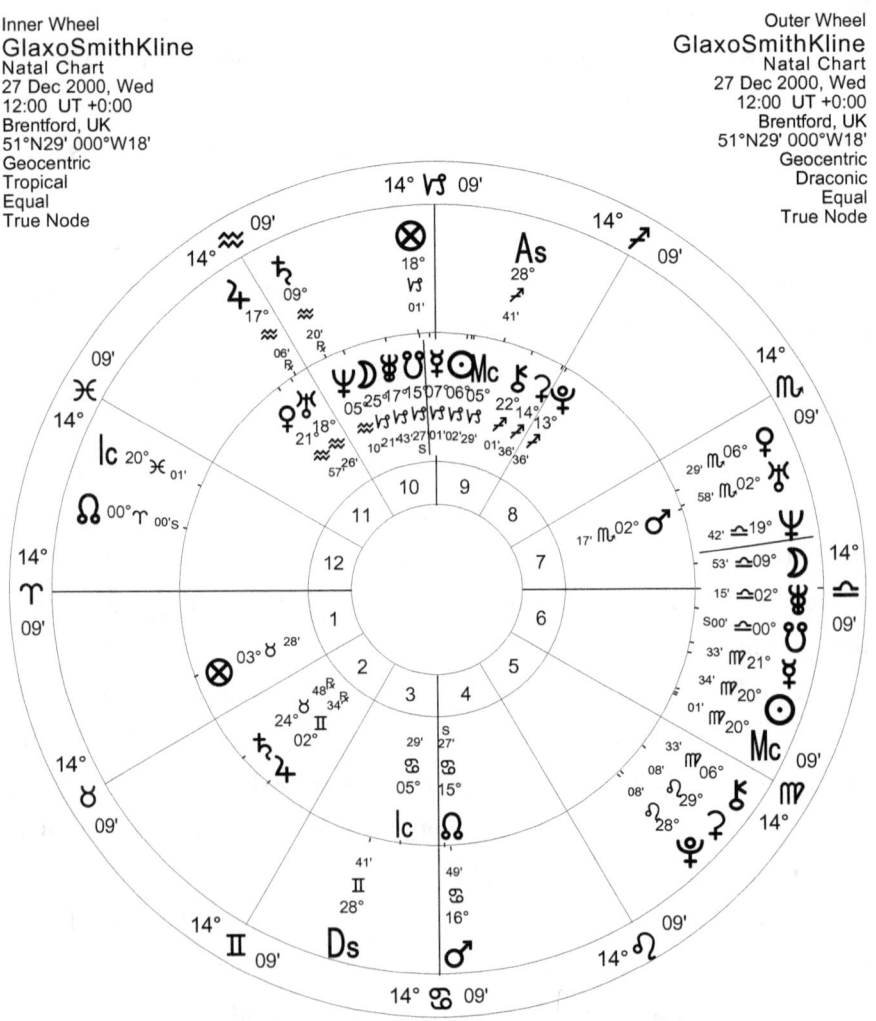

draconic chart. The tropical chart is highly cardinal with an abundance of Capricorn placements, which you would expect of a leading corporation, among which is asteroid Hygeia, associated with health and sanitation but also drug abuse and fear of doctors. South Node's involvement in the Capricorn stellium is not auspicious given the obvious connotation that GSK's glory days appear to subsist in its past, so there is much to prove in the present and future. Jupiter – linked to ability to heal – is in detriment in Gemini, not a happy condition for a pharma company, though chart ruler Mars and Uranus are strong in their signs for research and innovation, respectively.

The draconic natal chart is much more descriptive of GSK's purposes. A heavy Virgo presence is entirely appropriate for a healthcare company with Mercury in its strength, Sun, MC and Chiron (associated with 'wounds'). Not only that, but in the natal biwheel, Virgo is brought to the 6th house, chart domain of health. But there's still the association with South Node albeit out of sign in Libra. Chart ruler Jupiter is in a better condition in Aquarius. GSK's 'soul' chart of higher healthcare aims is at odds with the tropical horoscope's focus on business and status (as indicated by all the Capricorn energy).

In the synastry of tropical and draconic, interaspects highlight company purposes and potential challenges. Tropical Neptune and draconic Saturn (both associated with medicines) are conjunct in Aquarius – drawing together exacting rigour and pharmaceuticals. And draconic Uranus is exactly conjunct tropical Mars in Scorpio, merging innovation and research themes, but close to draconic Venus now in detriment in Scorpio (all square the draconic Saturn-tropical Neptune conjunction in Aquarius). The tropical nodal axis draws in draconic Part of Fortune at the South Node which again speaks of past triumphs, migrating to North Node and draconic Mars in its fall in Cancer, an unfortunate hint of problems related to the proper expression or use of energies.

Chasing the Dragons: An Introduction to Draconic Astrology

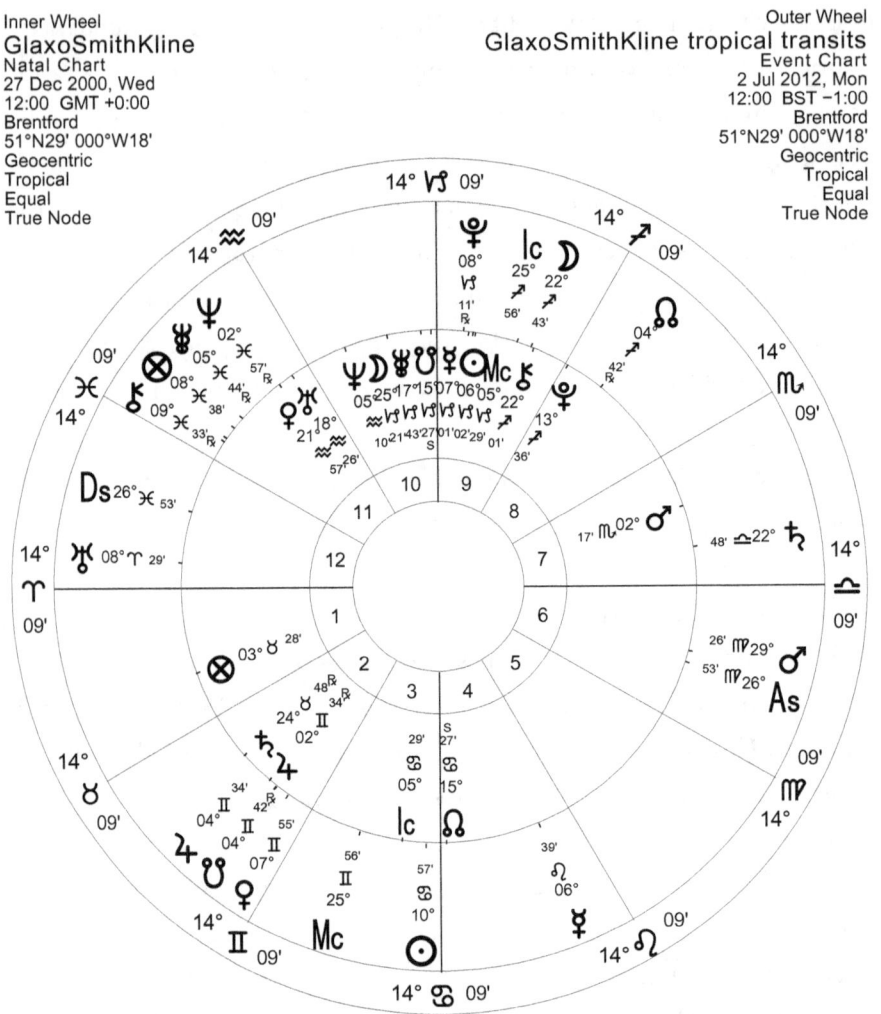

We now turn to the event charts for 2 July 2012 when GSK confessed all and agreed to settle for $3 billion, starting with the tropical transits with the nativity. I have allowed wide orbs to reflect the inevitable build-up to the press announcement, especially for the outer planets.

Trouble is plainly indicated, starting with transiting Pluto (exactly square transiting Uranus in Aries) in a conjunction cycle with natal Sun in Capricorn and opposing draconic Sun, pulling in the entire tropical

Capricorn stellium including MC (and IC below in Cancer). Pluto here brings convulsion where there is fault or corruption (think back to what happened when Pluto ingressed Capricorn in 2008: a global economic crisis arose as a result of predatory lending to low-income homebuyers and excessive risk-taking by financial institutions which had accumulated monumental debts).

Even if we did not know the context, we would expect a seismic occurrence in the company in the approximate time frame.

Transiting North Node is sufficiently close in separation to natal Pluto in Sagittarius in the 8th house to indicate a period of potential transformation in the sign of justice and in the house of hidden things and discovery, under a Jupiter return opposite in Gemini (in fall) with transiting Jupiter exactly conjunct transiting South Node – perhaps a chance to start again and put things right. There are other chart indicators to find.

In the draconic transits biwheel, we are looking for signs of literal crisis but also for a greater understanding of the spiritual significance of this period as affecting company purposes.

The draconic transiting Sun-Pluto opposition shifts to the 1st and 7th houses, with Pluto in its opposite sign of Taurus in the 1st and Sun in Scorpio, Pluto's sign. The opposition pulls in natal Mars in Scorpio and natal Part of Fortune in Taurus. This is a strong representation of what we know, of crisis and financial penalty, given the signs and aspect. From a spiritual perspective, this potential and major setback is a chance to start afresh in a detoxified state.

Draconic exalted Mars and Ascendant close together in the 10th conjunct the natal Capricorn stellium via natal Moon suggest that the company at this time is likely to abide by the law and recognise its deviations – apparent from its capitulation to the US Department of Justice and the $3 billion settlement. Capricorn brings the power of authority and status quo 'adopted' by the company.

Chasing the Dragons: An Introduction to Draconic Astrology

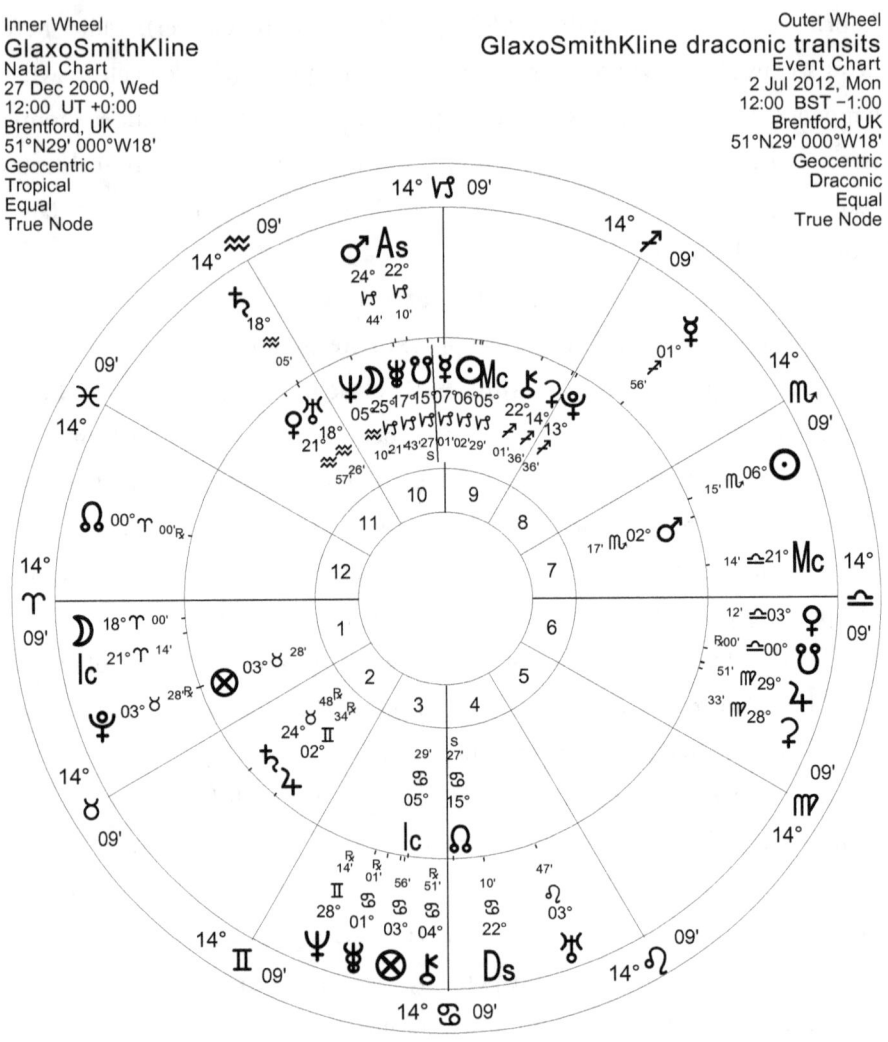

Significantly, draconic Saturn is exactly conjunct natal Uranus in Aquarius in the 11th, a powerful message that a company change is both enforceable and necessary. This Saturn is still innovative and forward-thinking, but demands order, probity and some caution: a new cycle is suggested by the conjunction.

Another indicator that the company has a chance to rise from ignominy is the opposition of draconic Mercury in Sagittarius in the 8th to natal Jupiter in Gemini in the 2nd: the mutual reception helps to counter the detrimental condition of both planets in the chart houses of values and shared responsibilities.

The striking oppositions between the natal Capricorn and draconic Cancer stellia, drawing in draconic Neptune in late Gemini and tropical IC in Cancer, suggest a requirement to re-embrace and re-accommodate the past (and by implication its values and approaches): the oppositions point to a chasm between past – highlighted by Cancer IC – and present which cannot work well for the company.

Hygiea is among the Capricorn and Cancer stellia. And while Chiron is plainly in the draconic Cancer stellium, next to Part of Fortune, in the tropical Capricorn stellium it stands apart in Sagittarius square draconic MC, as if separated from the core purposes of the stellium. I won't make too much of this but it's worth noting.

While the tropical transits are graphic of a convulsive event, the draconic transits more plainly identify one of the major likely problems, a disconnect with its heritage and nurturing traits (Cancer).

Chapter Six

Draconic synastry

We have examined plenty of synastry of self tropical and draconic charts. Now we shall focus on the synastry of two people in relationship. In all likelihood you are already familiar with this technique and have examined the tropical natal charts of couples to discover possible strengths and weaknesses in their union. This can also be done draconically, i.e., by comparing the draconic natal charts of two people. In my own practice, I have discovered that tropical synastry is more than adequate to assess the health of a bond. But the draconic analysis can serve as a clarifier and under-scorer of themes that may not always be strongly indicated in the tropical chart.

Once again, we seek the 'headline news' in the draconic chart. The draconic assessment aims to understand the effect that one life has on another, and vice versa, and what purposes may be served by the union in the evolution of either party. It is less concerned with the 'strengths and weaknesses' of the tropical, more so on the value and purpose (though difficulties may be shown) of a relationship. The history of either individual plays a key role in this understanding, and it is always fascinating to discover how the pasts of two people impact on either one in a blending of energies.

This is a big subject in itself. It can include draconic midpoint composites of couples. But for our purposes I am using just two tropical-draconic synastry case studies to introduce the approach.

Chasing the Dragons: An Introduction to Draconic Astrology

Harry and Meghan: each other's awakener through Uranus

Prince Harry (second son of Prince Charles and Diana, Princess of Wales) and American actress Meghan Markle married on 19 May 2018 in St George's Chapel at Windsor Castle in the United Kingdom. Subsequently they were made the Duke and Duchess of Sussex. Initial public enthusiasm for the union soon gave way to various controversies and general media hostility, though they retained and retain vocal supporters. In 2020 the couple withdrew from undertaking official royal engagements. This was a prelude to their relocation first to Canada, then California. At time of writing, they have two children.

In a controversial US TV interview with Oprah Winfrey in March 2021, the Sussexes claimed that racism within the British royal family had contributed to their effective defection. Among other things, the Duchess' estranged relationship with her family of origin, and with her father Thomas Markle in particular, triggered sensational newspaper headlines and litigation. Harry's low opinion of print tabloids became much more evident. He held them responsible for the premature loss of his mother in a car accident in Paris in 1997 as she and her boyfriend Dodi Fayed were being pursued by paparazzi.

Before we look at the draconic synastry, let's examine the tropical.

Meghan's Uranus in Scorpio is conjunct Harry's South Node (taking in his MC and Saturn) in opposition to his North Node, Moon and IC and her Chiron. This rich brew brings the influence of the awakener and game changer (Meghan's Uranus) to his realm of family and heritage with probable effect on his public profile (MC). Her Chiron's involvement links them in shared pain through family, evident in their respective life stories.

If we have any doubt of the transformative effect that she is likely to have on Harry's life, her Aquarius-Leo nodal axis makes an exact t-square to his strengthened Pluto in the 10th house in Scorpio. This is a powerful 'destiny' relationship (nodes in the 1st-7th houses of self and coexistence)

Draconic synastry

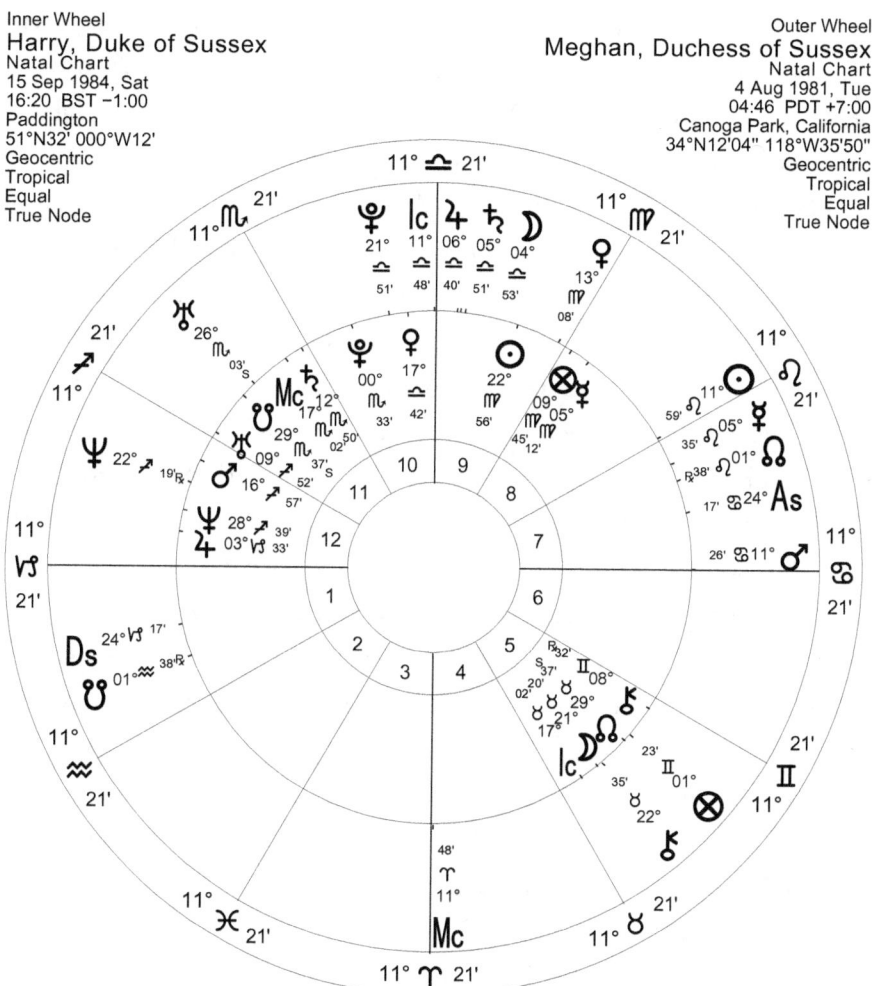

whose nature is passionate and delving, addressing what may be at fault both in themselves and the world, with the peril of extremism or relentless questioning. Her Pluto conjunct his Venus in Libra in the 10th clarifies that she not only triggers change but that this process alters her through relationship. Her Venus is widely conjunct his Sun in Virgo in the 9th, forging a strong bond between them, though over-sensitivity to what others think could be problematic

It is significant that at the time of writing both have broken with their families of origin. While the reality of their respective situations may be more complex than can be reflected here, the synastry wheel suggests major problems for both of them of a familial kind.

Her Mars in Cancer opposite his Ascendant is sexually charged but, in other ways, warns of likely war-footings with the world and likely tensions within the bond. The positioning of her Mars in the synastry wheel marks her as major instigator in the union and the doorway to new social worlds for Harry. All this is reflected in the public record.

If we flip over the charts and place Meghan's chart as the inner wheel (not shown), we find her Uranus and his South Node brought to the 4th house, domain of family, opposite his Chiron and her Moon in the 10th. This suggests much galvanic and exciting energy as a starting point in their relationship, but emotional volatilities are likely in struggles between her need for renewal and his for stability and practicality (Chiron in Taurus). Her Moon moved to 10th raises her public profile through the relationship.

The theme of Uranian awakening is underscored in the draconic synastry. Meghan's Cancer-Capricorn Uranus-Chiron opposition now takes in Harry's draconic Sun in Cancer in the 9th house. This describes her 'disruptive' effect on his very self and on family relationships. His life is very much bound up with her 'outsider' energy; they merge as a power couple of a challenging kind. Leaving aside the public controversies and critical media commentaries, there is no question that a spiritual purpose of this pairing is to awaken each other and reset emotional and familial coordinates – and in a literal way, too: the Uranus-Sun conjunction in the 9th house may be construed as family relocation overseas.

Even more stark is Meghan's 5th-house draconic Ascendant in tight conjunction with Harry's draconic Moon (dispositor of his draconic Sun and her draconic Uranus) in Pisces, indicating a strong emotional bond which may at times risk dependency. The past is a big theme of this union

Draconic synastry

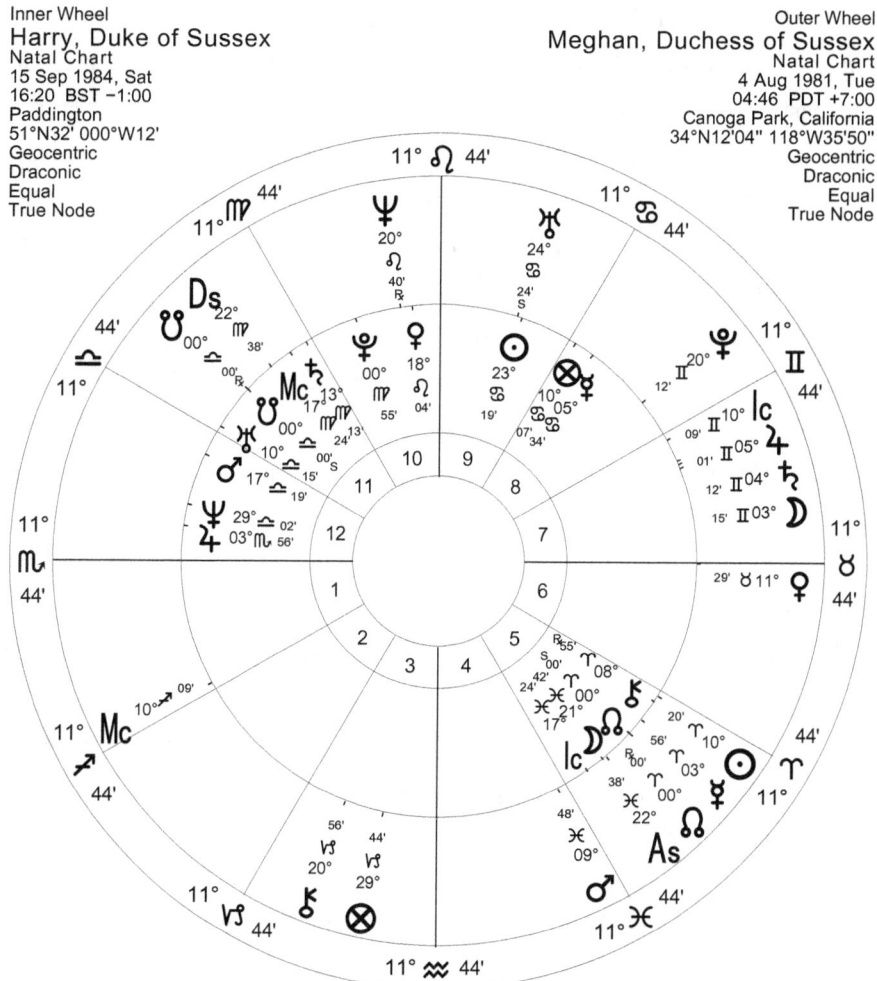

(his Moon conjunct IC) embracing many different matters and issues: Pisces strains against borders and barriers, seeking a new space which may be spiritually elevated or delusional, depending on the self-awareness of the people involved.

Meghan's draconic Ascendant (conjunct her Mercury and Sun and his Chiron) is sufficiently close to the pair's draconic Aries North Nodes to be of significance, albeit out of sign: the new space the couple seek for themselves is suffused with cardinal, proactive energy. Opposing this is Harry's draconic MC-Saturn conjunction in Virgo, his public role or status, which via Meghan's draconic Descendant pulls in the South Nodes and past conditions. Conflict and pain are part of the 'rupture' between past and present, and her Pisces Mars opposite his Saturn is a reiteration.

Yet a total dislocation with families is not inevitable or irreparable. Oppositional energies invite compromise or accommodations in time, where there's a will.

In straightforward terms, the couple must create their own joint 'heart expression' (5th house). This implies that there are redundant or life-denying factors in each other's past that require rejection (amplified by the Sun-Uranus conjunction in Cancer in the 9th). It's as if Harry and Meghan needed each other to make a breakaway. The romantic connection between them is suggested by the Venus-Neptune conjunction in the 10th in Leo, the sign traditionally associated with the 5th. Where this new journey takes them precisely is not the concern of this analysis, only that a 'liberation' was required.

To delve further, examine the tropical and draconic natal charts of both to discover individual life purposes and see how these may work out/manifest within the soul purpose of the marriage.

Queen Elizabeth II and Prince Philip, Duke of Edinburgh: an abundance of conjunctions

The UK Queen and her husband Prince Philip were married for 73 years, the longest union in British royal history, before his death at nearly age 100 in April 2021. This is a very brief look at their synastry – I would encourage you to draw up their respective tropical and draconic natal charts, examine each of their life purposes as outlined in this book, and then put together their tropical and draconic synastry biwheels.

By most accounts theirs was a passionate marriage based in part on a profound understanding of each other's very different constitutional roles, even if Philip chafed against his secondary status as consort in the early years of the union. The pragmatic Taurus Queen dealt with his Gemini sense of activist masculinity by granting him authority over the royal household into which be introduced many innovations, as Victoria's consort Albert had done before him. He encouraged the royal family to open up to the television public and he led the way in renovating the royal estates. Though much criticised over the decades for his many faux pas and likely indiscretions, Philip was viewed as stalwart in his loyalty to the ceremonial and formal roles of the Queen as Head of State.

No matter what crisis they faced together – whether the assassination of Mountbatten, the tragic death of Diana, the marital and many other scandals of their four children – the couple maintained in public a stoic, neutral pose, rarely if ever displaying personal feeling beyond Philip's odd quip or flash of temper (his Sun-Mars conjunction in Gemini is a sharp-shooter).

There are countless books and articles examining the charts of the Queen and Prince Philip, so here I am only looking at the purposes found in their synastry. Always examine the tropical synastry biwheel first for major themes.

Philip's North Node is taken to the 10th house in Libra, associating his destiny through marriage with high estate, in a supportive semi-sextile to the Queen's Saturn-MC in Scorpio. Meanwhile his Venus, which disposits his North Node and is close to his MC, conjoins the Queen's Sun in the 4th house, bringing together a medley of themes such as union, family, status, the Queen's self and marriage in earthy Taurus. Note the strong Venus-relationship presence allied to status in these aspects and placements.

Royal histories chronicle that as a young girl Princess Elizabeth was instantly attracted to Philip, which is supported by their electric Uranus-Venus conjunction in Pisces. Uranus (Philip) needed as much freedom as possible while Venus (the Queen) will have sought more in the way of

Chasing the Dragons: An Introduction to Draconic Astrology

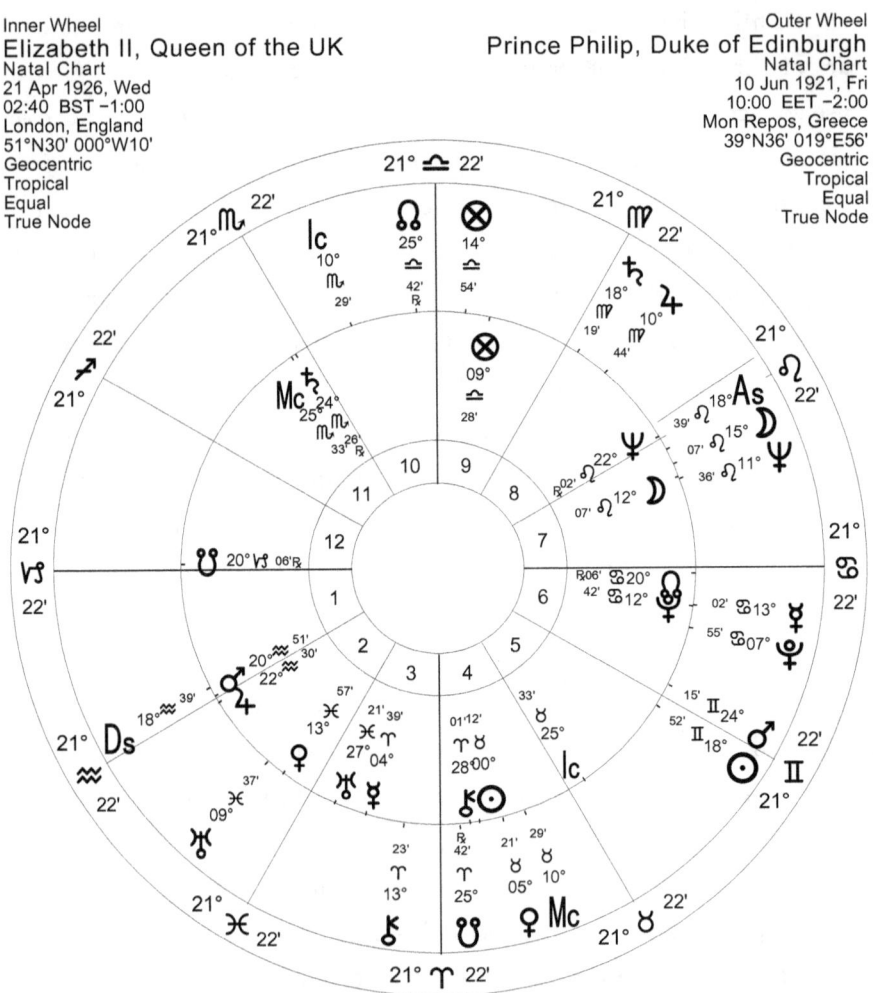

constancy, though mutable Pisces brings a degree of flexibility or tolerance (of the need for his own life and interests, for instance). His Virgo Saturn opposing her Venus brings further complication – it is not difficult to imagine that behind closed doors he could be highly critical if not overbearing at times.

An abundance of Leo in the 7th house makes for a richly textured marriage, but it is the Cancer energy that goes to the heart of this synastry. The Queen's North Node in Cancer in the 6th (but sufficiently close to the cusp to incorporate the 7th) is widely conjunct Pluto, both conjunct Philip's Mercury and Pluto. Pluto here brings tremendous resilience, stamina and willpower to her sense of purpose and to their union (by virtue of the aspects). Cancer bestows nurturing and protective themes while the 6th house locates the union in a zone of the chart that is about daily life, work and wellbeing – it is one of the houses that seeks to bring support.

This may be regarded as having a dual meaning. At one level the couple bring a tremendous support to each other through thick and thin. At another, the 6th is the place of service, and in the known context of their lives, the Queen and Prince Philip together were defined by the idea of service to the state, even if in resplendent style. A lot of their own concerns or desires had to be secondary to what was asked of them by the state. Cancer places them in the family, their own and that of the nation.

Many conjunctions are a feature of both the tropical and draconic charts, a sure sign of shared purposes and joint enterprise. It's also worth comparing tropical and draconic biwheels. For instance, Philip's draconic Ascendant point is brought to the Queen's tropical Ascendant point (see their tropical synastry biwheel) in a tight conjunction in Capricorn, a graphic indicator that one of his life purposes – shared with the Queen – was to uphold stately duty and responsibility before other considerations. And the Queen's tropical Part of Fortune at 9° Libra in the 9th is exactly conjunct Philip's draconic Venus in the 1st which speaks for itself of glory through marriage.

And, most remarkably, his draconic Sun in Scorpio sits tightly conjunct the Queen's tropical Saturn-MC, merging his very being with the planet of her authority, status and public responsibilities. I am certain you'll find other interaspects.

But back to those draconic synastry conjunctions – and I'll mention just a few key ones. First among them is Capricorn brought to the 4th house. It's entirely appropriate that Britain's longest reigning monarch

Chasing the Dragons: An Introduction to Draconic Astrology

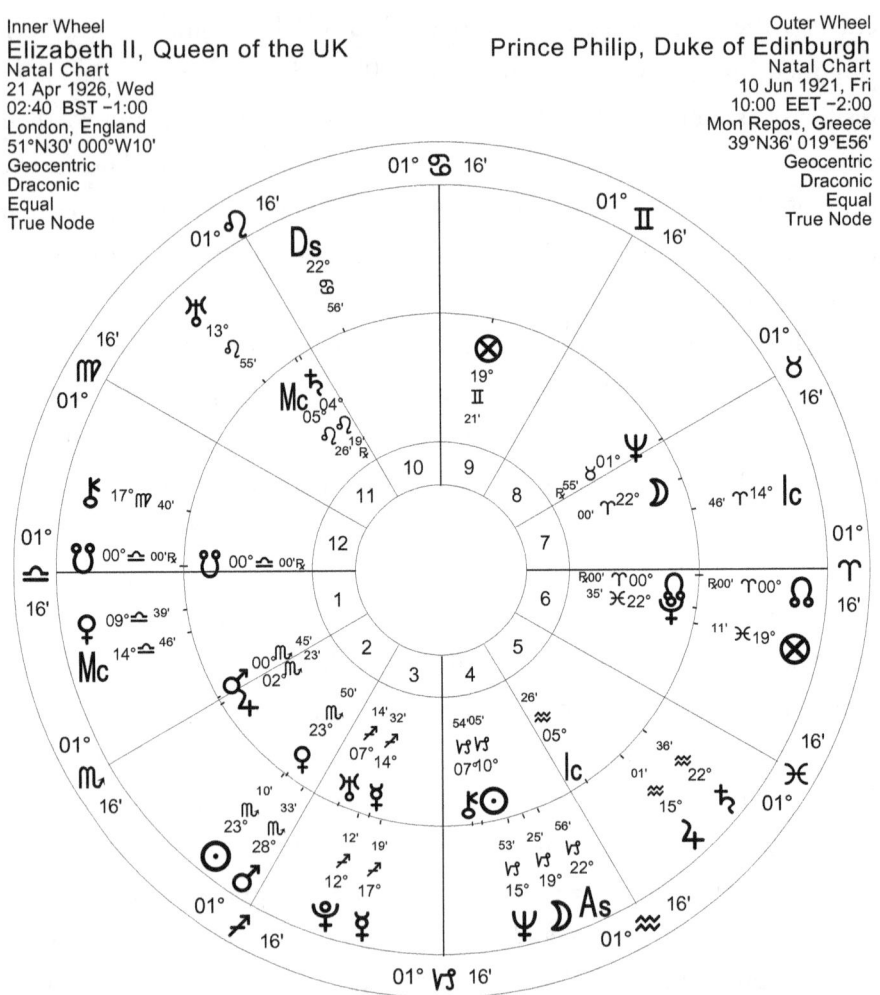

should be a draconic Capricorn whose ruler Saturn (planet of longevity) is disposited by the Sun. Her Sun conjoins Philip's Moon and Ascendant via Neptune, consolidating joint enterprise through state roles (Capricorn) in the chart zone of family and land. We see here a supportive merger of two people that speaks more literally than the tropical of what we know.

His draconic Sun in Scorpio exactly conjoins her Venus with co-ruler of the sign (his) Mars close by: a classic aspect of a strong union and one that is passionate.

It becomes more apparent that it is Philip's part to electrify and help renew the Queen's profile and sense of duty (his Uranus conjunct her Saturn/MC in Leo). We saw in the tropical biwheel that their Plutos were close together in Cancer in the 6th, which has a generational reason and theme. But in the draconic, his Part of Fortune conjoins her Pluto in Pisces in the 6th, near to the nodal axes on her Ascendant-Descendant line: prosperity and power merge in this interaspect in a chart zone (6th) that favours rigour and discipline but, in a sign (Pisces, a realm of mystique), that's not always comfortable with this life approach. Perhaps this sums up the dilemma Philip found himself in during the marriage, trying to square his military spirit with the nebulous nature of constitutional monarchy. Yet this is where fate has placed him, a male Alice in Wonderland.

Note also that while in the tropical synastry Mercury-Mercury are square, Aries to Cancer – reflecting their very evident different ways of thinking and expression – in the draconic the planets merge in conjunction in Sagittarius, drawing in her Uranus and his Pluto, all in the 3rd house. This shift in interaspect suggests the much wider canvas of life they had to occupy but one that required a huge amount of discipline to handle: Mercury in Sagittarius (and in Gemini's domain of the 3rd) has restless and outspoken features, yet in this synastry it also tells of a meeting place of shared philosophies or beliefs, and of immersion in the world, which helped to bind the couple together.

This draconic interaspect italicises how together the Queen and Prince Philip were capable of rising above personal differences of perspective or bias to present a united front to the world, and for the most part to be exemplars of a faith and ideals that cut across national borders. At a personal level, shared draconic Sagittarius energy suggests the capability of growth together through multifarious experiences which benefited how they were perceived by various publics (as an 'august' and worldly couple). But it's worth reiterating that Sagittarius in Gemini's zone of the

3rd implies the need to relate to the public at a down-to-earth level and restrain perceptions of excess or remoteness – which can be the peril of Sagittarius. Views may differ on how successful they were at this, but as a pair they were perceived as no-nonsense, borderline plain and simple in their tastes (as far as royalty permits) and tending to frugality.

Chapter Seven

Six draconic case studies from my files

In this final chapter I present six examples of draconic analyses conducted with clients or colleagues. All have generously granted me permission to publish the reports I wrote for them, and all have written commentaries of varying length and in different ways in response. This gives an opportunity at the very least to see how my reports are approached and presented – and I would encourage the three-step habit. Draconic analysis is best built through a process starting with the tropical chart – skipping to the draconic first will in all probability lead to a misunderstood chart because the tropical acts as your foundation of understanding. These commentaries also help to ground the astrology in the reality of the subject: I can vouch for the fact that none of the individuals showcased is ever likely to hold back on what they really think, and that includes my publisher, Margaret Cahill.

There is a formulaic quality to my reports in the way they are presented – I always start with the natal Moon phase of birth, for instance – but in every other way, the reports are bespoke. Computers may produce the graphic charts, but none has any say in what is written.

It's also worth pointing out that mostly I read for people I do not know personally. Marie Davis below is an example of this. I knew absolutely nothing about her life. Only when she responded could I see that the astrology had worked for her. Others in this section I do know personally. It is not a difficult exercise to compartmentalise what is known and what is not and to yield just to the astrology. Always test the astrology, treat each chart as an experiment, let it speak as unhindered by opinion or personal knowledge as you can. Or else the analysis becomes a projection and is therefore worthless.

The reports have necessarily been edited down to focus on essentials. So, welcome to these six experiments....

Anne Whitaker

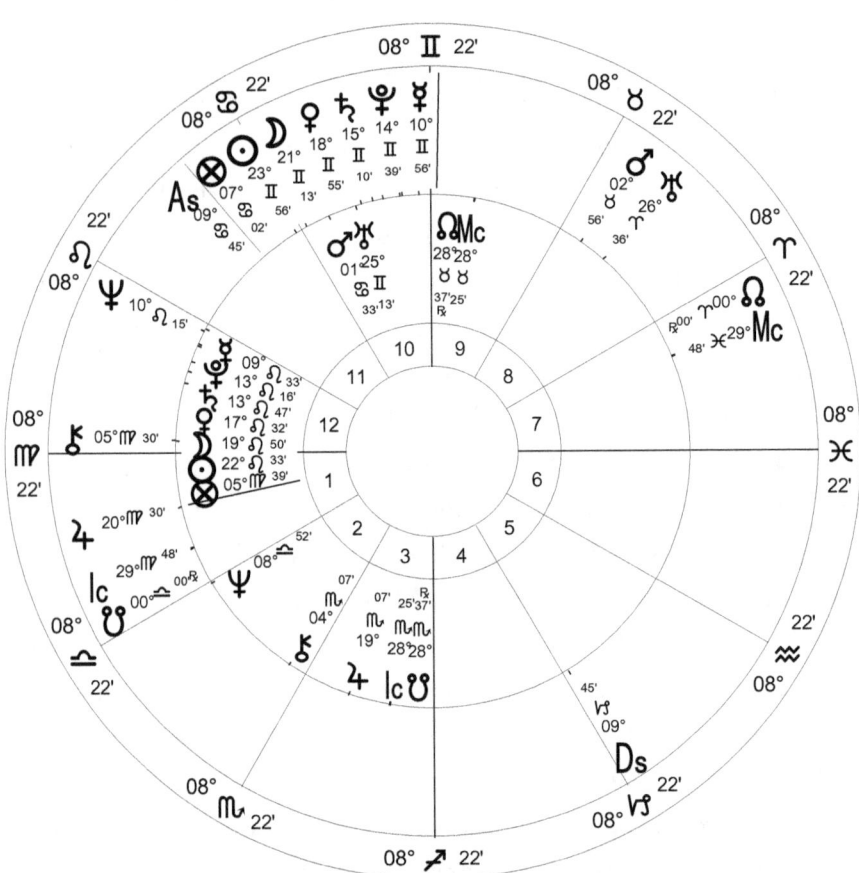

Anne is an astrologer, author, essayist and teacher. I edited her latest book Postcards to the Future: Mercurial Musings 1995-2021 *so I know quite a lot about her. She chose to place her commentary after her draconic report. As this is the first of the analyses in this chapter, I have kept in certain fixed passages that appear in all my reports designed to explain what I am about to do next.*

The Report

Dear Anne,

Step 1: the structure of your tropical birth horoscope

In this stage I look at your tropical birth horoscope to identify how it is structured e.g., what is the elemental balance – earth, air, fire and water. The structure often gives a background clue as to one's life potential and purpose. Some of the information below may already be familiar to you, but it is now oriented to the overall message of life purpose.

You were born under a Balsamic Moon just prior to a New Moon in Leo. The Balsamic has been likened to hibernation or withdrawal from the world before metaphorical winter ends and spring dawns (New Moon).

In reincarnation terms, it is the 'hermit' who brings to bear all that she or he has acquired over many lifetimes (not as a hermit). But you don't have to believe that. Another approach is to say that the Balsamic will incline you to withdraw from the world from time to time to collect your thoughts or simply to allow other perceptions and insights to percolate to the consciousness. The 'sanctuary' – which is any place you regard as free of the madding crowd or energy-sapping people – is your customised place of sanity and recovery.

This trait is re-enforced by the Moon's presence in the 12th house as part of an amazing super-conjunction of planets in Leo – the 12th being the domain of the last life cycle and of the sanctuary or closed environment. This stellium brings together a vast array of energies focused on specialist purposes – so, it will be the case that you excel in some particular way even if the 12th slows the sequence to some extent.

In practical terms this will incline you to seek the company of engaged but spiritually evolved people. Or if 'spiritual' is problematic to you, towards people of contemplation, sensitivity and some unorthodoxy. The Balsamic quietens and diffuses (but does not alter) the nature of Leo (the creative exhibition of ego) – as indeed does the 12th itself as natural domain of

Pisces (the creative exhibition beyond ego). And this Moon can signal the characteristics of a visionary blessed, if not with second sight, then with immense worldly shrewdness.

Such a Moon can be fully involved in the worldly world, drawing on a vast reservoir of karmic memory to negotiate transient, material challenges.

Balsamics often undergo major transformation during the life and are quietly very resilient. Leo, which is the symbol of the heart and self-expression – also of structured approaches and management – supports this process: Leo in the 12th radiates memory, abstract truth and universal spiritual themes. At least it does where the individual is receptive to finding the good and the truth in the world.

Structurally, your chart is highly Fixed which describes depth, resolution, determination and persistence, though stubbornness may also be present. A Fixed chart is excellent for maintaining an inner equilibrium and holding onto values and standards.

Fire has the chart majority among your elements, enriching receptivity to inspiration and heart-felt creativity. Fire at best purifies and refines. Air is not so well represented: there could be some need to consciously work towards communicating your thoughts and towards levels of objectivity in certain life areas against impulse or bias.

Cadence is strongly represented. Traditionally this is regarded as a weak house modality, but this is to ignore its vital role in the actual world. The cadent chart is that of the thinker, the analyst, the reflector or philosopher and teacher. Without cadence we have thoughtless action and impulsiveness. It is part of your life purpose to recognise connections to make sense of the whole. At another level, you may be a guide or teacher, given that the 9th house is the home of your Midheaven exactly conjunct North Node in Taurus.

On which point, Taurus is the sign of value and values. This has material and spiritual resonances. Part of your life purpose is to address moral questions as well as to turn the discoveries of research and exploration

(South Node in 3rd-house Scorpio) into practical expressions. Identifying value is part of the process of discovering truth (which in this matter is not a relative term) and what may be valued, a process of discrimination and application of higher learning (9th house).

Jupiter (natural co-ruler of the 12th and ruler of the 9th) widely opposite this conjunction of node and point accentuates the themes of wisdom and teaching in their best manifestation: the opposition is part of a loose t-square whose apex takes us into the heart of 12th-house Leo in your chart, the place where past and present become borderless and may be distilled, resolved, synthesised and turned (through conflict and attrition) into 'pearls' or focused lessons. Much struggle and pain lie as backstory.

So, a teacher you are of sorts – this much could be discerned even if I didn't know you. In draconic analysis one assumes the best!

Note that Part of Fortune is also to be found in the 12th but in Virgo, the cleanser, the analyst, fault-finder general. Virgo in the 12th widens the sign's application to health beyond the body to include spiritual health and what may be required to heal a dislocated or questing soul.

It is so close to your rising point in Virgo that we have here another part of life purpose: you excel as a guide as well as teacher. The one plots a course, the other provides lessons.

Mars is its fall in Cancer as it sits in the Equal 10th close to Uranus in Gemini. This Mars feels its way while this Uranus thinks its wayward way. Gemini Uranus is rebellious, independent, pioneering and of course astrological, using intellect and surface rationality. A strong combination of approaches in the house of life direction.

Also, your Uranus is the lead planet of the chart's shape, the Bowl. This Bowl tenants the eastern half of the chart – so bringing an astrological or pioneering perspective is part of your lot in the sign that rules communication and teaching.

Chasing the Dragons: An Introduction to Draconic Astrology

Step 2: your draconic chart

We now move to your draconic (draco) chart before we compare this chart with your tropical birth horoscope. The draconic is not an alternative to your birth chart but a supplementary – it draws attention to higher energies and purposes which will help (or have helped) you reach fulfilment. Sometimes they highlight things only hinted at in the tropical birth chart. Very occasionally the draco chart suggests a huge challenge to alter approach for success.

The striking first difference is that this chart is Mutable. Your Fixed nature remains intact but to raise your game, gifts of expression and communication need development. The mutable chart is a mediator, a teacher and communicator amongst other things.

Amplifying this point is your draco elemental change: the majority element is now Air. Air has to do with communication and intellectual approaches – in the sense of use of the rational mind in the delivery of information. Draco Air far outweighs the other elements. Water comes second at half the value, embracing intuitive and emotional energies. Tropical Fire demands Air.

Naturally, your draco chart remains heavily cadent.

All the Leo planets move to draco Gemini, bringing the communicator to all that we have said about the 12th and Leo in your tropical chart. The teacher is indicated in the tropical chart. But the draconic leaves no room for doubt.

Draco Part of Fortune moves to Cancer ruled by Moon which itself is disposited by Mercury in Gemini: feeling and mind combined.

Mars is no longer in fall but is in debility in Taurus, next to Uranus in bold initiatory Aries which Mars rules: the progress to realisation and fulfilment is not easy yet is fed by a 'young' and eager energy; it cannot be made blasé or dull by mere experience. Indeed, struggle has the perverse effect of rejuvenating the character.

North Node naturally is in Aries, its fixed position in the draconic chart, but it draws in a Pisces MC which reflects Neptune's themes while embracing the guide or even guru of the 9th. Traditional house ruler Jupiter moves to Virgo in the 3rd, where detailed and literal work must be done to feed the broader themes of your life – in another way, this is the teacher of primary through to tertiary, 3rd to 9th.

Step 3: the birth and draconic synastry of self chart

All of the above remain true to you. Here, we refine the focal points as to life purpose(s). In this comparison, I look to see where planets in your birth chart sit in relation to planets in the draco chart. This may repeat some of the information above. There are important indications, confirmations and clarifications here.

1) All of your draco Gemini planets are moved to the 10th as a strong suggestion that the role of teacher and communicator of 'wisdom' (tropical 12th) is yours. Tropical Uranus first conjoins draco Sun under Gemini's third decan ruler, Uranus (in modern Western astrology). This strongly marks you as an original and pioneering communicator and 'awakener' with your person underlined as the source (Sun). Tropical Mars in Cancer, close to Gemini Uranus, blends themes of feeling and intellect – this is not just about scholarship. Gemini also brings in writing, journalism.

2) Draco Neptune in the 12th is almost exactly conjunct tropical Mercury but actually implicates the entire tropical Leo stellium, linking to the value/values theme in your tropical chart. In obvious terms, the planet which naturally rules this chart house and is therefore accidentally domiciled, Neptune, brings its themes to your tropical Leo in the 12th as described above. Neptune spiritualises and allows a blending of many levels and experiences in order to create hyper-truths which could be described as essences of the soul that arise from disparate experiences.

3) Draco Jupiter shifts from the communicator 3rd to the personal in the 1st in Virgo, bringing us the exacting teacher-guide in your personality. The

draco nodal axis falls 1st to 7th linking person and mediator or counsellor (both you, draconically). This mediator can help people who wish to transition in some way. Jupiter links to tropical MC and NN in Jupiter's 9th.

4) Rising draco Chiron is exactly conjunct tropical Fortune in Virgo. This shifts the tropical theme of value and values to the 'autobiographical', in which you draw on past hurts and experiences to illustrate and amplify. Virgo is purity of recollection, integrity. Also, of healing. Both are sextile draco Ascendant in Cancer in 10th. This links the personal to the public in some way.

5) Note that draco Mars, though in detriment in Taurus, is in the 8th as ruler of the house's cusp. This sign may slow Mars' progress, but the planet comes into its strength through a major life change. Helping this process is Mars' conjunction with draco lead planet Uranus in Aries, making a virtue of sudden or unexpected change in the life as impetus. Another part of your life purpose is to help others 'transform' – and it could be said that this is only possible through the example of your own transformation.

6) The biwheel hemispheric Bowl shifts from eastern to southern in the main. Part of your lot is to talk directly to the world in the role of communicator-teacher-guide, no matter what you feel!

Anne Whitaker's commentary on her draconic report:

You write: 'Indeed, struggle has the perverse effect of rejuvenating the character...'

Never was a truer word said about a person! I don't have Saturn/Pluto conjunct most of my Leo planets for nothing.

You have provided plenty of rich food for thought in the substance of the report. I liked the three-stage model: this makes it quite easy to follow the Life Purpose theme without unnecessarily cluttering it up with other stuff from the person's character/life pattern.

Nothing in what you said about me was either jarring to what I already know about myself or news to me. What is interesting, however, is how the draco chart really does strongly underline what I can look back and see very clearly at this later life stage: there was always a very definite central vocational path. This was fed by several tributaries, each of which had to be followed individually along the way: writing (in every vocational context), Adult Ed, social work, psychiatric work, counselling/therapy...and ultimately the practice of astrology which has drawn all the tributaries into one deep flow.

This shows up *so* clearly in that mega-Leo stellium shifting to Gemini by sign, and 10th by house.

In my natal chart, asteroid Urania is at 20° Virgo [not shown] in the 1st house. It really made me smile to see draco Jupiter sitting exactly on that point; teacher of astrology, anyone?! Furthermore, when I was 27 and a total astrology dismisser (from the dismissers' usual base of no real knowledge of the subject), I had an encounter in a launderette in Bath, England, with astrologers who took me home with them, read my horoscope in depth – and told me I'd end up becoming an astrologer myself – or something very like it. That year, my progressed Sun was crossing the natal Urania /draco Jupiter point...Fate? Discuss...

The *exact* conjunction between the natal 12th-house Part of Fortune and Draco Chiron in Virgo, was for me the most striking item. I can see so clearly from this peaceful place in my later life how a profound, deliberately made choice early in my twenties to commit to the struggle to derive insight and clarity from deep pain provided by family, Fate and its inevitable outworkings in my younger life, has fed all along into the work I have done with people in various contexts for the last 50 years.

The Wounded Healer archetype really has been a dominant force throughout. So, it was actually very moving to see that affirmed so strongly in draco.

Thank you, Victor, for your clarity and insight.

Chasing the Dragons: An Introduction to Draconic Astrology

Margaret Cahill

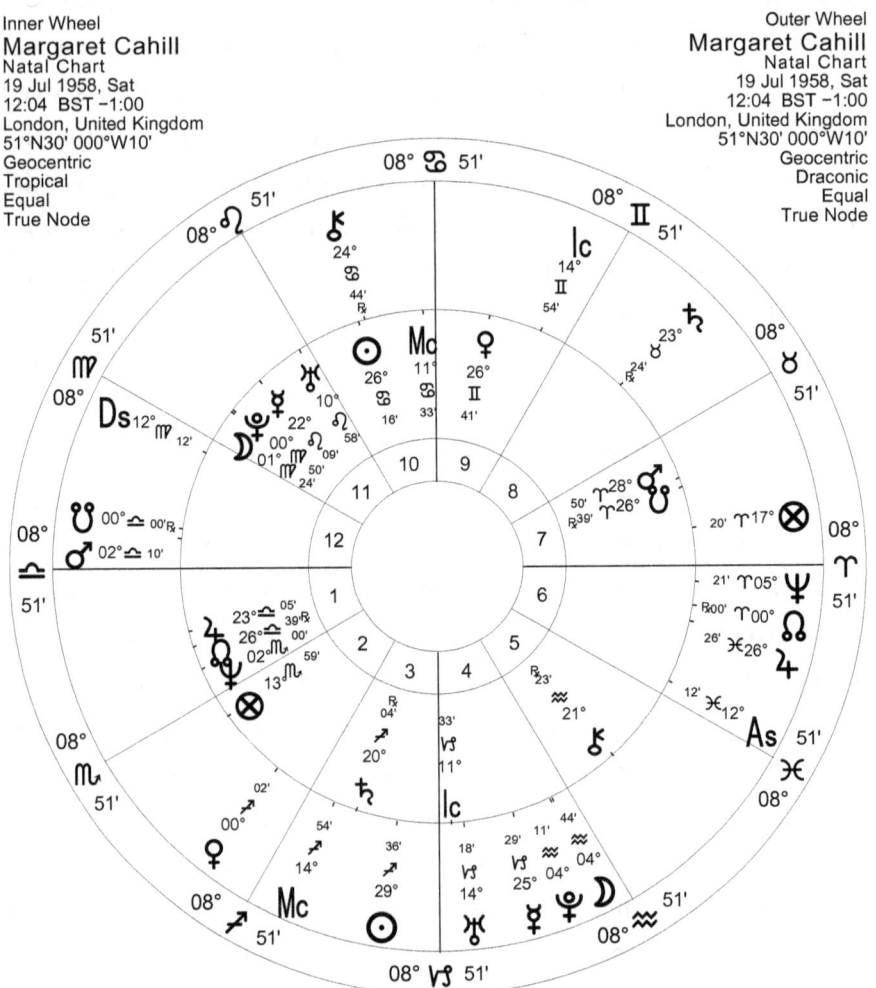

Director of The Wessex Astrologer, publisher of this book, Margaret is an author in her own right. Aside from that I know little about her life other than that she has a partner and children – and she loves the sea, judging by the photos she posts on Facebook. Margaret interposes her commentaries in the report, placed in bold and brackets.

The Report

Dear Margaret,

Step 1: Your tropical chart

Highly cardinal which is proactive and blessed with initiative. This is complemented by a New Moon in Virgo conjunct Pluto in Virgo in the Equal 11th house, intensifying analytical skills almost to a point of relentlessness: you will find it hard to rest until everything you undertake is to your satisfaction. Though perfectionism is no bad thing in itself, it sets high personal and professional bars, especially with placement in 11th, domain of ideals and professional associations. **(Margaret's comment: 'I often don't realise I'm doing it, but other people can get irritated because of this... especially authors!')**

The Locomotive chart pattern has Mars as its lead in Aries in the 7th house conjunct South Node. This ties life progress to relationships and the struggle or challenge to maintain independence within joint enterprises of any kind. The nodal axis echoes this theme with North Node in Libra in the 1st, the traditional Aries zone: the destiny point brings joint or shared enterprises into the chart realm of balance. The South Node in the 7th conjunct Mars in Aries as noted already presupposes a very independent backstory either in this life or in past lives, one that may have struggled to accept help or to acknowledge the contributions of others – a warrior of sorts who takes no prisoners and leads the way. This default may exist within you, yet life as presented asks you to redirect egotistical energy into shared or negotiated ventures.

Chart ruler Venus is found in Gemini in the 9th disposited by Mercury in Leo in the 11th triggering themes associated with the 9th: church, publishing, high ethics, etc. Everything you do must be driven by heartfelt passion; anything less will not engage you. **(Margaret's comment: 'Haha. "I'm bored" was my favourite phrase as a child. It drove everyone mad, and my family wondered whether I'd ever find a career/partner that**

Chasing the Dragons: An Introduction to Draconic Astrology

I wouldn't get bored with. Fortunately, I now have both...') Saturn's opposition to Venus can suggest early life struggle to find your way in life: with Gemini and Sagittarius each in its opposite chart domain, there may have been a struggle to find a practical expression to high ambitions or ideals or to 'scale down' so that people understand you or your work. **(Margaret's comment: 'So true....')**

The nodal axis forms an exact t-square to Sun in Cancer in the Equal 10th. The nurturer in you is pronounced with likely professional expression (as well as in private life), one requiring the nodal theme of negotiation, compromise to some extent and the sharing of energies. The t-square draws in Mars, Jupiter and Neptune by conjunctions to the nodes, linking personal expansion to the extent to which you can harmonise very powerful and contradictory impulses within you: this won't have been easy, but sets you up for potential success with awareness of the advantages of evolution through cooperative effort.

MC in Cancer with Sun reiterates professional potential through nurturing, though with IC in Capricorn this journey may have started against limitation or authority rooted in family or heritage. This can be a wellspring of strength either through personal struggle against authority or sign of a hereditary advantage as IC ruler Saturn is in Sagittarius in the 3rd. **(Margaret's comment: 'I had real problems at school as I didn't fit into the aggressive grammar school curriculum very well – always got "C, could try harder" in my reports so felt like I never lived up to anyone's expectations – especially my own.')**

Overall, communication and relationships handling are the central themes of this chart.

Step 2: Your draconic chart

Much more a mutable chart with cardinality demoted. This does not mean you should cease to be initiatory or fearful of taking the lead, only that in your progress, you will be required to apply greater flexibility and versatility to make substantial progress. **(Margaret's comment: 'That is the Great Work in Progress, I think and definitely part of the soul journey.')**

Pisces rising shifts chart rulership to Neptune and Jupiter in the 1st. Jupiter's draco position is a promotion thanks to old astrology – blessing advancement where your spiritual or creative energies are engaged and where old barriers or ways of doing things are replaced by more inclusive or reinvented models. Pisces seeks to dissolve and identify fundamental trends whatever the manifestation, to understand what drives self or society.

Draco Neptune in Aries connects through conjunction tropical cardinal get-up-and-go with Piscean tendencies, so it is part of life challenge to break barriers, forge new visions, spiritually or creatively. In best manifestation, a highly developed and high-minded sensibility combines with a fairly hard-nosed readiness where instincts are engaged. Note that Jupiter's move from tropical Libra to draco Pisces blends the value of cooperative effort with a heightened understanding of the dynamics of relationship. This potentially lifts you from the struggle to contain ego within any kind of relationship to a reflex of empathy and caring – the next stage from conscious synthesis of 'me and you'.

Sagittarius Sun underscores the strength of Jupiter in the chart and all the themes associated. The passion identified in the tropical points to the draco 9th-house Scorpio Venus – this of course includes publishing and practical or communicable expression with Saturn in draco Taurus in the 3rd.

Mars' shift to Libra merely repeats what is apparent in the tropical but adds a nuance: not only finding a balance between 'you and me' but preserving 'me with you': in other words, retaining independence within any kind of bond without loss of goodwill or intimacy, depending on kind of relationship. Life does not ask you to 'lessen' sense of personal impetus and sovereignty, but to preserve **(Margaret asks: 'protect myself?')** against life situations presented which may either seek to overwhelm you or which gull you into thinking you can have total control. This may arise in personal or professional situations. As a challenge it can be a hard call. (**Margaret's comment: 'This is really true. I am psychically and emotionally very easily overwhelmed and have to consciously protect myself. That in itself takes quite a lot of effort which is why having a good relationship is incredibly important – that 1st/7th house axis nourishes me when it's good and destroys me when it's not.'**)

MC/IC in Sagittarius and Gemini further emphasise the domain of acquired knowledge and communication as likely career options. Tropical Virgo energy moved to Aquarius retains powerful analytic skills and instincts, applied draconically to new ideas, innovation. Surf the future. Mercury in draco Capricorn tells of the need to apply rigour to tropical intellectual passion (Leo), a business sense (11th) and immense practical considerations (Capricorn). (**Margaret's comment: 'Yep.'**)

Step 3: Synthesising tropical and draconic

1) Draco MC/IC fall in 3rd-9th axis in Sagittarius/Gemini, taking in by wide conjunctions tropical Venus and Saturn, focusing on communication and knowledge as points of passion and practical challenge. It is part of your life challenge to accommodate complex expectations in practical ways while retaining the integrity of your beliefs and knowledge. This theme will recur throughout life so that excessive idealism or ruthless pragmatism do not dominate your thinking. Finding a balance is key. (**Margaret's comment: 'Yes – walking on a knife-edge springs to mind.'**)

2) Draco North Node in 6th brings challenge in the area of health or work and is a springboard for caring initiatives, especially for those without a voice or who are under-represented. Draco Jupiter in Pisces and Ascendant in 6th serve to emphasise. Personal health/wellbeing may serve as a basis for learning or teaching. (**Margaret's comment: 'Very definitely. I have a few soapboxes that have to be kept under fierce control.'**)

3) Draco Mercury-Chiron opposition takes in tropical Sun in 10th. This binds in biography to career and thinking: personal life experiences/

pain will help inform work and may inspire some ventures in the hope of enlightenment. The Cancer-Capricorn axis in 10th-4th applies nurturing to home and career tied to practical realties. Balancing the personal and professional is another challenge. **(Margaret's comment: 'For sure. And that is asking a lot of a partner who might hope for some level of domesticity from me, which I must admit I don't really have.')**

4) Draco Uranus joins tropical IC/MC, signalling the need both to find your own path perhaps against family expectations or inclinations and to innovate in your life/career. There may be an enhanced interest in the power of heritage, family, roots etc. and a desire to find better life approaches. **(Margaret's comment: 'My mum introduced me to astrology at a very young age (8, I think?) when she received Linda Goodman's book on Sun Signs for her birthday. Needless to say, I was glued to it from that point onwards. Mum's second experience of cancer took her on a completely unconventional route in terms of treatment, so I grew up with familiarity of anything complementary and alternative; that early exposure has definitely influenced my own attitude towards health.')**

5) Note that draco Aries energy highlights health, work and relationships through the 6th and 7th houses as areas for particular breakthroughs in your knowledge and effect on the world. **(Margaret's comment: 'I wrote a blog during my treatment for lymphoma which was a great spiritual outlet for me but was also used on other platforms to help support others going through the same treatment.')** With draco Neptune close to Descendant, there is a powerful, spiritualising life theme, especially among those you work with.

6) Draco Saturn in Taurus in the 8th drives you to find practical ways to self-empowerment strategies of any kind, especially in relationships given Venus' opposition in the 2nd.

7) A recurring theme in your biwheel is the need to balance very powerful conflicted forces within the self. Tropical and draconic planetary/point

degree distance of difference falls into the quincunx which has the nature of allowing difference in this life without always the need to change one's own perspectives or nature, a 'live and let live' philosophy. This may come naturally to you. Or it may be immensely difficult at a reflexive level. (Margaret's comment: 'Difficult for sure. I'm still learning that 'live and let live' thing!')

Margaret's final comment: 'There's also something about courage here… somehow the Mars/Neptune opposition square the Sun is very unstable and I can get myself into situations of potential conflict without meaning to – usually in the process of defending something then not knowing how to follow it up. The nodes in both charts are a perfect reflection of my inner confusion – not necessarily knowing when it's appropriate to intervene or when not to. And then having the courage to carry it through if I do.'

Six draconic case studies from my files

Marie Davis

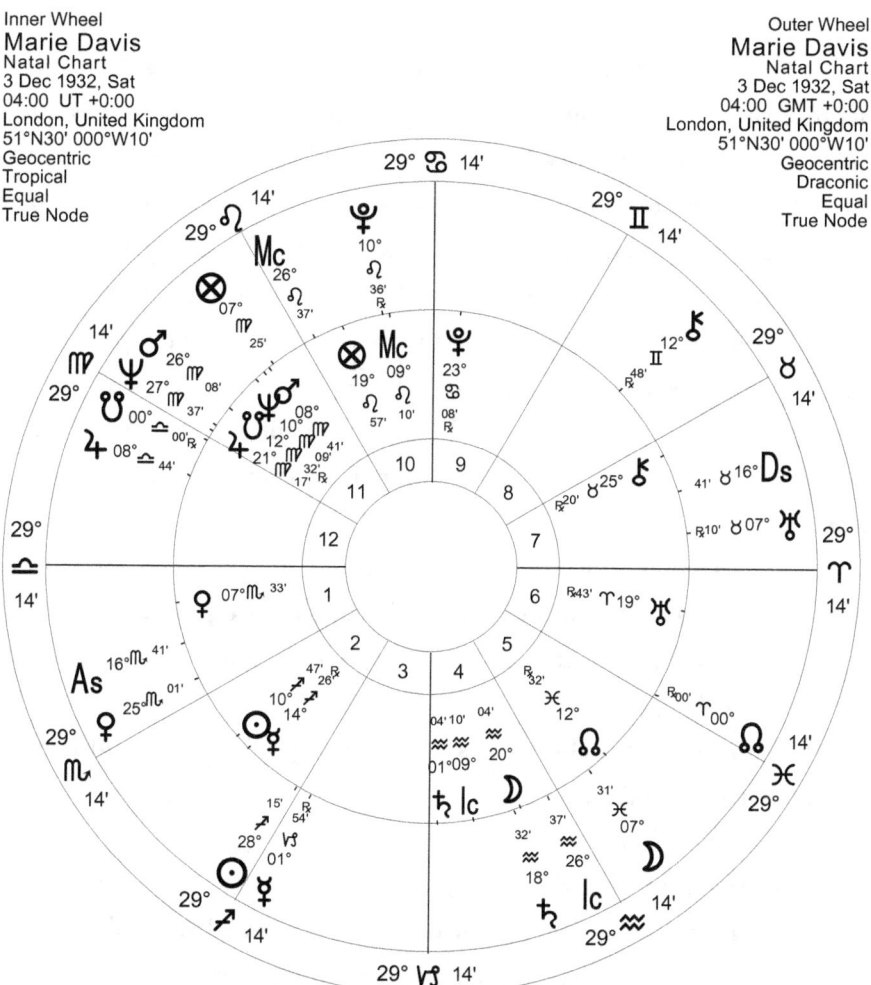

As indicated at the start of this chapter, I knew nothing about Marie's life other than that she was aged around 90. She came to me as a client via Margaret Cahill who did not supply me with any personal information about her – and I didn't ask, except for birth data. A little while after I sent her the draconic report, I heard from Margaret that Marie was delighted with it. Because Marie is not entirely au fait with emailing, Margaret was happy to summarise Marie's commentary following a phone *conversation. In this instance, I'll start with the commentary, followed by the report.*

Margaret's summary of Marie: Marie Davis wanted to share her story because she said that her draconic report allows her, for the first time in 89 years, to hold her head up high and not be frightened; for the first time she feels whole and can accept herself as she is, despite having had many chart readings in the past. She says that she completely disappeared into herself for three weeks to absorb the implications of the report, which made her look at herself and realise that she had grown up with horrendous fears: fear of the war; of being Jewish; of not trusting people; fearing intimacy because of childhood abuse; of being ugly; of being uneducated due to having to care for her brother and sister; of being worthless.

At 17 Marie was married to a Jewish businessman and she worked long hours in the restaurant he owned. He would regularly say, 'Prove yourself to me' but nothing she did was ever good enough, so she continued feeling worthless.

Having been told she was psychic at one point she started reading cards for friends and was amazed to find she was very accurate – but even that hasn't given her any confidence.

Marie's husband died several years ago and for the first time she can explore exactly who she is in relation to herself and also her family. She says that since reading the report she has stopped trying to control her children and grandchildren and has released them to their own destinies; she leaves them in peace now, whereas previously she would phone them constantly to check that they were okay. Her tinnitus is much better, as is the banging in her head, which used to be constant. She describes herself as the oldest teenager in town and is looking forward to living her fullest and most productive life in the time she has left as she feels she has wasted so much of it feeling bad.

The Report

Dear Marie,

Step 1: the structure of your tropical birth horoscope

You were born under a Crescent Moon in Aquarius, a lunar phase often indicative of a dynamic person who wishes to be fully engaged with life – as opposed to someone who waits for things to happen. There is a powerful can-do quality to your character that brings with you high expectations – no life can fulfil all these, but the trying and the anticipating preserves your fervour, eagerness, spirit and positivity. There is always a new challenge ahead of you even if you're not certain what it involves or even what it is precisely.

Aquarius orients you emotionally to be of broad use to humanity – perhaps politically but just as likely in different ways, such as through group or collective actions, and this is one clue to life purpose. We'll explore this more below. Aquarius enables you to stand back from situations to evaluate needs and not get too emotionally involved: it's quite likely that you regard emotional involvement in the problems of others as an obstruction to making progress, and it is most unlikely that you'll tolerate having personal boundaries breached.

However, this is not indicative of a lack of compassion: on the contrary, it is probable that you have had to nurture and care for a great many people given that Moon sits in the 4th house, the traditional zone of 'family' and nurturing. While others flap about, you keep your cool and take the initiative in finding solutions.

Your Moon is ruled in modern astrology by Uranus which sits in Aries in the 6th house, the domain of service, work and health. And it is aligned constructively with your Moon. This adds to the sense of an enhanced personal initiative, and your approach is enthusiastic about new ideas and even controversial ones; but certainly, you will be open to innovation, alternatives and unorthodoxy. The 6th cares for others in its most positive manifestation, and you are drawn to people who are in need or are vulnerable. Uranus here could suggest many different jobs or areas of work covered by you. Saturn in old astrology rules your Moon and the two share the same sign in the 4th house: this tends to mirror the Uranus rulership in that while you can operate within traditional structures you will adapt the 'rules' as you see fit, make your own mark, and encourage or pioneer new notions.

The 'service to others' theme of your chart is underlined by your lunar nodes – these are points in the sky where the pathways of the Sun and Moon meet periodically; they are not actual celestial objects. The two nodes sit across your 11th and 5th houses in Virgo/Pisces. This suggests a powerful practicality in you, one that may be sharply critical on occasions but driven to be of direct use to others. It could be said that you were born with these characteristics.

The North Node – known also as the destiny point – sits in Pisces in the 5th: in essence this sets the challenge not to get lost in micro-managing or details, and to seek the larger picture, the higher thought or dream. There may at times have been a tendency to lose sight of the wood for the trees. Pisces encourages you to create 'missions' in life that are expressive of your passions or dreams, and this can be difficult because Pisces is drawn as much to the misleading or confusing as to spiritual truths or artistic abstractions. Pisces also can be too self-sacrificial at times.

So, embedded in your destiny in this life is a need to bring balance between personal needs and other people's needs.

Your South Node – representative either of a past life or default characteristics which arise from instinct – in Virgo is conjunct Neptune which rules your North Node. This is a double whammy of Neptunian energy which in its higher form is spiritualising, compassionate, sometimes self-sacrificial, committed to missions of care or healing or artistic expression. It could be said that this is a direct invitation to rise above the detail or mundane considerations and allow your spiritual or artistic

Six draconic case studies from my files

self to reign over you in some way. In literal terms this can include many interests, from photography to psychic/clairvoyant expressions. You will thrive in collectives yet with the North Node in the 5th house, the artistic or spiritual theme must tap a personal gift or passion – otherwise there's the peril of feeling that you have neglected the self to help others.

Interestingly, the nodal oppositional axis forms squares to your Sagittarius Sun and Mercury in the 2nd house. This chart domain governs finances, lifestyle, value and values, among other things. Jupiter rules Sagittarius and your Jupiter is in Virgo in the 11th house, not always the happiest of signs for this planet. Virgo is focused on the detail, Jupiter on the larger canvas; Virgo is careful and cautious while Jupiter is expansive and adventurous. You may have felt this tension in your life, especially over finances (extravagance could be a problem). But this position does enable you to perfect a craft or technical skill (or even one's self-expression as a writer).

Neptune's proximity to Mars in Virgo does suggest a perfectionist (either over detail or conduct or both); and a constructive alignment to your Venus in Scorpio in the 1st house is favourable for relationships, sense of style and working with all sorts of different people at once. This Venus deepens passions and focus, orients you to make lengthy commitments – Venus actually rules your chart through Libra rising so charm and a pleasing aura are among your blessings. However, your rising point (or Ascendant) is right at the end of Libra, so it is entirely possible that you are a Scorpio rising or a hybrid of Libra and Scorpio in the makeup of personality: this combines a diplomatic and entrancing persona with higher levels of intensity and focus than usual. People in general warm to you and find you magnetic.

Mercury in Sagittarius is good for intellectual attainment, drawing you to philosophy, education possibly and other higher learnings and leanings. Whether you have been entrusted to handle money for charitable purposes or in some other way you have held fiduciary duties I cannot know, but these lie within your competence. You may also have made a mission to raise money or to campaign for better use of money to serve certain humanitarian purposes. These are not inevitable, but again could be said to be within your gifts.

Structurally, your tropical chart shows a fine balance of fixed and mutable energies which tells me that you are neither particularly stubborn nor over-compliant. If Scorpio is rising, it could be that in certain matters you become uncommonly resolute.

Fire is your lead element, indicator of a driven personality, one 'fired' with inspiration and enthusiasm. Air is also strong, enhancing communication, self-expression and a capacity for objectivity. With 'succedent' energy strong, you are likely to be a very good manager of other people's projects/businesses; or turning ideals into practical ventures.

Note well that your Part of Fortune (a point that suggests a focus for fulfilment) is in Leo in the 10th alongside your Midheaven (or career point). No matter your caring and compassion, there will be a powerful need to use work and other life areas as part of your heart expression, and it is your fate to shine in your own light (more about this below under draconic). If you do not, dissatisfaction will be palpable. You require attention (though this does not make you an attention-seeker) and recognition; you do not want to be faceless. You have a message to the world that requires dissemination.

Leo ups your courage, passion and ability to manage. The Sun rules your Fortune and Midheaven, so Sagittarian themes are relevant here – such as adventure, higher learning, dissemination of information, teaching, etc. Not all of these will apply, but Sagittarius' embracing and fiery energy feed career or duties – it is part of your fate to enlighten others with your vivid example.

Step 2: Your draconic chart
Your draconic chart is more 'fixed' though not at the expense of mutability. In other words, it will help serve you towards self-fulfilment to show even

Six draconic case studies from my files

greater resolve and determination in pursuit of aims while not becoming unbending in all matters.

Water is now the majority element (but only just ahead of fire) and is not a major change from the tropical chart: however, it is a cosmic hint to make the most of empathetic skills and to be open in your feelings.

Scorpio now clearly rises and there is no fusion with Libra here. Scorpio is a 'fixed' sign, one that is capable of great focus because the underlying energy tends to be built on a deep and personal passion – this is an encouragement to look deep into the self and find that thing which truly expresses you, whatever it is. Scorpio is motivated as much by belief as passion and applies tremendous focus to get to the truth or to realise a dream. It is this side of your nature, the believer, the truth-finder, that is accentuated in your draco chart.

With Scorpio rising but Mars still in Virgo (Mars co-rules Scorpio with Pluto), this is a strong indication of caring through a specialised skill of some kind, perhaps medical or pharmaceutical although not inevitably.

Draco Sun stays in Sagittarius – so the instinct to educate, enlighten, to treat life as an adventure is part of the journey to self-fulfilment – but now Mercury moves into Capricorn though remaining close to Sun. This does suggest a capacity for leadership and taking the initiative: but also, a need to turn high ideas (Sagittarius) into practical expressions (Capricorn). In the domain of the 2nd house, we return to the themes of value and money – and moral values. This could suggest work of a benevolent kind involving finance, as one possible interpretation. Capricorn does tell me that holding something in trust to help others is a life theme.

Draco Jupiter moves into Libra which marks an improvement on its tropical position in Virgo. This elevates the value of charm and diplomacy as vehicles for gain, whether financial or benevolent. It is entirely possible that financial or other impediments can be exceeded by negotiation, persuasion, joint or collective actions. The concentration of energy in the 11th house takes us into organisations, collective action, ideals and interconnectedness, with the repeated theme of specialism of some kind with Mars and Neptune still in Virgo, focused on management and critical evaluations.

Draco Moon has moved into Pisces in the 4th house, the most sensitised and sensitive of lunar placements. There exists as potential within you to be both highly rational (tropical Aquarius) and preternaturally aware of your environment, able to pick up on what's not said, on unseen trends and other energies that many other people cannot detect. You may have spiritual or psychic gifts, in addition. Such sensitivity can come at some price if you do not maintain personal boundaries.

Draco Saturn stays strong in Aquarius underlining two sides of you, the rational and non-rational, the openness of mind to alternatives and the unorthodox but not at the expense of order. The 4th house could suggest heavy family responsibilities or duties related to the nurturing of others.

Venus stays in Scorpio so see above in tropical. You are encouraged to make commitments and to use powerful empathetic energies to understand and care for others, particularly against problems or obstructions. Venus is in a happy alignment with North Node, suggesting that working with others, relationship of all kinds, the pursuit of beauty and related themes are significant for you.

Pluto

An important planet that I did not touch on in tropical is Pluto – it is important because it co-rules your draco birth chart and therefore has a lot of weight. In your tropical chart, Pluto is in Cancer in the 9th house – this tells me that the care and nurturing of others is integral to your life, past or present. This trait is part of a core values system in you, a world perspective of a philosophical nature. Cancer is associated with the 4th house where Saturn and Moon are found – so family, care, clan values, roots mean a great deal to you. From an early age, the need to get things done via cooperation with others will have been felt as a major theme.

Six draconic case studies from my files

And it is probable you have undergone a number of significant changes in family/relationships – which were not always welcome. You have at times, reluctantly, had to accept and adapt and in so doing have grown.

Pluto's move into draco Leo, in the 9th house, is a message from the chart that what you have achieved in your life under the terms of Pluto in Cancer has something to do with a perspective or philosophy that should be radiated to the world. This could be through teaching or books or some other means of media communication. The 9th house is the domain of publishing, higher teachings and philosophy: it is the zone of Jupiter. It is also the zone of Sagittarius, your tropical birth sign. This is a strong tie-up of energies pointing to radiating from the self (Leo) your lessons of transformation (Pluto) out to the world (9th). The underlay of this is your experience of relationships, care and nurturing (Cancer).

Step 3: the birth and draconic comparison chart

All of the above remain true to you. Here, I *refine* the focal points as to life purpose(s). In this comparison, I look to see where planets in your birth chart sit in relation to planets in the draco chart. This may repeat some of the information above. There are important indications, confirmations and clarifications here.

1) In respect of the last observations that I made above under draconic, it is significant that your tropical career point (Midheaven in 10th house) is now conjunct draco Pluto. Pluto's shift from tropical 9th to 10th houses (the latter, the zone of life direction) is a strong indicator that something to do with teaching/publishing/dissemination is part of your life purpose: what you have to say to the world has a transformative energy, and this arises from your personal experiences, radiating from the heart.

2) Draco Pluto/tropical Midheaven conjunction is very widely opposite tropical Moon/Saturn and draco Saturn. This is a complex mix but in essence suggests possible early struggles with authority or father figures and likely family problems/restrictions which helped shape your

perspectives. Draco Saturn on tropical Moon in Aquarius in the 4th house is a sign of early life affliction as an essential part of purpose development. There may have been emotional deprivation or deficient nurturing in early life or other restrictive energies. However, because Saturn is in one of its signs (Aquarius), there is an increased likelihood of overcoming these obstructions.

3) Tropical Part of Fortune in Leo is widely conjunct draco Midheaven in the 10th house, another indicator that it is important that something arising from your heart (or passion) is central to self-fulfilment. This could be creative or spiritual, but it is for you to identify this. I can only outline its nature.

4) Draco Moon in Pisces now sits on your tropical North Node. Moon is also opposite tropical Mars, Neptune, South Node and draco Part of Fortune. Sensitivity is acute, especially to the needs of others, and it is probable that it has been vital to balance competing energies or else be overwhelmed by demands made on you. This will not have been easy. The Moon is the nurturer – it has been your lot to be 'parent' to so many people in some capacity. Pisces helps to raise your sights beyond the moment or mundane demands: Pisces helps to find a spiritual purpose to these experiences and in the process transmute them into lessons. Draco Moon and tropical North Node sit in the 5th house, the domain of Leo. If you consider that draco Pluto sits in Leo, you have a strong indicator here of the need to radiate to the world the energy you dedicated to others in the past. How this is done is a matter of personal choice, but suggestions have been made above. As an aside, Moon in Pisces on North Node also suggests advanced psychic gifts, or an advanced sense of empathy.

5) Tropical Jupiter widely conjunct draco Neptune in Virgo. An aspect of care and specialised skills.

6) Draco Venus in the 1st in Scorpio exactly opposite tropical Chiron in Taurus in the 7th. Another aspect of care and sensitivity. In this instance

the 'wounds' of others draw you in, partly because you can personally relate to those wounds.

7) Draco nodal axis draws in draco Jupiter into the 12th house in Libra. Growth through many negotiations with others, a powerful charm factor. This is rooted in spiritual lessons on the theme of compromise and cooperation. Your draco Pisces Moon is of the 12th house, marking you out as highly spiritually developed in potential – manifesting as readiness to receive higher learnings.

In summary: your draco analysis advises consideration of reaching out to the world with your life lessons, perhaps informed by a specialist knowledge. Whether this is done through writings or talks, or some other means, is a matter for you to decide if you recognise the foregoing. Very best wishes.

Stephen Gawtry

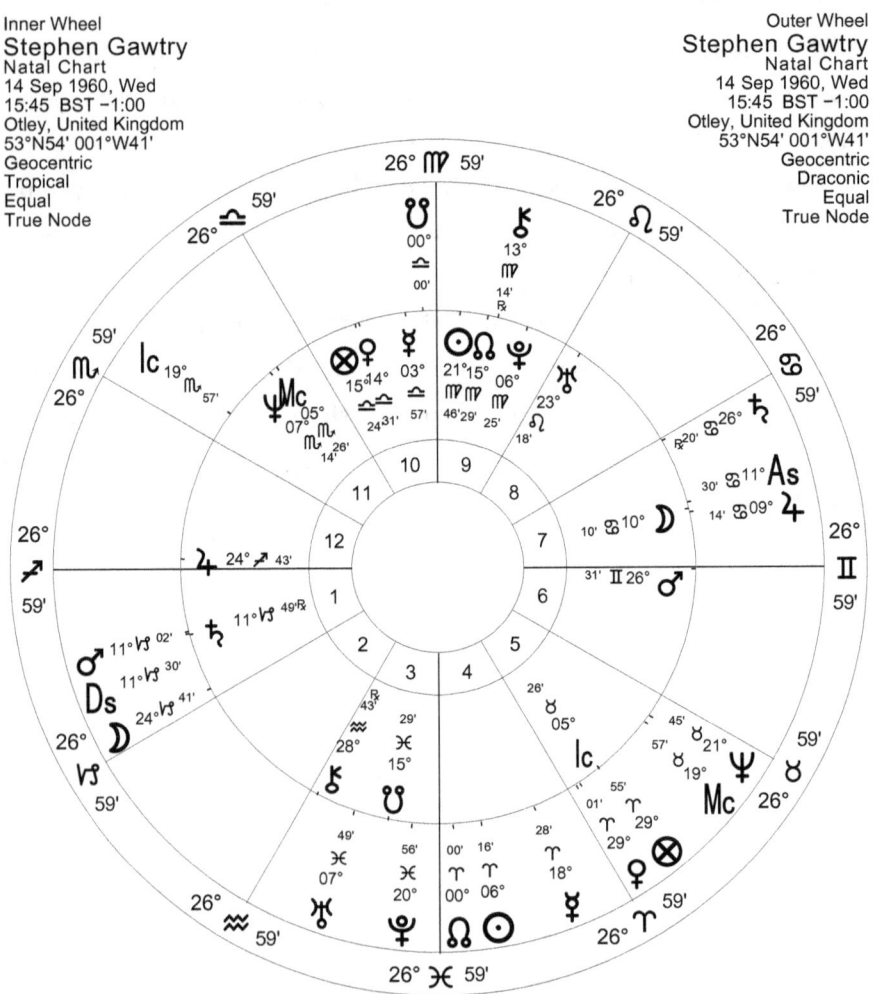

All I knew about Stephen before I examined his charts was that he is the Managing Editor of Watkins Mind, Body, Spirit *magazine and that he is Margaret Cahill's partner. This locates him in media and publishing. His commentary on his draconic reading was concise:* '**It hits the nail on the head**'.

The Report

Dear Stephen,

Step 1: Your tropical birth chart

You were born under a Third Quarter Moon in Cancer, a phase likened to autumn in its spiritual experience. The life will feature most probably a huge shift or change in philosophy, often in the middle years, in which you separate yourself from old ideas or roots to live your life more in accordance with new ideas and values. This may be a gentle transition with no confrontation with people who represent the 'old' life or a dramatic one where people challenge your moving on. This may have happened already, is happening or something that occurred later on in life, perhaps in your 50s-60s. This is not about getting older in itself, more about realisations from experience. By nature, you will be inclined to be constantly reassessing how you live your life. Instincts are vibrant and often there will be a strong artistic, creative or spiritual component to the nature. This Moon is strengthened in Cancer, elevating nurturing and protective instincts oriented to close relationships and mediation.

Your chart shape is known as a Locomotive, so called because your main planets occupy about 240 degrees of the chart in a fairly even pattern, mainly in the southern (or top half) part of the horoscope. There will be active engagement with the world but not necessarily at a cost to personal life because there is powerful representation in the interior area of your chart. The Locomotive lead planet (or 'engine') is Mars in Gemini in the Equal 6th house on the Descendant – this bestows a highly questing, restless energy which thrives in competitive worlds and orients you to media, a high need for self-expression, a great need for intellectual or mental stimulation and a likely low boredom threshold.

A strong Jupiter in its domicile opposite Mars will add to a combative nature and embracing, intellectually curious persona – the mind is open to new ideas, experiences and adventure, and much will be gained from setting personal targets throughout the life or else risk inertia. Feet up in slippers is not you. Mars-Jupiter are part of t-squares which suggest that unusually turbulent or restless and driving energies are best directed towards practical and analytical expressions (Sun in Virgo) in the areas of higher education, publishing, languages, etc (9th house).

With Venus, Mercury and Part of Fortune in the 10th house, a strong basis for advancement of ambition is through partnership and the finding of a soulmate. With Venus elevated in the sign it rules, this need is accentuated, underscored as the apex point to the Moon-Saturn opposition which can be an indicator of earlier-life relationship struggles and/or tendencies to feel isolated or emotionally restricted. But bear in mind that both Moon and Saturn are in their own signs which is more than a hint that earlier life hindrances can be overcome.

Neptune conjunct MC in Scorpio can be an ambivalent combination in that there is both high sensitivity to the world around you, which enhances one's sense of reality (almost to a psychic extent), and a tendency to feeling at a loss, confused or somehow up against a capricious fate. In the material sense it may incline you to photography, film, sea, etc. This should be treated as 'existential' in that the usual material markers of success or achievement will mean little to you. In reality, this quite challenging aspect is best handled by actively developing a likely innate interest in spiritual (or artistic/abstract) areas of life and harnessing this energy to one's professional connections (the 11th). Neptune/MC are well aspected to your Moon in the 7th, another pointer to partnership, mediation themes already addressed above with Libra in your 10th.

Structurally, your chart is mutable and cardinal, expressive of leadership, self-initiatory and versatile and flexible energies.

The nodal axis across 3rd/9th in Virgo/Pisces orients you to writing or teaching or dissemination on related themes with the challenge to turn spiritual or artistic (or other 'abstract' areas) into practical manifestations which guide or educate. Difficult or painful experiences may have focused your mind on the need for accuracy, truth and correct detail.

At heart, your tropical chart is that of some kind of explorer and 'warrior' (of the spiritual kind) whose purpose is to uncover, discover and widen other people's understanding.

Step 2: Your draconic chart

A striking difference from your tropical chart is that your draconic is definitively cardinal. This is an urging to develop pioneering/leadership qualities. Life will present you with challenges to strike out alone or on one's own initiative, usually against opinion or circumstances. An absence of air in the draco chart suggests that there will be a struggle to find your voice or to overcome some kind of obstacle to full self-expression, most probably in younger years. This struggle – if recognised and negotiated – is the springboard to a strength in the areas of intellect and communication. With tropical South Node in Pisces in the 3rd, there may have been a challenge to make discrete many different awarenesses and feelings – this theme may be echoed or amplified by the absence of air in the draco chart.

Another striking feature of your draco chart is that Aries is now highly dominant, embracing Sun (close to North Node), Mercury, Venus and Part of Fortune. Ruler Mars is 'promoted' from tropical Gemini to its exaltation in Capricorn. This describes someone born to pioneer and break new ground through career (10th) and through education/publishing and other 9th-house associations.

Fulfilment is more likely to be found the more you act on inner personal urgings or dreams or ambitions. But this can create tensions with partners/allies (draco Venus is demoted to Aries). The shift of Mars from Gemini to draco Capricorn re-enforces the suggestion that career or part of life purpose finds fulfilment through intellectual questing and communication, often with the component of mediation or representation.

Although draco Moon and Saturn are 'demoted' to their opposite signs on the 1st to 7th axis of personal relationships, the mutual reception is another indicator (as in the tropical) that there is sufficient strength to overcome certain challenges to personal and shared equilibrium. This life area does suggest that it is part of life purpose to work actively on relationship enhancements against certain earlier-life obstacles.

The shift of Neptune/MC to Taurus (from its opposite sign in the tropical) repeats a theme already identified in this analysis of the wisdom in finding practical expressions for quite complex and sometimes abstract awarenesses within you. There may be the challenge of your tending to complicate life in trying to synthesise too much, resulting in muddle. The draconic chart wants you to address matters of literalism, practicality, value and results while also engaged in much inner inquiry and delving.

Achieving balance between immense inner drives and outward results is a big theme of your draco chart – this may be thought to be a common enough challenge, but it is highly italicised in this chart.

Step 3: The tropical and draconic comparison chart

1) With tropical Cancer Moon conjunct draco Jupiter (both planets dignified and exalted respectively in Cancer) and draco Ascendant, in the 7th, there is much fulfilment to be found in partnership and acting in concert with others such as friends – growth comes through partnership(s) of any kind, and most probably through feminine energy in the main. This is part of your life purpose, to learn to share your life. Though this may be seen as a common purpose to humanity, life situations will have served to address problems in either forming or maintaining relationships, especially indicated by draco Ascendant exactly opposite tropical Saturn: early life situations may have set up a fear of sharing your life, such as an overwhelming authority figure limiting your emotional range. Even so, the oppositional planets in the 1st to 7th houses are all strong which indicates a

robust attitude to problems and challenges, especially when you are acting in concert.

In another sense, negotiation through life is blessed i.e., learning not always to have your own way entirely.

2) Draco nodal axis conjoins tropical Mercury in Libra in the 10th: this emphasises talents of communication and intellect working in partnership with others in career, supporting point 1 above. With South Node on this Mercury, most likely communication or learning took a slow route to fruition for whatever reason.

3) Draco Pluto in Pisces exactly opposes tropical Virgo Sun, 3rd to 9th. This complements the Moon phase you were born in, Third Quarter, and the theme of constant change and self-questioning. Pluto wishes to perfect and so does your Virgo Sun, but in entirely different ways, giving rise to a constant state of dissatisfaction with performance, your lot in life or other people's work. This striving for perfection, if recognised, is not in itself a bad thing, but is unrealistic and does not take into account the many imponderables of life as well as the subjective nature of perfection. It is likely you have found a way to balance these powerful forces so that you do not yield always to impulses, but here it is presented as a life challenge, allied to fulfilment.

4) Draco Aries' wide stellium is brought to the 4th and 5th houses, the traditional realms of Moon and Sun. The pioneering potential in you will have had to find its identity or freedom despite or because of family or cultural expectations. The great emphasis of Aries does suggest some kind of 'fight' to self-realisation and the potential of considerable impact. This is allied to creative self-expression and manifestation of your 'passions' – there is a great instinct for constant renewal and fresh, new things – and it is in this approach that the greatest fulfilment can be found. Life will have presented you with challenges to focus attention on this championing and expression of all that's new and pioneering.

Sue Brayne

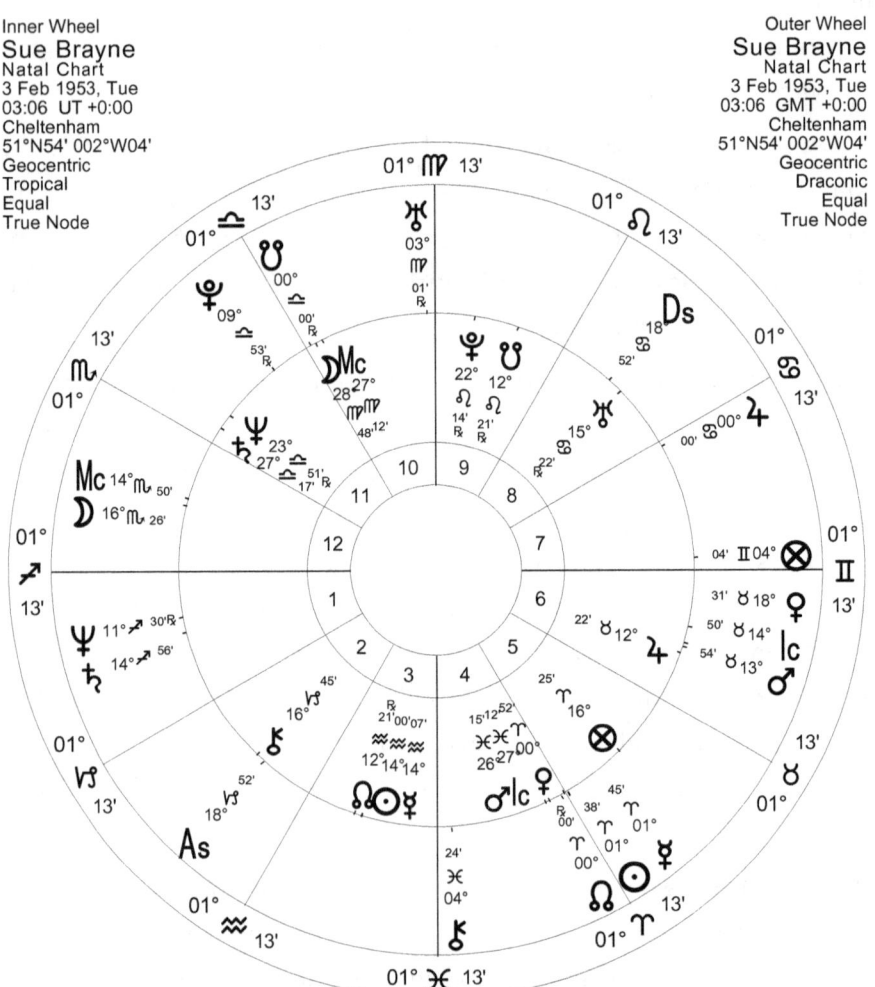

Sue and I go back many years. She has lived a life of infinite variety and continues to do so. She survived a light aircraft crash, and this terrifying experience turned her mind to questions of mortality. She has conducted end-of-life research, led workshops on this theme and written books on spirituality, consciousness, death and dying. She is also author of the innovative Granny Mo *picture book series for children which addresses death issues, and she hosts podcast interviews with pioneers and*

Six draconic case studies from my files

practitioners in spiritual and therapeutic work. She is currently studying astrology. Her commentaries on her draconic report are interposed in bold and brackets. I appreciate that she was prepared to clarify or even question certain observations. Website: Suebrayne.co.uk.

The Report
Dear Sue,

Step 1: The structure of your tropical birth horoscope
You were born under a separating Full Moon in Virgo conjunct MC in the Equal 10th house, associated with full expression of talents: Full Moon orients you to a desire to understand the dynamics of relationships while Virgo drives you to identify 'components' of human bonds with the capability of dispassion and a certain impersonality. (**Sue comments: 'Yes, I do feel the ability for dispassion'**) Virgo is a health sign, so this drive has to do with the search for perfection – and with the link to MC, it is highly probable that a part of your adult life has sought to help others optimise self-understanding and relationship. (**'Yes, my life has been about helping people to understand who they are.'**) Full Moon sees the Moon at maximum light from the perspective of Earth; likewise, you seek to shed light on all themes that interest you, often from a very critical perspective. (**'Perhaps analytical rather than critical, although this also resonates.'**) This journey may bring into your life a number of different partners (business or intimate) each of whom presents you with a stepping-stone to greater self-understanding (**'Agree with number of different partnerships acting as stepping-stones to greater understanding.'**) How to manage a relationship of opposites (Sun opposite Moon) is of especial interest and how to find a working synthesis for happiness – this may not be a grail you reach, but there is the aspiration and the learning as compensation. (**'Happiness is not my goal but learning about it is!'**)

The tropical chart is highly mutable – adaptable, versatile and reasonably flexible though with Sun in a fixed sign, obstinacy or high resolution may be evident when the mind has settled on a perspective. (**'Yep!'**) Elementally, there is a fair balance, but water is the minority which suggests an ability to detach from situations of emotional intensity (which may be useful in working with other people) and a certain coolness or avoidance in the face of emotional intensity. (**'I can easily detach emotionally.'**)

Angular and cadent energy is well represented marking you as proactive and blessed with communication skills (**'Communication – writing and verbal – is essential for me.'**)

Sun is in the 3rd house, domain of Gemini the communicator, in Aquarius with Mercury cazimi – 'in the heart of the Sun' but for seven minutes (17 minutes of orb is the usual maximum): Mercury is thereby enhanced, adding beneficence to communication skills such as writing and speaking. (**'That's what I do!'**) Aquarius also opens the mind (Mercury) up to pioneering ideas, futurology, unothodoxies etc and these themes may be the subjects of communications. [**'I speak and write about consciousness, mortality, death and dying.'**)

The Seesaw shape of your chart complements the Full Moon character, the dealing with opposites. This Seesaw in your case, divided between northern and southern hemispheres, sees a struggle between private and public worlds as if there is a basic irresolution in you as to which should be the main focus of life. (**'I protect my private life yet feel drawn or even hauled into the public domain, but don't relish recognition.'**]

The nodal axis takes South Node from the 9th house in Leo to North Node in Aquarius conjunct Sun/Mercury in 3rd. South Node is widely conjunct Pluto – arguably out of orb – but sufficient in proximity to be considered: very intense or challenging experiences derive from earlier life (**'This life was a massively bumpy ride when I was younger.'**) or past lives as focal points of your interests: Pluto brings to you these experiences but the association with South Node imports also a desire to understand and move on from them towards a dispassionate understanding, in the direction of North Node. The Sun-Mercury-North Node conjunction in the 3rd impels you to intellectualise experiences for greater clarity – intellectualisation is not necessarily a 'scholarly' process, but more to do with picking apart 'experience' into cause-and-effect processes before seeking to express your understanding (the 3rd). **('I have written and spoken about my experiences as a process of making sense of them.')** Pluto almost always works through pain and trauma as a starting point of epiphany, and this may be evident in this life or past lives. **('Certainly in this life.')**

The 10th Moon-MC in Virgo opposition to 4th Mars-IC (including Venus just in Aries) does set up a challenging focal point in the life, between the search for perfection **('Perfection is one thing that doesn't resonate.')** and the potential understanding that perfection may be elusive. This applies to career, family, emotional life, attitudes to authority, parents. **('I would say that I am more dispassionate about these issues than involved with perfection.')** Venus is detached from the Pisces energy, bringing a strongly independent spirit in relationships, an ability to cut away if you feel your independence is being compromised. **('Yes, definitely'.)** Mars conjunct IC bestows tremendous energy where interest is engaged, possible unresolved anger towards family or parents (but not necessarily) and a need to discover practical or accurate ways (Virgo) to express much in the way of Piscean nebulous or muddled feelings and attitudes. **('My healing journey involved training as a psychotherapist.')**

Saturn-Neptune conjunct in the zone of Aquarius in Libra (11th) enlarges your social world, you may be forever seeking 'partners' to work with. This conjunction mirrors the dichotomy in your views of relationship, a place where either ideals and practical realities may merge in a greater understanding of joint enterprises of any kind or clash as expectations collide with hopes or dreams. **('I have worked solo for the past thirty-odd years, and when I have joined groups or partnerships, they have never worked out – although I would still love to find the perfect fit.')**

Part of Fortune in Aries in the 5th is a tropical indicator that doing things your own way, breaking new ground and so forth, is the best life approach. Chart ruler Jupiter in Taurus in the 6th blesses work on health and wellbeing, especially where high ideas are brought to point of practical application. Black Moon Lilith at the top of your chart in Virgo relates to the 6th house, raising perfectionist tendencies to daily life or work. Lilith is disposited by cazimi Mercury which links care, perfectionism, work to communications, writing, speaking etc: tropically, this is a major life purpose, to bring into the light what you know from crisis or other challenging experience. (**'This is bang on!'**)

Step 2: Your draconic chart

Cardinal and fixed energies are now elevated. This does not mean you should be less flexible or adaptable, but rather to have greater faith in your ability to act alone, to pioneer new things and to act with great resolution where you are motivated. Initiating new ideas or projects is part of life purpose. (**'Yes!'**)

This is repeated more emphatically by the Sun now in Aries next to Mercury and North Node: boldness, courage, independence are keys to success – especially in the realm of your intellectual interests and expressions, such as writings. (**Yes!'**) Tropical Aquarius spurs you to delve into unorthodox ideas, but draco Aries is a call to espouse your learning with confidence and courage. Dispositor Mars is in detriment in Taurus in the 4th which builds in challenges to your Aries energies – perhaps family or practical considerations or comforts may complicate your independence, and it is part of your fate to isolate what may be regarded as your 'inner warrior' from doubts, fears or compromises. This won't always be easy. (**'It hasn't been.'**)

South Node/Pluto's move into Libra identifies a spiritual starting point as part of karma or purpose: relationship is identified as a major area of painful or difficult experience; also, as a place to evolve from towards a greater sense of your own power (North Node in Aries). (**'Yes, I agree with this.'**) This does not mean you are evolving to be 'alone', but acting singly, especially over perspectives, knowledge and communications, is crucial. What you have learnt from relationships informs your acquired wisdom, which takes us back to your Full Moon and the interest in relationship dynamics (**'Relationships have always been rather complexing for me – in personal life and professional career, I have not attracted emotionally solid, dependable people, which I would like to do!'**)

Draco Moon-MC are in Scorpio. Tropical Virgo seeks mental understanding. Scorpio also seeks this but through powerful emotional connection and opening up to life areas which may be regarded as dark or morbid or 'mysterious'. (**'I thrive on talking and writing about life and death!'**) You are encouraged to 'open up' to those life areas that may be regarded as challenging. These explorations take you away from the Taurus certainties opposite, but these do act as ballast to counter any tendency to obsession or phobia which is always a Scorpio risk. Dispositor Pluto in Libra includes 'relationship' as a theme of exploration, and this may involve an emotional engagement you find difficult. (**'Personal relationships have always been challenging for me.'**)

Uranus in Pluto's domain in Virgo echoes the theme of unorthodox approaches to matters related to the 8th – be this spirituality, death or sexuality. Jupiter is promoted to its exaltation in Cancer, urging you to play the nurturer in your dealings with others, however this is expressed. A recurring theme is the engagement of emotion or empathy in your dealings. (**'Yes, I have developed this over many years of dealing with personal crises.'**)

Elementally, water is raised in importance which sets the challenge to acknowledge emotional needs and realities and to empathise with others as a key to your own better self-understanding. This is involved in soul purposes.

Draco chart ruler is now Saturn moved from Libra to Sagittarius (conjunct Neptune): an urging to pursue higher knowledge, usually through scholastic study, in pursuit of understanding. **('I have two MAs and am constantly engaged with higher learning and knowledge.')**

Step 3: The tropical and draconic synastry of self comparison chart

1) Relationship understanding in its many forms is strongly highlighted in the self-synastry. First, draco North Node is exactly conjunct tropical Venus in the 4th: it is part of life challenge to work on relationships to an advanced extent towards greater understanding; and in the personal sense, to retain independence within bonds of partnership and family. **('I relish my independence yet want partnership.')** Second, draco Black Moon Lilith in Libra conjoins tropical Saturn-Neptune: Lilith seeks out what one tries to avoid or fears while Saturn and Neptune approach the Libran themes of union from different perspectives, as 'rules' and as a spiritual reality, respectively. If we suppose that in early life or past lives, 'relationship' was a place of great difficulty **('I believe it was.')**, in this life the grail is to acquire a liberating better understanding from an independent perspective. **('I have lived alone for most of my life'.)**

2) Draco Venus is shifted to the 6th conjunct draco IC and Mars, and tropical Jupiter, all in Taurus. A strong indication that you are empowered as a 'carer' and exponent of wellbeing and good health (especially in matters of relationship). This may also be your source of income (Taurus). **('Yes, true.')** Finding practical applications is imperative. The relocation of draco Scorpio MC-Mars to the 12th in opposition factors in other considerations of care, but of a spiritual kind, which includes transitions, death, confined conditions. In all these approaches a balance between reality and over-immersion is required, so that knowledge may be applied in a workable way towards wellbeing. **('Running death cafés may be an expression of this.')**

3) Draco Aries energy cuts across 4th and 5th houses, taking in the zone of passion for your independent expression. There will be a 'nurturing' trait to this expression, a desire to protect and elevate others. **('Yes, I enjoy empowering people to find their own unique expression.')**

Six draconic case studies from my files

4) Note that the draco Sun-Mercury/Pluto opposition is shifted to the 5th/11th axis: only when passions are engaged will you feel able to express your truth as relates to Pluto matters, such as spirituality, death and the nature of crisis. What you learn in your own way is what counts of value, not group think in the main. (**'Absolutely, agree!'**)

6) Draco Ascendant-Descendant draws in tropical Chiron and tropical Uranus in the 2nd-8th houses axis, Capricorn-Cancer. You are fated to be an authority in matters connected to emotional wounds or fears, but also matters related to the 8th which includes mortality. (**'Yes!'**) Cancer is on the 8th-house cusp, the nurturer, the comforter. With draco Descendant conjunct tropical Uranus, you are drawn to pioneers, the unorthodox, astrology, people of science, especially as pertains to the 8th house. Once again, a balanced approach works best for you, between formal understanding and emotional recognition. One without the other leads to incompleteness. (**'It's been a struggle to find this balance – it's getting easier as I get older.'**)

7) Draco Uranus sits at the top of your chart conjunct tropical Lilith and draco Chiron, a reiteration of the above. In essence, you are a pioneer and an awakener in spirit designed to expose what is hidden and painful. (**'How true.'**) For the most part you will be drawing on life stories including your own (**'I write and communicate about people's stories to help others to have a deeper understanding of themselves.'**)

Alex Trenoweth

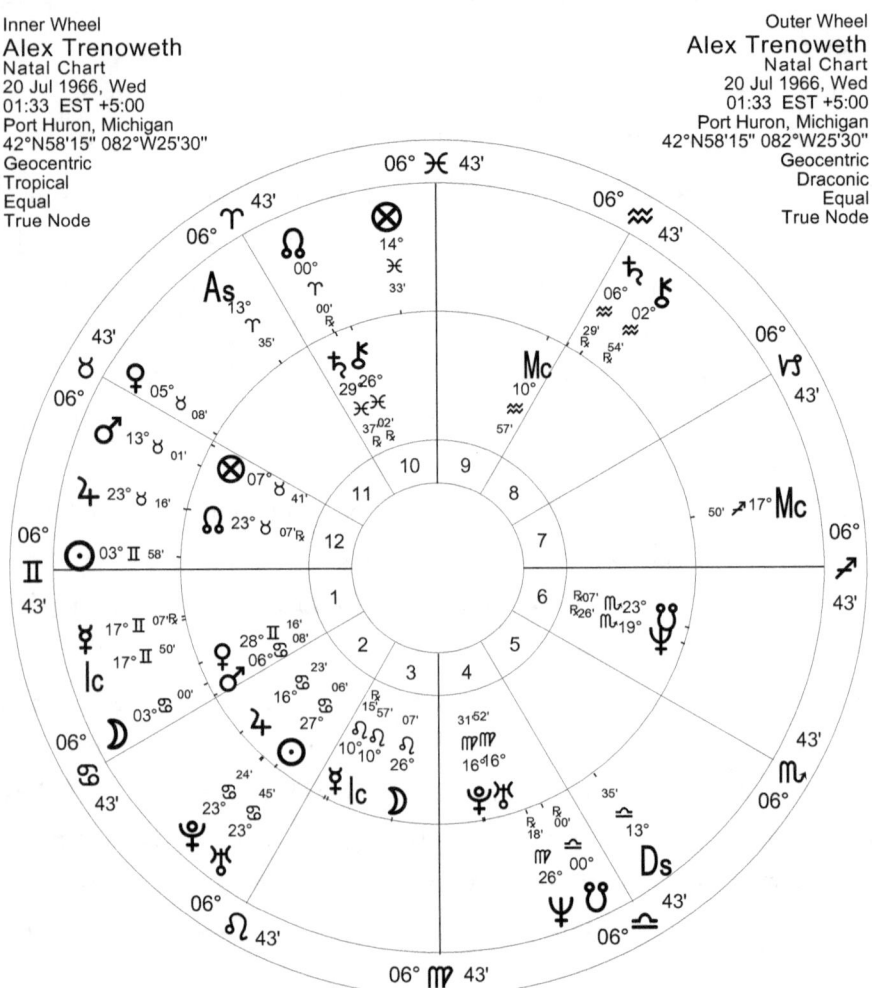

Alex is one of the leading lights of astrology and an author – her book Growing Pains *pioneers research into Jupiter-Saturn patterns in children's education. And her latest book is* Mirror Mirror: The Astrology of Famous People and the Actors Who Portray Them, *published by The Wessex Astrologer. She is also a very active 'player' in the world of astrology, having run the Institute of Vedic Culture annual conferences in Kolkata, India, and is presently CAPISAR President and Ambassador*

Six draconic case studies from my files

for India for ISAR, Principal of the Rohini School of Astrology, etc. She is also a professional schoolteacher. Alex's commentary follows the report. More about her at Alextrenoweth.co.uk.

The Report
Dear Alex,

Step 1: the structure of your tropical birth horoscope
You were born under a separating dissociate New Moon in Leo starting in Cancer at point of exactitude, blending nurturing and theatrical or egoic self-expressive energies. This bestows enormous enthusiasms, especially for new things, people new to things and young people, with a radiant quality in yourself. Leo bestows management skills and a need for appreciation. The Moon in the 3rd as Sun ruler is at the apex of the t-square of the Scorpio-Taurus nodal axis, 6th to 12th: these are zones of care, wellbeing and spiritual immersion. The Moon in the 3rd, among other things, orients you to communications and teaching. The t-square draws on very wide learning and experiences as basis of teaching or communications.

The Locomotive chart pattern – which endows you with a memorable way of doing things – places Saturn as lead planet in the last and problematic degree of Pisces in the 10th close to Chiron. Saturn as a definer and Pisces as a place without definition introduces a wayward element to life direction so a vast variety of occupations may be expected as you seek to find berths.

Saturn-Chiron plays to self-esteem issues and your own authority: confidence and lack of confidence ebb and flow in Pisces so that you are not always certain of your own power or authority. This may be discomforting, but the trine to 6th-house South Node and Neptune in Scorpio suggests that this ambivalence can work well in matters to do with care of others and wellbeing, as well as daily work. The struggle to reach definitive, dogmatic or inflexible ideas about life and the world can mean that you retain an open mind on many subjects or at least a readiness to entertain parallel perspectives in the avoidance of fixation.

Neptune's conjunction with South Node brings the themes of spirituality, addiction or avoidance of reality into your default, either through family, early life experiences or past lives. In this incarnation or life, there is the driver of dealing with realities or finding practical expressions for ideals, though with the complication that North Node in Taurus is in Neptune's realm, the 12th house. This sets up another struggle to find reality in a place where reality has little purchase in the ordinary sense: somehow you must trust your instincts to find your way to truth as opposed to wishful thinking. Life will present you with situations where distinction between what's real or false is required for personal progress. This is part of life purpose.

Structurally, your chart is highly fixed-mutable, a healthy blend of flexibility and resolution. Air and water are strong, communication skills and empathy are well developed. Earth is in the minority suggesting a struggle at times with practicalities. The strongly angular trait of the chart in mutable signs favours situations where you must improvise, adapt and bend to some extent.

Venus and Mars out-of-sign conjunct in Gemini-Cancer respectively adds another 'ebb and flow' quality to life, this time within the self and relationships: mind and heart may frequently be at odds, though the conjunction encourages a blending of the two through experience: the square to Saturn sets you on an ambivalent attitude to authority or to power issues within relationship with the likelihood of conflict.

Jupiter, the guide and higher teacher, is exalted in Cancer in your 2nd trine 6th-house placements. Nurturing others is suggested as a channel of personal growth. The placement of Uranus-Pluto in the 4th in Virgo is problematic of family or heritage matters yet the focal point of a Minor Grand Trine and a loose Kite pattern: disruptive or painful family experiences are paradoxically a source of strength to you or can become so.

Chart ruler Mercury exactly conjunct IC ingrains you with tremendous curiosity and a questioning nature: mental activity is enhanced, lending

Six draconic case studies from my files

gifts in teaching, research, use of language and/or mathematics. You will be a wide reader and well equipped to work from home. MC in Aquarius in the 9th is excellent for higher teaching, higher education and higher forms of knowledge which seek to bring together disparate worlds.

Stage 2: Your draconic chart

Cardinal and mutable energies are more emphasised, encouraging you to find soul purpose through proactivity and resolution, if not already. Do not fear your power. Aries rises replacing Gemini: in communications such as writing and speaking, boldness and pioneering energies are better rewarded. Chart ruler Mars is its detriment in Taurus though supported by conjunction with dignified Venus in the 1st house: this is a complex mix of masculine and feminine energies placing a fundamental/basic/grassroots challenge in your nature to express yourself with more focus/intention: Taurus can still your dynamism, perhaps for reasons of security. At times you hold back in feelings or position yourself rather than act. Finding your boldness is part of your life purpose.

Sun in Gemini emphasises communication, teaching and mental skills as key abilities. Emphasising this is Mercury promoted to its dignity in Gemini conjunct IC which reiterates what is apparent in your tropical chart: enhanced mental and teaching skills driven by endless curiosity, experiment and playfulness.

Saturn, too, is promoted to its old sign of Aquarius, as lead planet of the Locomotive: this lends a forward-thinking energy to your career efforts twinned with a tendency to lay down the law, to uphold rules and impose order.

Neptune is now separated from South Node by sign in Virgo, encouraging you to apply a more detached and critical intelligence to matters where fantasy or avoidance of reality may pertain. With Aries North Node in the realm of Neptune opposite and still drawing in planet

Neptune, this is a clearer message of finding your own reality against any muddle, fantasy or avoidance beliefs.

Draco MC in Sagittarius draws you to higher learning, teaching, universal ideas and beliefs, overseas, as ingredients of career direction.

Cancer's shift to its natural home of the 4th where Pluto and Uranus sit makes clearer the theme of family disruption or source of challenging experiences. The Moon is promoted to its dignity in Cancer also but in the 3rd. The Minor Grand Trine that points to Uranus-Pluto is Gemini in nature, a communication aspect pattern. This and the Moon's position is an encouragement to use family or heritage as a communication theme or to embrace it in some way as part of identity.

Stage 3: The tropical and draconic synastry of self comparison chart
1) Draco Jupiter in Taurus is exactly conjunct tropical North Node in the 12th, a classic indicator of the teacher-cum-guru of sorts. It is your soul purpose to enlighten others through practical actions, to guide, enlighten and expand horizons. Positioned in the 12th, this Jupiter cuts across boundaries, mixes and merges, drawing on so many different themes. The exactitude of the aspect is significant.

2) Draco North Node in Aries is taken to the 10th house and out-of-sign conjoins tropical Saturn and Chiron in Pisces. Prominence is in your potential as an authority and pioneer but only after struggles to identify what is true as opposed to muddled or ambiguous.

3) Draco Moon in Cancer conjunct tropical Mars; draco Uranus-Pluto conjunct tropical Sun in Cancer; draco Neptune-South Node out-of-orb conjunct tropical Uranus-Pluto in the 4th: all these aspects are variants on family or heritage/ancestral themes and suggest difficult memories and experiences too complex to explore here. It could be that part of your life challenge is to explore and express these feelings/thoughts, especially with draco Black Moon Lilith opposite tropical Sun (Lilith addresses what is hidden or feared). At the top of the chart, Part of Fortune in Pisces

conjoins Lilith, encouraging discovery, revelation, exploration. The draco nodal axis now finds its apex in the 1st house in draco Moon/tropical Mars: this raises family or nurturing responsibilities as personal issues and is best handled by taking charge of relevant situations.

4) Draco Mercury rises exactly conjunct IC in Gemini opposite MC in Sagittarius in the 7th: like draco Moon, this relates very much to your person and interests, and links career direction to teaching or acting as an intermediary or negotiator. MC here draws you to specialists, experts, 'gurus', scholars and the like.

5) In summary, the most significant aspect is Jupiter on North Node.

Alex Trenoweth's commentary:

Thank you for this amazing analysis.

Currently I am a schoolteacher and astrologer, but I have had many jobs in the caring industry such as working with the elderly or with people with disabilities.

As a child, I was a reluctant reader, and I was under observation for learning difficulties owing to a severe bout of meningitis (which I was not expected to survive) when I was 9 months old. I found it difficult to focus and had a habit of wandering around the classroom chatting to everyone. I could memorise large chunks of text quickly so I pretended I could read and fooled everyone for quite a long time. My teacher came down hard on me and made me stay indoors at lunchtime practising my letters and even threatened to not let me go home until I read an unfamiliar text that was probably way too difficult for a six-year-old. Then one day, I stopped resisting and started reading on my own. My mother tells me I completely changed. Suddenly, I was a bookworm and read absolutely everything. By the time I finished high school, I read the library's entire collection of classic literature.

Saturn in Pisces did indeed lead me to struggle to find a focus at university. I began university studies as pre-med with the view to become a psychiatrist. A year of training rats and pigeons in a behavioural Psych lab, plus intensive statistics, pretty much finished that ambition off. I did find a placement teaching sign language to children, so the year wasn't a complete waste. I took a year out of university to try to discover my true passion which I thought was becoming a lifeguard (how Saturn in Pisces is that?). I did return to university the following year as a journalism major. Then I re-kindled a love of writing fiction and became a creative writing major. By my third year, I decided I needed an interdisciplinary major and chose American Studies which involved History, Literature and the Arts and as a double major, creative writing. I was assured these majors would lend themselves easily to teaching (I entered the teaching profession as an English teacher). I also accumulated a lot of minors (journalism, sociology, psychology and history). The result was, as you noticed, a wide field of learning which I am grateful for every day that I teach children.

My natal Mercury and Gemini links do make me insatiably curious—and very easily distracted. I collect jokes, trivia, stories, anecdotes and I love memes and clever word play. But there's another side to me that can become completely lost in intensive research, writing or reading (I think this is the Neptune in Scorpio in the natal 6th house).

As I don't relate to my natal Cancer Sun at all, I'm delighted to have draco Sun in Gemini. In fact, I'd say my life is divided neatly into two halves: I'm mixed race, I have two completely compartmentalised careers and I even have a different first name for each career. The vastness of the field of astrology has kept me suitably entertained for the past 30 years. The downside of so much Mercurial energy is that I can be extremely anxious. Years of cognitive behavioural therapy have helped me manage this, but I do suffer from the occasional relapse that I've accepted I will always be susceptible to. I would say a lot of the anxiety does come from self-esteem issues and a general feeling that I can't do something well enough to warrant adequate approval.

From the early days of my studies, I understood I needed a focus for astrology too. I think that is the lesson my experiences at university gave me. I looked to my natal Jupiter for help. With Jupiter on its exalted degree in Cancer, I knew that as long as my focus was on children and families, I'd be absolutely fine. And so, it is.

I knew my natal Neptune needed to be used wisely or I could fall into addiction and other bad habits. Alcoholism and drug abuse runs far back in my mother's side of the family (though not my mother herself). For this reason, I avoid any type of over-the-counter or prescribed drug unless absolutely necessary (not even aspirin). Instead, I channel a huge amount of energy into music. As none of my family is a musician, it was as if I somehow intuited how important music would become to keep me from drifting into substance abuse. Films also hold my interest, and they fulfil the need to collect trivia, too. Both of these interests are Neptunian in nature and are far more productive and healthy than the alternatives. I do consume alcohol but have strict rules around when and how I use it.

I can see exactly how the draco Mars in Taurus can be a problem: people continuously underestimate me because I may appear to be content and slow-moving and perhaps even lacking in ambition. But with the insight of the draco chart, I can see how I actually function. I just act all calm and content (Mars in Taurus) but then when bored, I come in with a surprise attack (Venus in Aries). I have indeed made many bold moves that have shocked people.

In terms of the 'teacher-cum-guru' with draco Jupiter in the 12th conjunct the North Node, I would say that my one true talent is knowing what people are good at and suggesting something fulfilling for them to do or helping them improve on their weaknesses. And I actually love teaching.

Allow me a chance to exercise some Gemini energy by telling a story. Once there was this five-year-old boy in my class who clearly didn't understand what odd and even numbers were. I could see how frustrated and upset he was getting so at break time I taught him by counting some footballs together. He came back to the lesson so pleased with himself and wanting to show off his new skills. Years later, I saw him in the shops (I never say hello to former students unless they speak to me first). I quietly stood behind him at the checkout and his order came to £8.69. He turned to me and said with a sly grin, 'And that, Ms T, is an odd number.' I was so glad I didn't have a bottle of gin in my hands.

The draco North Node in Aries in the 10th does rather neatly show how I honed my scattered interests into something useable. Thank goodness it counteracts some of the Mercurial energy. I've written two quite unique astrology books and I now know that I can teach any age group or any subject, both achievements are very useful.

The challenges of the draco 4th house have indeed played out with an extremely messy divorce complete with an ex-husband who quite simply took everything but the liabilities from me. I was left with no option but to re-build my life in my mid-thirties as single mother (of three Aries children) with good qualifications, but yet stacking shelves in Sainsbury's because my American degree was pretty worthless in the UK. The shitty council flat we lived in wasn't even in my name. However, whatever Pluto destroys, it also re-builds and I am grateful that my life now in no way resembles the misery of twenty years ago. I did take control and once again put my nose to the grindstone to train as a teacher whilst studying to get an MA degree. I eventually cleared all my debts, finished three various degrees, bought my own home and have done some rather spectacular feats within the astrology world that I would say took a lot of people by surprise.

But I still have the habit of wandering around the classroom chatting to everyone.

Epilogue

What might be the soul purpose of this book? Do books have souls? I doubt it, but I have a soul (that's my working presumption; a rebuttable one, to lapse into legalese). To find the draconic purpose of *Chasing the Dragons* – which may seem obvious, to educate people on an astrological technique – as mediated through my nativity we must consult the charts. Perhaps there's an underlying theme to find beyond the overt intention...

It so happens that I have a book 'conception' time – the moment that my publisher Margaret Cahill first suggested to me that I write this book. The contract was signed a few weeks later. But on 8 September 2021, at 13:48, she sent me this private message on Facebook: 'Have you thought about writing an introductory book on draconic?' I am paraphrasing. How can I be certain of the precise time? Because messages on Facebook are date- and time-stamped. I read the message the moment it arrived as Margaret and I were in text conversation. I decided to draw up the tropical chart for this moment in conjunction with my own natal chart – given that without me the book would not happen.

It's not complicated. This is a Yes chart to the question: Should I write this book for Margaret Cahill? The transiting Great Benefic Jupiter (retrograde) is in a conjunction cycle with my Ascendant in Aquarius (personal expansion), disposited in the modern system by natal Uranus in Leo in the 6th (self and work), with transiting Uranus in a conjunction cycle with my Mercury in Taurus in the 3rd (zone and planet of communication). Uranus represents astrology, among other things, as does Mercury in old astrology. My natal Uranus is also conjunct progressed Sun

Chasing the Dragons: An Introduction to Draconic Astrology

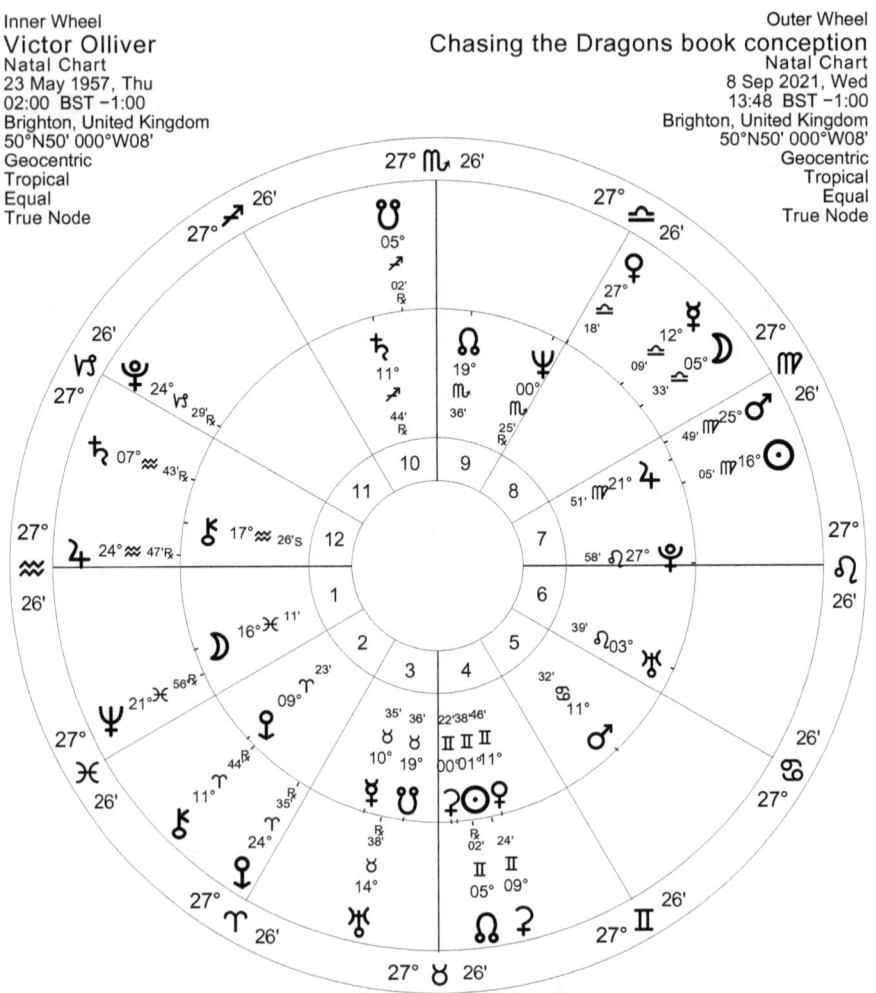

at time of writing, and in summer 2022, a progressed New Moon in Leo occurs exactly on my Uranus. Goodness knows how that will manifest. The multiple Uranian themes express a pioneering and/or independent proactivity. And back to Jupiter on my Ascendant: be reminded that this is the planet that the Babylonians associated with the deity Marduk who placed the Great Dragon in the lunar nodes in the first place.

Transiting Sun in Virgo in the 7th is approaching natal Jupiter (preparatory stage of a partnership) while transiting North Node (retrograde,

Epilogue

remember) approaches conjunction with my Sun in early Gemini: a 'destiny moment'.

So much for the tropical. What about draconic purpose?

The first of the draconic charts has draconic transits placed on my tropical birth chart for the moment Margaret messaged me. We have established in the tropical natal/transits chart that the project looks beneficial, but now what of its 'soul purpose'? Let's see. The most striking conjunction is draco Sun exactly conjunct my Mars in Cancer in the 5th

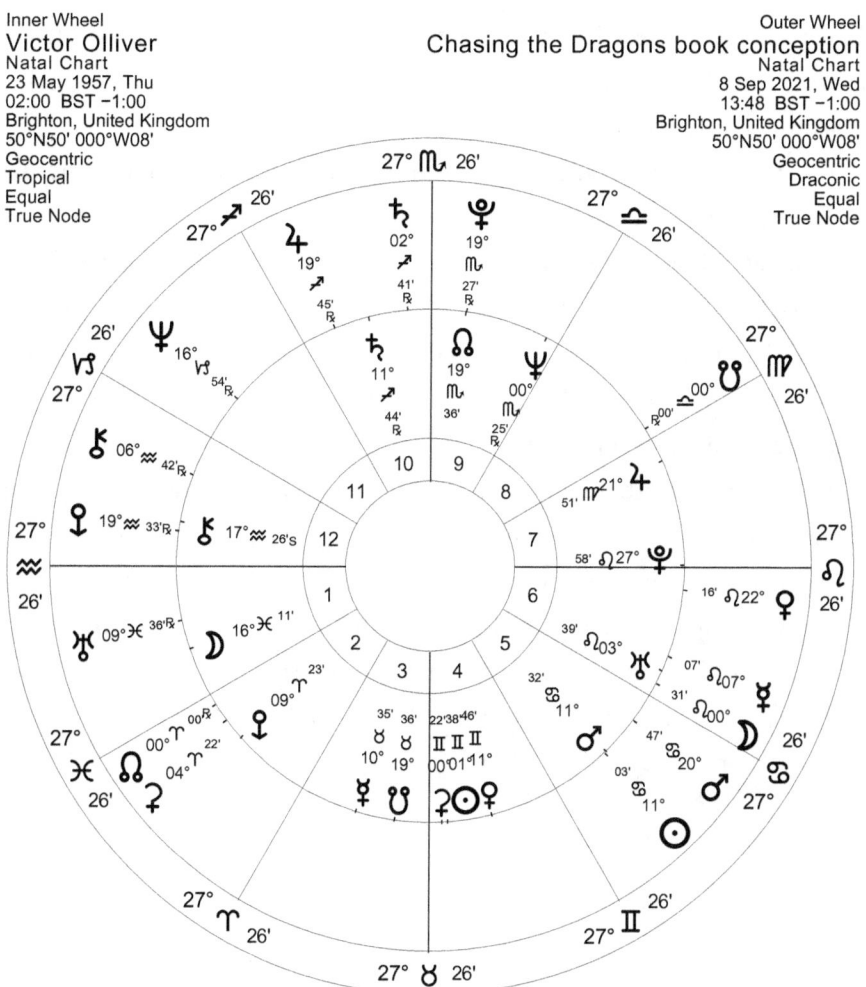

(zone of personal passion and creativity). Mars is the trigger or the fuel of action. Moon disposits this Sun/Mars aspect – and what is this book about but Moon-based astrology. Draco Moon is in Leo (self) in 6th (work) applying to conjoin my Uranus (astrology). This Moon is very close to my progressed Sun (not shown) on Uranus. One major purpose of my book is to explore the role of memory, reflex and past in the life – lunar themes.

Up in the 9th (zone of publishing and higher knowledge) we find draco Pluto exactly conjunct my North Node in Scorpio (just nine minutes out). This is a powerful destiny indicator of change and transformation at personal and effect levels. Whatever else is going on in this chart, the energies are delving to reveal that which is hidden (very much the part of draconic in relation to the tropical).

Draco Jupiter – planet of publishing – and Saturn in Sagittarius, are shifted to the 10th house of career direction.

What might be revealed by the purely draconic biwheel, natal and transits?

This is not a chart to micro-analyse. The ultimate soul chart needs to speak plainly or not at all. The Cancer Sun rises now which is promising for my prominence and the two Moons are close together in the 1st binding Leo's creativity with lunar themes. But the primary detail is transiting Uranus in Pisces in the 9th conjunct draco Neptune. Astrology (Uranus) is brought to a spiritual or soul place (Neptune and Pisces) in the zone of publishing and higher knowledge (9th). That's it in a nutshell. In case of doubt, both draco North Nodes (always at 0° Aries) sit in the 9th house, marking this as the place for cardinal launch and breakout.

Welcome to *Chasing the Dragons*.

Epilogue

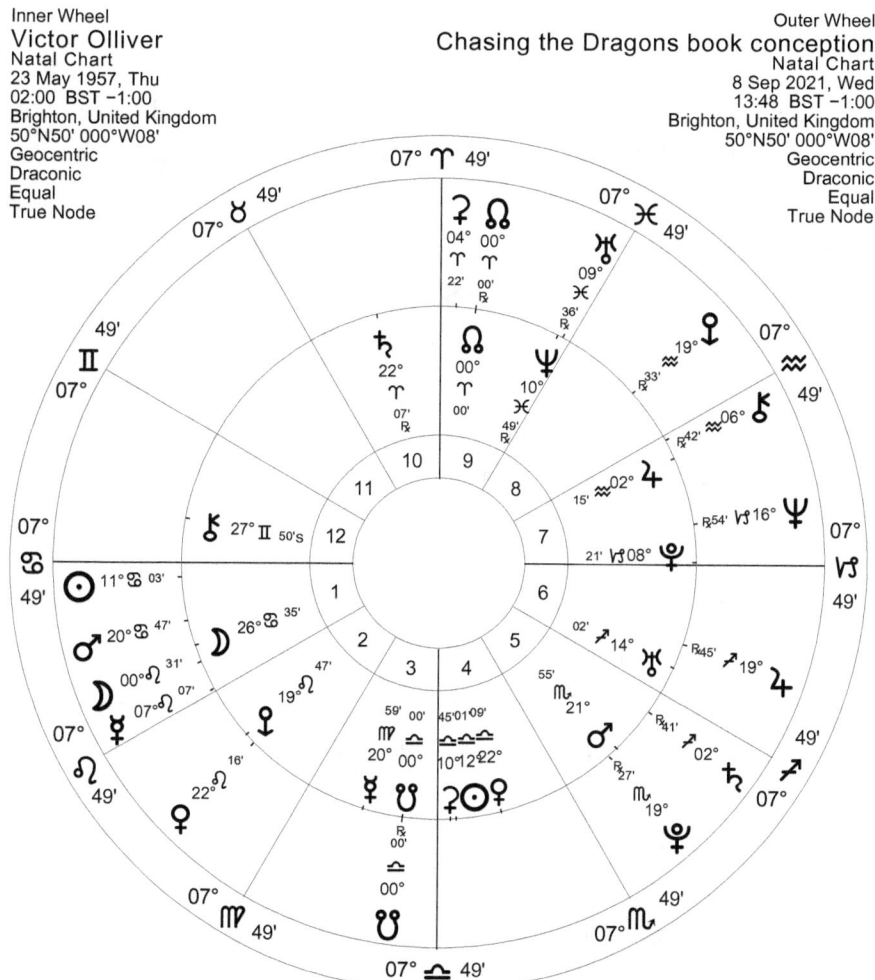

About the author

Victor Olliver has edited *The Astrological Journal* – published by the UK-based Astrological Association – since 2014, having obtained a diploma with distinction from the Mayo School in natal and mundane astrology. A popular teacher of draconic astrology he has presented many webinars in various parts of the world, including the UK, South Africa, Canada, the USA, Australia and Turkey, and is a high-profile draconic consultant with many clients. He is also the Media Officer of the Association of Professional Astrologers International which sets professional and ethical standards in astrology and astrological schools.

Before turning to astrology Victor had a long career as feature writer, editor, radio broadcaster (working with Lorraine Kelly and Anna Raeburn among others) and interviewer, winning two Periodical Publishers' Association awards for his celebrity interviews and travel journalism. His work has appeared in *The Times*, *The Sunday Times Magazine*, *Marie Claire*, *Woman's Journal*, *Australia Women's Weekly*, etc. He has held senior editorial posts at IPC Magazines, Mirror Group and DMGT.

Subjects of his profiles and interviews include Elizabeth Taylor, Gore Vidal, John Travolta, 8th Earl and Countess Spencer, Joan Collins, Hugh Hefner, Meryl Streep, Lauren Bacall, Raquel Welch and other luminaries. He covered the Cannes Film Festival for several years.

Originally, he trained for the England and Wales Bar, and was called to the Bar in the early 1980s as member of the Middle Temple. He has never practised as a barrister, however.

Victor is the author of the *Lifesurfing...*series of annual astrology forecast books. His comic novel *Curtains* is available on Amazon.

He is based on the south coast of England. His websites: victorolliver.co.uk and draconicastrology.co.uk.

www.ingramcontent.com/pod-product-compliance
Lightning Source LLC
Chambersburg PA
CBHW062027220426
43662CB00010B/1502